D1001066

TEACHING REFLECTIVELY IN THEOLOGICAL CONTEXTS

Promises and Contradictions

TEACHING REFLECTIVELY IN THEOLOGICAL CONTEXTS

Promises and Contradictions

Edited by
Mary E. Hess
Stephen D. Brookfield

KRIEGER PUBLISHING COMPANY
MALABAR, FLORIDA
2008

Legal acknowledgments

The course material on p. 97 of this book is reprinted with permission of John Wiley & Sons, Inc., and originally appeared on pp. 60–61 of Stephen Brookfield and Stephen Preskill's book *Discussion as a Way of Teaching: Tools and Techniques for Democratic Classrooms* (San Francisco: Jossey-Bass, 2005).

The figures on p. 51 of this book are reprinted with permission of John Wiley & Sons, Inc., and originally appeared on pp. 100 and 102 of Parker Palmer's *The Courage to Teach: Exploring the Inner Dimensions of a Teacher's Life* (San Francisco: Jossey-Bass, 1998).

Portions of Chapter Ten originally appeared in an earlier version in *Listening: Journal of Religion and Culture*, Vol. 39, No. 3, Fall 2004, pp. 441–451 as "Better off for all that we let in: Being Catholic while teaching at a Lutheran Seminary" and are reprinted with the permission of the journal.

Portions of Chapter Twelve originally appeared in an earlier version in *Theological Education*, Vol. 41, No. 1, 2006, pp. 77–91, "What difference does it make? Digital technology in the theological classroom" and are reprinted with the permission of the journal.

Original Edition 2008

Printed and Published by
KRIEGER PUBLISHING COMPANY
KRIEGER DRIVE
MALABAR, FLORIDA 32950

Library of Congress Cataloging-in-Publication Data

Teaching reflectively in theological contexts : promises and contradictions / edited by Mary E. Hess, Stephen D. Brookfield. — Original ed.
p. cm.
Includes bibliographical references and index.
ISBN-13: 978-1-57524-284-2 (alk. paper)
ISBN-10: 1-57524-284-2 (alk. paper)
1. Theology—Study and teaching. 2. Teaching—Religious aspects—Christianity.
I. Hess, Mary E. II. Brookfield, Stephen D.
BV4020.T43 2008
230.071'1—dc22

2007046058

10 9 8 7 6 5 4 3 2

CONTENTS

QUESTIONS ARISING FROM PRACTICE

REALIZING PROMISES AND CONFRONTING CONTRADICTIONS

ACKNOWLEDGMENTS

Our deepest thanks goes to the Board of Directors of Luther Seminary, who first made available the funds for collaborative faculty development which empowered the junior faculty teaching and learning reflection group.

Mary thanks Stephen for agreeing to come on this journey to the "strange land" of theological education in the first place, for sharing his wisdom and humor with a group of colleagues in the early years of their teaching, and most especially for the mentorship and guidance he's offered in the writing of this book. She thanks her colleagues at Luther for their willingness to write for this project and their keen interest in making Luther a good place in which to teach and learn. She also thanks her family—Eric, Alex and Nathaniel—for crazy energy, staunch love, and substantial patience while she worked on the project; and Theodora Braun, for opening her home and in doing so creating a wonderful space for reflecting and writing on this project.

Stephen wishes to thank Mary for inviting him to join the Luther group, for being his coauthor and coeditor, and for so skillfully steering this project to completion. He also wants to thank Luther Seminary and the members of the junior faculty reflection group—Rolf Jacobsen, David Lose, Alvin Luedke, Frieder Ludwig, Jan Ramsey, and Matt Skinner—for two years of fascinating conversation and coauthorship. Finally, Stephen wishes to thank The 99ers—Colin Selhurst, Molly Holley, and Kim Miller—for their support and encouragement during the writing of this book.

INTRODUCTION

Stephen D. Brookfield and Mary E. Hess

Stephen writes:

Genuine dialogue is a rarity in life, something to be treasured when it happens and lamented when it ends. This book grows out of the experience of genuine dialogue eight of us enjoyed over two years at Luther Seminary in St. Paul, Minnesota. In 2002 I was approached by Mary Hess (then assistant professor of educational leadership) to run a session for faculty at Luther on discussion as a way of teaching. That initial session was part of the seminary's ongoing commitment to the Lexington Seminar project, and from my perspective it was well attended and seemed to generate energy and interest amongst participants. A few weeks after this session I was contacted again by Mary, this time to sound out my interest in meeting with a new faculty conversation group. The group comprised seven untenured faculty at the Seminary and its function was to serve as a venue for focused, but relatively unstructured, conversation about the day-to-day realities of teaching each of the seven members had experienced. I was invited to serve as a kind of resident consultant who would inject into the group's conversation some perspectives on teaching and learning that were those of a nonseminarian unused to Luther's culture. My task was not to run the group, but rather to be a catalyst for conversation. I was told that I would be expected to meet with the group once a month for an hour.

The idea for this group grew, at least initially, out of the pragmatic need that one of the junior faculty members had to complete a unit of Clinical Pastoral Education (CPE) prior to being ordained. As a seminary professor, the idea of taking long hours out of regular teaching duties to travel to a hospital setting was not very appealing. On the other hand, most of the junior faculty felt a clear need to process the experiences they were having in their teaching, and the structure of a CPE group—several peers engaged in practice assisted by an experienced guide—had a degree of resonance and interest for them that was energizing. Serendipitously, the Board of Directors at Luther had just authorized the expenditure of additional funds for focused faculty development, and thus the group was born.

I agreed to this proposal and, at the end of our first year together, we learned we had money to sponsor another year of monthly conversations. During this year we welcomed a new member (Kelly, who subsequently left the Seminary and was unable to be part of the book) and were pleased that various group members were awarded tenure. When the two-year experience of monthly conversation ended I suggested that our meetings had been so rich that perhaps there was a book that could be produced that captured some of the collaboration we had enjoyed during the group's existence. To my surprise I found myself volunteering to be a coeditor on this book.

My surprise came from my professional identity. As a professor of education I had never held a permanent, or even adjunct, position in a seminary. Although I currently work in a diocesan Catholic university, most of my life has been spent in resolutely secular institutions in England, Canada, and New York. I had imagined that seminary teaching had its own specific dynamics and complexities and that the topics that seminary faculty would choose to talk about would be so grounded in theological practices and biblical texts that there would be little I could offer. Yet, after two years of regular meetings I was struck by how familiar were the problems and tensions that the group wished to explore. The crucial importance of building a trustful relationship between teacher and taught was one theme to which we returned again and again. The importance of modeling for our students the ways we grappled with difficult texts and the contradictions of practice that were uncovered (for example, that sometimes the best way to help students deal with contingency is not to offer them immediate help in this task) were remarkably familiar to me.

As our conversations progressed I realized that what I had imagined as the emergence of seminary-specific teaching problems was not happening. Instead, the problems and questions raised were those familiar to all teachers of adults: How do we model struggling to learn new material when we feel ourselves to be well-versed in that material after years of studying and teaching it? How do we know that students are learning and changing in the ways we hope for them? How do we judge when our interventions are appropriate and when they are getting in the way of students' learning? How do we build trust with students when we ask them to do things (such as question deeply held beliefs) that they experience as attacks on their personal credos, even their faith? These were the kinds of problems familiar to teachers across the disciplines and ones with which I had grappled for years.

The structure of the monthly conversations remained the same over the two years of the group's life. The group would meet without me for the first hour during which time they discussed the best and worst experiences they had enjoyed and endured during the preceding month. I would join them for the second hour of conversation during which time we would focus on more general dynamics of teaching. What was particularly striking to me as I joined the group each month was the moral culture the group established in remarkably short order. Without exception, the meetings were characterized by a respectful tone and a commitment to the kind of intersubjective understanding—the genuine attempt to appreciate another's point of view in the way it was framed by the other and to follow its logic—identified by Habermas as the hallmark of communicative action.[1] I did not expect this and was, quite frankly, surprised by it. As I observed the thoughtfulness of participants' contributions, the ways they made space for each other to speak, the manner in which they paid careful and close attention to each other's comments, and the way they proved ready to reappraise ways of thinking about seminary teaching that had been taken for granted, I realized I was witnessing a rare event—the evolution of something close to Habermas's ideal speech situation.

Until that time I had always thought of the ideal speech situation as something of a dialogic unicorn, a mythical creature that stalked the magical pages of ancient mythologies but something one would never expect to see in the flesh. Yet here was a group that met all of Habermas's conditions of the ideal speech situation—"that (a) all relevant voices are heard, (b) the best of all available arguments, given the present state of our knowledge, are accepted, and (c) only the non-coercive coercion of the better argument determines the affirmations and negations of the participants."[2] In other words, the Luther Seminary group was one in which everyone contributed, everyone strove for the fullest possible understanding of the different perspectives offered, and everyone was ready to give up their position if a better argument was presented to them.

Lest this sounds as if the group was one distinguished by an earnest intensity let me say that the group members' gentle humor was one of the most appealing features of their conversations. There was a consistent, gentle ribbing of each other, as well as much self-deprecating puncturing of any tiny bubbles of ego that members saw emerging in themselves. This consistently enjoyable group conversation, which ensured that laughter was always a predictable element of our afternoon meetings, impressed me immensely. My assumption that Lutherans were models of somber and sober solemnity was completely jettisoned—I had no idea some Lutherans were so funny! Who knew such a rich stream of comedy coursed through the veins of these seminarians! Many times I felt guilty about getting paid my consultancy stipend for doing something I was enjoying so much (though not guilty enough to refuse to cash the check).

All of us involved in those conversations have our own memory of them, and it may be that for others these were far less revealing, provocative, and enjoyable than they were for me. But the fact that the group enjoyed each other's company was illustrated by their readiness to socialize outside of these afternoon meetings. We enjoyed dinners and parties together, some involving just group members, some involving members and their partners. What made this group work so well together, aside from the unpredictable element of the chemistry of personality? I feel it had nothing to do with me since, by all accounts, the hour-long conversations they held each month before my joining them seemed to be just as enjoyable and helpful for them—if not more so—as the time when I was present.

I do think that it was crucial that all group members were untenured, so no one member exercised any positional authority over any other. Consequently, there was no favor to be gained by one member parroting or obsequiously echoing the views of another member who occupied a position of power in the seminary. No one could increase chance of being granted tenure by comments in the group, nor was there any self-imposed pressure to refrain from critiquing another's position for fear of offending someone who would be voting on tenure in the future. I thought often of how important this positional equality was to the group's functioning. It may be that they would have behaved in just the same way if members of their future tenure committee had been in the room, but my instincts tell me that there always would have been a slight second-guessing of the impact a comment might have on those individuals. As it was, anyone could speak freely on any subject and could describe in great detail what they felt were errors and misunderstandings in their practice with no fear of future retribution or negative consequences.

Second, the group was fortunate in having as members individuals who exhibited the dispositions and attributes identified as crucial to good conversation in several analyses of teaching through discussion.[3] They were models of openness, always ready to consider a perspective that challenged their own. They were genuinely interested in what each other had to offer. They were committed to equity of participation and would frequently draw into speech members who had been relatively quiet up to that point in the conversation. On the other hand, they never made anyone feel that by not speaking they were somehow letting the group down. Group members were comfortable with the recognition that on different subjects different people would have different perspectives and also different amounts of comments to make. Overall, the kind of hospitality and humility that Palmer claimed are the foundations of good dialogue was, I contend, much in evidence.[4] Hospitality and humility will not, in and of themselves, ensure that good conversation ensues. However, without them good conversation will most definitely not occur. In Palmer's terms, hospitality makes possible the painful things without which no learning can take place, "things like exposing ignorance, testing tentative hypotheses, challenging false or partial information, and mutual criticism of thought."[5] In the Luther Seminary group there was a sense of hospitality towards each other, towards me as outside consultant, towards the expression of challenging ideas, and towards the person who joined the group at its halfway point.

Two other dispositions merit special mention. The first of these is curiosity. Participants were intensely curious about what each other thought and how each other taught, particularly when discussing how to respond to predictable rhythms of learning (for example, students being unwilling to think critically about their core beliefs). This curiosity was demonstrated in a constant willingness of members to ask questions of each other and of the awareness of the more extroverted members that it was important to make space for the quieter, more introverted members to voice their own opinions. Participants were also quick to show appreciation for each other's presence, particularly when something one person said helped another member come to a new understanding of a situation that had long been frustrating. Thanking each other for the way their comments had helped them see an old problem in a new light, or for suggesting an action, exercise, or technique that promised to ease a difficulty or tension, was a regular feature of the group's conversation.

Each member of the group no doubt has drawn a map of the territory we traversed, and each of us will remember certain themes as standing out in starker relief from others. From my perspective, the five most common themes that kept surfacing in our deliberations were (a) the importance of faculty modeling for students behaviors and dispositions they desired to see exhibited by students, (b) the benefits of team teaching, (c) the predictable nature of students' resistance to critical thinking, (d) the importance of seeing your practice through your students' eyes as often as possible, and (e) the broader cultural inhibitors to attempts to change practice. Modeling was a theme that emerged at the very first session I attended, largely (at least, as I recall) because of my own interest in it. One of my teaching mantras is that faculty must model in front of their learners an engagement in every learning task that students are being asked to undertake. This is most important when the learning carries an element of risk, but is something that should happen regardless of the level of unfamiliarity or difficulty involved. Many times our conversation circled back to this theme, at first because of my relentless (and no doubt annoying) insistence on its importance, and later because different members of the group began to raise it.

One of the dimensions of modeling that was most frequently discussed was the difficulty of providing for students examples of collaborative learning, respectful disagreement, and peer critique, when most of us are forced to teach solo. There are ways one can get around this problem, as when one models a conversation with oneself—but there is no doubt that it becomes much easier to model good discussion when two or more teachers provide a live example in front of students. When we explain to students that we are trying to talk to our teaching colleagues in ways we would like students to engage with their peers, it becomes much more realistic to expect this kind of conversation to happen in students' small groups. Without this kind of modeling, we often ask the impossible of students—to engage in respectful disagreement and peer critique around controversial and sometimes deeply felt issues, without ever providing them with an example of what that looks like and how we try to deal with the complexities and roadblocks that inevitably arise. It is no surprise to me that a concern with modeling surfaces in all of this book's chapters, but directly in chapters 5 through 8.

This emphasis on the importance of faculty modeling critical conversation in front of students is one aspect of the second theme I kept noticing—the benefits of team teaching. It may be that I'm engaging in an act of distorted recall to serve my own interests, but I do remember many times when we were discussing working with student groups and preparing them for ministry with parish groups that would benefit from critique or that contained deep disagreements that needed addressing, when one of us would say, "It would be so much easier to teach this method to my students if I could teach this course as part of a team." Along with the benefits of team teaching modeling, there also emerged an agreement that team teaching was an important element in teaching reflectively. I was asked to expand on my own ideas regarding the ways peer feedback comprises an important lens of critical reflection (several group members knew my book *Becoming a Critically Reflective Teacher* in which I discuss this),[6] and it was often remarked that the Luther Seminary untenured faculty group itself functioned as a team teaching once-removed model. The group treasured this aspect of its activities, I believe. They knew that they could bring to the monthly group meeting a problem that they were struggling with in class that week and receive some helpful feedback. At various times I suggested trying out the three-role conversational protocol in *Becoming a Critically Reflective Teacher*,[7] but no one deemed this necessary. And they were correct in their estimation—the group was already functioning in the empathetically critical way that process describes. Additionally, and no less importantly, the group was also a source of emotional sustenance for its members. Even if no easy resolution of the problems brought to it were offered, the fact that others in the group clearly struggled with the same problems was reassuring to those who felt they were alone in facing a particular difficulty. This appreciation of the group's support, and the more widespread utility of team teaching, are apparent in chapters 7 and 9 in the current book.

The pedagogic problem I recall as being the one most frequently addressed was a predictable one—how to get students used to thinking in dichotomous ways, and, socialized to look for the correct answer from their teacher, to engage first in multiplistic, situational reasoning and then to realize that faced with an array of ideas, answers, or practices all of which seem to have value, we nonetheless have to choose one of these as the one that is most appropriate in a particular situation. This dynamic is as old as teachers have been working with students and as pedagogically ubiquitous as the need to breathe. If I had been asked to predict what problems the group would spend most of its time talking about, this would have been one of them (the others would have been how to deal with the culture of entitlement where students seem to expect an "A" in return for showing up regularly in class and how to find the time to teach well enough to secure favorable teaching evaluations from students while meeting the college's expectations regarding scholarly publication for tenure).

Time and again we returned to ways of working through the same contradictory dynamic—on the one hand, how to provide a classroom climate that was perceived as sufficiently safe and supportive by students so that they would be ready to venture into the uncharted waters represented by challenging spiritual beliefs that they viewed as constituting an important part of their identity; on the other hand, knowing when skillfully to remove the security blanket of always providing a ready, teacher-approved response to a parish situation, or correct interpretation of a text, and to encourage students instead to grapple with the problem of crafting their own responses and creating their own meanings.

The problem with this dynamic is, of course, that it has no resolution, no point of balance that can be attained. One of my own responsibilities within the group was to point this out. I have long ceased to measure my success as a teacher by how well I attain the right point of balance between seemingly irreconcilable forces. The point about irreconcilable opposites is that they are opposites. The only way any kind of synthesis or productive praxis is achieved is by giving up the notion of perfect equilibrium and accepting that a state of more—or less—congenial tension is all one can hope for. I don't claim anything as profound as wisdom, but if I were forced to declare what

I had learned about teaching after thirty-six years in practice it would be that there are some contradictions that can never be resolved and that recognizing this is not defeatist or pessimistic, but rather an accurate acknowledgement of necessary complexity. From educating students to confront problems in pastoral counseling, to encouraging them to create their own meanings and interpretations of scripture, the hardest thing is to help them confront the fact that ultimately the choice of action or meaning is theirs and theirs alone. We can model our own grappling with these issues and support them in their own struggles, but at some point we need to let go. How we might work through this dynamic is explored skillfully and pragmatically in chapters 1 through 4.

A fourth metatheme that surfaced was an awareness of how many of our own assumptions regarding the best conditions for learning, and which of our actions students would find most helpful, needed checking. Many times a rich vein of conversation was opened when one of us would ask simple questions: "How do you know your students think that?" "Why do you think they feel that way?" "What do they do that tells you they're interested or bored?" Then we would produce an array of actions and behaviors that, on closer inspection, could usually be interpreted in a number of different ways. The purpose of such conversations was not to determine who was right or wrong, but rather to get into the habit of focusing on *students*' actions and behaviors and their connection to learning, rather than those of teachers. One specific technique we repeatedly talked about was the Critical Incident Questionnaire (CIQ), the one page, anonymous feedback form completed by students once a week and reported to them by the instructor at the next class.[8] Some of the specific ways this technique was used, and some of the insights it gave rise to, are mentioned throughout this volume.

Finally, an issue our conversations bumped up against repeatedly was the way in which organizational and cultural forces in the wider society, in the culture of theological education, and in the specific practices of the seminary itself, constantly circumscribed what was possible. To take an example already mentioned, if team teaching was agreed to be a desirable teaching arrangement allowing faculty to model dialogic dispositions and practices in front of students (thereby improving subsequent student-to-student conversations) it did not take long to confront the bureaucratic, financial and psychological obstacles that made this practice difficult. Truly dialogic team teaching in which all faculty plan, conduct, and debrief classes together, is far more time consuming than solo taught courses in which only one person makes decisions. Logically, then, one should arrange for those who do team teaching to have a lighter teaching load. In practice, this is not often the case. In fact the converse is sometimes true—if you co-teach a course with a colleague the inference seems to be that you're only teaching half a course, since the labor of one teacher is now deemed to be split evenly between two. Given that it's highly unusual for someone team teaching a course to be granted a half course or whole course release to allow for the extra effort involved in teaming, this usually means that those committed to team teaching end up taking the extra time and energy out of their own personal life for no extra remuneration. In effect, their commitment to team teaching a course means they expend the labor involved in teaching the equivalent of one and a half or even two courses, but get credit for teaching only one. It is to the examination of these wider cultural inhibitors, and how they might be challenged, that we devoted the final chapter of this volume.

One last thing that bears mentioning about these conversations is that for much of the time they had no agenda. This does not mean that they were without focus, meandering, or perceived as irrelevant. In fact the opposite was true. What was talked about in the second hour was usually framed by the incidents and dilemmas disclosed in the first hour. The conversations thus exhibited an organic development that felt much more authentic (to me, at any rate) than conversations where we had been told beforehand what to focus on. It was not as if we had to look for topics—how to initiate students into a critical and informed skepticism without appearing to undermine their faith, how to introduce students to complex ideas in an accessible way without oversimplifying these to the point of absurdity, and how to bring quieter students into classroom discussions without humiliating them in front of their peers. Other topics available were how to judge when metaphor, humor, narrative, personal disclosure, and so on were being used appropriately and when they were shading into egomania or self-indulgence, what to do when students seemed to resist our best efforts to engage them, or when one individual or group of students tried to bludgeon the rest of the class into agreeing with a particular view. Topics emerged spontaneously and naturally out of the weekly sharing of best and worst moments of teaching. As the two years progressed we introduced more sessions in which we committed to read or think about a particular topic beforehand (such as how to assess student learning), and one person would be designated for leading the discussion that month. But my own recollection is that this did not happen until we were into our second year. Consequently, I would argue that these focused discussions on prearranged topics were framed by the first year's conversations.

Conversations that are useful, reassuring, provocative, enjoyable, stimulating, humorous, insightful, and animated—how many of those do you have in a lifetime? And how many, in particular, do you have within the walls of an educational institution? So many of our discussions with colleagues are about decisions regarding students' progress (or lack thereof) and how best to meet institutional requirements, accreditation standards, or the expectations of the wider culture (not to mention the expectations of trustees and alumni). To talk about the actual process of teaching, with no pressure to produce a report of findings, compendium of best practices, or inventory of future projects generated is, in my experience, a rarity—even in schools of education where talk about teaching might be expected to be most prominent. To have participated regularly in such conversations was an absolute joy, and it is no surprise to me that as word spread amongst the Luther Seminary community about how much fun we were having several people reported feeling envious of our group. Had I been on the outside looking in I would have been envious too. After all, there was much to be envious of!

Mary writes:

I'd add only a few things to Stephen's introduction. First, I think he seriously underestimates the ways in which his presence—self-deprecating, gentle, collaborative, and particularly nonanxious—helped to create a space in which we, as junior colleagues, were invited to bring our best selves to the conversation. I think he's right that the fact that none of us exercised positional authority over each other made it possible for us to enter into the discussion with a greater degree of honesty and empathy. But I also think that Stephen's degree of distance from the most painful internal debates we faced in our institution made it possible for us to set them some small distance apart from us, too, and thus wonder with genuine curiosity about our teaching and our students' learning. He modeled that kind of curiosity in his evocative questions, and he brought his extensive experience and scholarly resources to the task of interpreting the events to which we were attending.

Second, I think that we are living in a distinctive moment within theological education, and that moment provides a fresh opportunity for these kinds of conversations to occur. Of the seven of us who began the group, four had been involved previously in Wabash Center workshops, and all of us had been the beneficiary of Lexington Seminar work with our school.[9] Both of these institutions have created room for theological educators to "wonder aloud" about the work in which we are engaged and to honor that work with specific time and space devoted to pedagogical inquiry. A large part of the gift of our time with Stephen, at least for me, was the rest and refreshment that came with setting aside two hours once a month to gather in a small moment of sabbath and muse aloud about the educational heart of our work together. Our previous exposure to such conversations made it possible to imagine that simply being present to our experiences—without a task-oriented agenda beyond that kind of attentiveness—contained the potential for real transformation.

Third, when we sat down and began to talk about this book project, we began with memories of our time together in the group and the stories that first emerged there. With no clear sense of mission beyond inviting other colleagues to imagine the potential for this kind of engagement, it has been striking to me to discover certain recurrent themes. From a theological perspective, I'd note that the Spirit was clearly breathing among us. As Stephen notes in chapter 1, there is a kind of formation that lives in the very fiber of our classroom experiences. I think all of us found that we could begin to see that formation as we began to try to "see through our students' eyes." Stephen's gentle, but persistent, efforts to invite us to do so led directly to sustained curiosity about how to shape environments that encouraged trust. All of our chapters follow that thread, some more explicitly than others. Given the larger world we inhabit, one in which trust is not in deep supply, I think it's crucial to recognize that developing trust and trustworthy spaces—at least in this moment, and in this seminary—is at the heart of theological education in the twenty-first century. Such a theme is echoed in a number of other recent books in theological contexts, and of course is at the heart of a faith that confesses an incarnate God. Given this commitment to an incarnational and deeply relational God, it is only natural that building such trust requires modeling the very postures, emotions, and ideas we seek to evoke and invite from our students. Planted deep within us are the truths we seek to express, and we can only do so by trusting that God will accompany us in our searches. It is my hope that the following reflections will invite you to listen deeply to your own experiences within theological education.

NOTES

1. J. Habermas, *Between Facts and Norms: Contributions to a Discourse Theory of Democracy* (Cambridge, MA: MIT Press, 1996).
2. J. Habermas, *Autonomy and Solidarity: Interviews with Jurgen Habermas* (London: Verso, 1992) (revised edition), 260.

3. See, for example, D. Bridges, *Education, Democracy, and Discussion* (Lanham, MD: University Press of America, 1988); S. Brookfield and S. Preskill, *Discussion as a Way of Teaching: Tools and Techniques for Democratic Classrooms* (San Francisco: Jossey-Bass, 2005); N. Burbules, *Dialogue in Teaching: Theory and Practice* (New York: Teachers College Press, 1993); C. Christensen, D. Garvin, and A. Sweet (eds.), *Education for Judgment: The Artistry of Discussion Leadership* (Boston: Harvard Business School Press, 1991); and S. Haroutunian-Gordon, *Turning the Soul: Teaching through Conversation in the High School* (Chicago: University of Chicago Press, 1991).
4. P. Palmer, *To Know as We are Known* (San Francisco: HarperCollins, 1993).
5. Ibid., 74.
6. S. Brookfield, *Becoming a Critically Reflective Teacher* (San Francisco: Jossey-Bass, 1995).
7. Ibid., 155 ff.
8. The CIQ process is first described in S. Brookfield's *Becoming a Critically Reflective Educator*, but introduced at length in chapter 1 of this volume.
9. The *Wabash Center on Teaching and Learning in Theology and Religion* and the *Lexington Seminar: Theological Teaching for the Church's Ministries* are both Lilly Endowment initiatives in support of teaching and learning in higher education and theological contexts. More information can be found online at: http://www.wabashcenter.wabash.edu/home/default.aspx and at: http://www.lexingtonseminar.org/.

CONTRIBUTORS

Stephen D. Brookfield

Since beginning his teaching career in 1970 Stephen has worked in England, Canada, Australia, and the United States, teaching in a variety of college settings. He has written and edited nine books on adult learning, teaching, and critical thinking, four of which have won the World Award for Literature in Adult Education (in 1986, 1989, 1996 and 2005). His work has been translated into German, Finnish, and Chinese. He has been awarded two honorary doctor of letters degrees from the University System of New Hampshire (1991) and Concordia University (2003) for his contributions to understanding adult learning and shaping adult education. During 2002 he was Visiting Professor at Harvard University. After ten years as a Professor of Higher and Adult Education at Columbia University in New York, he now holds the title of Distinguished University Professor at the University of St.Thomas in Minneapolis, Minnesota.

Mary E. Hess

Mary E. Hess joined the Luther Seminary faculty in 2000. Currently she serves as associate professor of educational leadership. Her BA is in American Studies from Yale, she has an MTS from Harvard Divinity School, and her PhD is in Religion and Education from Boston College. She is the author of *Engaging Technology in Theological Education*, the coeditor of *Belief in Media: Cultural Perspectives on Christianity and Media,* and a frequent contributor to the journal *Religious Education.* She directs the Open Source Religious Resources project, which is the developer of the www.feautor.org Web site, and consults regularly with both the Wabash Center for Teaching and Learning in Theology and Religion, and the Lexington Seminar: Theological Teaching for the Church's Ministries.

Rolf Jacobsen

Rolf Jacobson, associate professor of Old Testament, joined the Luther Seminary faculty in July 2003. Prior to joining the seminary, he taught at Augsburg College, Minneapolis. After graduating from Luther Seminary in 1991, Jacobson served for five years as associate pastor of Como Park Lutheran Church in St. Paul before continuing his education at Princeton Theological Seminary. Jacobson's publications center on the psalms, prophets, biblical theology, and the scholarship of teaching and learning in theological education.

David J. Lose

David J. Lose has served as a member of the biblical preaching faculty at Luther Seminary since July of 2000. In May 2005, he received the Marbury E. Anderson Chair in Biblical Preaching, and in July of that same year he was named academic dean. Between 1993–2000, Lose served as pastor at several Lutheran congregations in New Jersey. He received his PhD in homiletics from Princeton Theological Seminary, where he also served as a teaching fellow and visiting lecturer. Lose is the author of *Confessing Jesus Christ* (Eerdmans, 2003), as well as numerous articles on preaching, biblical interpretation, and theology.

Frieder Ludwig

Before joining the Luther Seminary faculty as associate professor of mission and world Christianity in 2002, Frieder Ludwig served as substitute chair of the church history department at the Ludwig Maximilian's University of Munich, Germany. Ludwig studied theology and history at Heidelberg University and the University of Birmingham and taught at the Universities of Bayreuth, Munich, Leipzig, and Jos (Nigeria). He has extensively researched church and mission in Tanzania, Nigeria, and India. He has also published and edited several books—three of them in English: *Church and State in Tanzania* (Leiden, 1999); *European Traditions in the Study of Religion in Africa* (edited together with Afe Adogame, Wiesbaden, 2004); and *History of Christianity in Asia, Africa and Latin America 1450–1990* (edited together with Klaus Koschorke and Mariano Delgado, Grand Rapids, 2007).

Alvin Luedke

Alvin Luedke joined the Luther Seminary faculty in July 2001. He earned a master of divinity degree from Trinity Lutheran Seminary, Columbus, Ohio, in 1982. In 2002 he completed his PhD in sociology with specialties in rural sociology and demography/human ecology from Texas A & M. He served as a pastor (1982–1988, 1993–1995) at two parishes and as assistant to the pastor (1988–1992) in a third parish, all in Texas, and as pastor at one parish in Minnesota (2001–2003). Luedke has written or cowritten numerous sociological studies. He coauthored the book *Demographics: A Guide to Methods and Data Sources for Media, Business, and Government* (2006). His recent articles include "Farm Financial Crisis—Challenges for Ministry among Small town and Rural Communities, Congregations, and Individuals" (*Journal of Lutheran Ethics*, 2003) and "Dynamic Population Change in Size and Diversity" (*Texas Almanac*, 2002–2003).

Janet Ramsey

Janet Ramsey joined the Luther Seminary faculty in 2002 as associate professor of congregational care leadership. Previously, she served churches in southwestern Virginia and was in private practice as a licensed marriage and family therapist. A diplomate in the American Association of Pastoral Counselors, Ramsey received her doctorate in adult development and aging from the Virginia Polytechnic Institute and State University in Blacksburg, Virginia. She is first author of *Spiritual Resiliency in Older Women: Models of Strength for Challenges through the Life Span* (Sage, 1999) and has written numerous journal articles and book chapters on aging, pastoral care, and forgiveness.

Matthew L. Skinner

Matthew L. Skinner is associate professor of New Testament at Luther Seminary. He is author of *Locating Paul: Places of Custody as Narrative Settings in Acts 21–28* (Society of Biblical Literature, 2003) and a contributor to the preaching commentary *New Proclamation, Year B, 2006: Easter through Pentecost* (Fortress Press, 2005). During 2006 and 2007 he codirected a consultation titled "Teaching Biblical Exegesis in Theological Schools," funded by grant from the Wabash Center for Teaching and Learning in Theology in Religion. He serves on editorial committees for the journals *Religious Studies Review* and *Word & World* and for the Web site *WorkingPreacher.org*.

CHAPTER 1

How Can We Teach Authentically? Reflective Practice in the Dialogical Classroom

Stephen D. Brookfield and Mary E. Hess

The last few years have seen something of a renaissance in the study of spirituality within academe. There have been broad analyses of the increase in religious pluralism on campus,[1] considerations of the implications of spirituality for student services practice,[2] and explorations of the meaning of spirituality in adult[3] and higher education.[4] As regards the practice of teaching, books by Palmer,[5] Apps,[6] and Cranton[7] have struck a chord with those who regard teaching as sacred work focused on the nourishment of the spirit as much as on the pursuit of more familiar objectives such as developing critical thinking. The two of us have been provoked and challenged by these works and have drawn on them as we seek to understand what it means to teach theologically. One of us works at a Lutheran seminary (Mary Hess), the other at a Diocesan Catholic university (Stephen Brookfield), but both of us believe that teaching theologically is something that can happen in a wide range of settings, some of which appear highly secular. In this chapter, we explore what it means to teach theologically in overtly religious higher education institutions, primarily seminaries.

What is the essence of teaching in theological contexts? Is it a matter of identifying promising practices that work well in contexts such as an undergraduate biology or mathematics class and then simply transplanting these practices to seminary environments? Or is there something inherently different about religion-based teaching? If the former is the case, then all we need to do is study processes such as the best size for small group discussion (five) or the optimal amount of time that lecturers should spend in uninterrupted talk (about 12 minutes), and then integrate these into our teaching of biblical texts or pastoral leadership. If the latter is true then we need to specify what about theological contexts is unique.

Both of the answers given above are correct. On the one hand, educators in theological contexts can benefit enormously from studying the general literature on postsecondary teaching and learning since this contains many insights and practices that can be adapted within seminaries, schools of divinity, and departments of theology. Chapters 9, 11, and 12 in this book, for instance, deal with the dynamics of evaluating student learning and using technology to enhance teaching and learning. All of these chapters explore practices and issues recognizable to many who do not see themselves as theological or religious educators. To take just one example, the considerable literature on classroom research and assessment describes examples such as the one-minute paper or the muddiest point that theological educators can use to gain an accurate sense of how their students are experiencing learning.[8] On the other hand, theological education has as central foci questions of spiritual identity, faith development, and pastoral formation. Theological teachers view their stewardship of learning as something of a sacred trust, a process distinguished by the movement of the Holy Spirit within all those involved. Such concerns are unique to theological education in a way that would not be paralleled in an undergraduate major in sociology or a doctoral program in biochemistry.

Two recent volumes on theological education illustrate the ways that theological education is like and unlike the rest of higher education. Warford writes of how "new student constituencies, multiple institutional commitments, and severe fiscal pressures, all occurring within a world of continuing change, present theological seminaries with challenges demanding meaningful response."[9] One could substitute schools of law, community colleges, state universities, and any number of other institutional descriptors for the term "theological seminaries" in

Warford's observation without changing its accuracy. Similarly, Brady Williams speaks of the "diverse learning styles, new ethnic and religious differences, new student expectations and market demands, age variations and diverse theological commitments" that make contemporary seminary classrooms "exciting and sometimes conflicted places."[10] Remove the word "theological" from this sentence and it could be uttered by instructors in almost any higher education setting.

So what makes theological education distinct? Perhaps the most common response to this question focuses on the concept of formation, the idea that theological teaching has at its center the development of a certain kind of personal quality, faith commitment, or spiritual sensibility. Winkelmes is typical in her contention that "seminary classrooms are perhaps the single most important and most feasible place for formation to occur" and that "if the work of formation does not happen in classrooms, then the special task and special value of seminaries is in jeopardy."[11] In the introduction to a Carnegie Foundation study of seminary classrooms and the pastoral imagination these foster, Sullivan argues that "the knowledge at the basis of clergy practice—religious knowledge—is directly concerned with how to *be* in the world, for religious knowledge is concerned with the significance of life in the most profound sense."[12] He holds that formation is at the center of seminary pedagogy and that in the process of formation "the student becomes a certain kind of thinking, feeling, and acting being."[13] Although the Carnegie study identifies four signature pedagogies of theological education (pedagogies of interpretation, formation, contextualization, and performance) it is the pedagogy of formation that is not found in other areas or disciplines. Interpretation, contextualization, and performance are part of disciplines as diverse as English literature, psychology, or social work, but few professors in these disciplines would argue that the task of formation is essential to their work. Professional educators would no doubt claim to foster a particular kind of professional identity but they would probably not see "engaging the mystery of human existence" as one of their tasks.[14]

Of course the concept of formation is problematic. Although widely employed by theological educators, those working in seminaries share no single interpretation of this idea. Indeed, the Carnegie Foundation study notes, "almost no one—even in Catholic communities who use this terminology most frequently—is truly satisfied with formation language."[15] Notwithstanding this level of dissatisfaction, we believe the concept is broad and malleable enough to capture two distinct emphases in theological teaching. First, formation focuses on the awakening and deepening of spiritual awareness. It is concerned with helping students explore processes of divine contemplation and faith development, often aided by teachers' own modeling and disclosure of their engagement in these processes. Second, formation focuses on the development of human qualities of empathy, compassion, and love deemed central to pastoral work. This second emphasis is not to be confused with learning particular skills of counseling, which is a crucial but separate theological endeavor. It is more a matter of spirit, of understanding and appreciating the essential humanity and capacity for love that manifests itself in those of different faiths, races, cultures, and ideologies.

What teaching approaches are central to these formative tasks? We contend that three pedagogic emphases are discernible in theological teaching: a commitment to continuously researching the pedagogic contexts in which we work and to responding publicly to what we learn from this research, a deliberate attempt to treat learners as adults with the attitude of respectful attention to students' experiences this implies, and modeling a public, critically reflective engagement in spiritually grounded learning. Each of these three processes in different ways allows teachers to attend to the formation of themselves and their students. Together they represent a pedagogic holism that treats emotional and mystical dimensions of learning as being of equal importance to its cognitive aspects.

I. RESEARCHING OUR PEDAGOGY

A commitment to assisting students' formation requires us to understand how those students experience the emotional and cognitive rhythms of learning and how they interpret our actions as teachers. Having some insight into what students are thinking and feeling in our classes is the foundational, first-order knowledge we need to do good work. Without this knowledge the choices we make as teachers risk being haphazard, closer to guesswork than to informed judgments. We may exhibit an admirable command of biblical texts or pastoral practices and possess a dazzling variety of pedagogic skills, but without knowing what's going on in our students' minds our knowledge may be presented and our skill exercised in a vacuum of misunderstanding. Theologically grounded teachers realize that most of their procedural decisions (what content to teach next, what examples to use to illustrate a complex idea, how to approach exegesis, who to call on in discussion, and so on) should be guided by an awareness of how students experience the classroom.

Getting inside students' minds is tricky. First, we cannot just ask students how things are going and expect honest responses, at least not if students are asked to speak these responses publicly or put their name to written evaluations. The power we have over students will ensure that any identifiable responses we get from them will be filtered through students' desire not to offend us and thereby arouse our ire. Students are understandably reluctant to be too honest with us. They may have learned that giving honest commentary on a teacher's actions can backfire. Teachers who say they welcome criticism of their decisions vary widely in how they respond when it is expressed. Consequently, students have an understandable reluctance to describe how they see the teacher's actions affecting adversely what happens in class. Even under the cloak of anonymity it feels risky to point out oppressive aspects of a teacher's practice. Rarely will students publicly raise questions about how teachers have unwittingly stifled free discussion, broken promises, or treated certain kinds of students with more deference than others. Given the egomania and power wielded by some academics, student paranoia is sometimes justified.

A cardinal principle of seeing ourselves through students' eyes is that of ensuring the anonymity of students' responses to any questions we ask regarding their classroom experiences.

When students have decided that you have earned their trust they may choose to speak out publicly about negative aspects of your actions. But early on in your relationship with a class you will only get honest criticism if students' anonymity is guaranteed. After students have seen you, week in, week out, inviting anonymous commentary on your actions and then discussing publicly how this underscores or challenges some of your assumptions, they start to believe that you mean what you say about the value of critical reflection. But saying you welcome critical commentary from students and having them believe you are two quite distinct events; between them lies a period of time during which you model consistently a public, critical scrutiny of your actions. The elusive and contradictory nature of trust and trustworthiness are explored in much greater depth in chapters 2, 5, 6, and 7 of this volume, though aspects of what these comprise are referred to throughout this volume.

A key element in theological teaching is making public students' anonymous comments and then responding to them so students can judge for themselves how seriously you take their comments. We would go so far as to argue that this is a central element of all effective teaching, irrespective of discipline or level. One approach we have used to engage in this process is the classroom Critical Incident Questionnaire (CIQ). Rolf Jacobson in chapter 5 also provides some detailed examples of how he uses this instrument. The CIQ is a single-page form that is handed out to students once a week at the end of the week's last class. It comprises five questions, each of which asks students to write down some details about events or actions that happened in the class that week. Its purpose is not to ask students what they liked or didn't like about the class, though that information inevitably emerges. Instead it gets them to focus on specific events and actions that are engaging, distancing, confusing, or helpful. Having this concrete information about particular events and actions is more useful than reading general statements of preferences.

The form takes about five minutes to complete and students are told *not* to put their names on it. If nothing comes to mind as a response to a particular question, they are told to leave the space blank. They are also told that at the next class meeting we will share the group's responses with them.

The questions are

> At what moment in class this week did you feel most engaged with what was happening?
>
> At what moment in class this week were you most distanced from what was happening?
>
> What action that anyone (teacher or student) took this week did you find most affirming or helpful?
>
> What action that anyone took this week did you find most puzzling or confusing?
>
> What about the class this week surprised you the most? (This could be about your own reactions to what went on, something that someone did, or anything else that occurs.)

Students are given the last five minutes of the last class of the week to complete this form. As they leave the room we ask them to leave the form on a chair or table by the door, facedown. After collecting the CIQ responses we read them looking for common themes. For a class size of 30–35 students this usually takes about 20 minutes. We look for comments that indicate problems or confusions, particularly if they are caused by our actions. Anything contentious is highlighted, as is anything that needs further clarification. Major differences in students' perceptions of the same activity are recorded as well as single comments that strike us as particularly profound or intriguing. These themes become the basis for the questions and issues we address publicly the next time we meet the class.

At the start of the first class of the next week we spend three to five minutes reporting to students a summary of the chief themes that emerged in their responses. If we have time we will type a one-page summary and leave copies of this on students' chairs for them to read as they come in. Most times we give a verbal report. If students have made comments that have caused us to change how we teach, we acknowledge this and explain why the change seems worth making. We try also to clarify any actions, ideas, requirements, or exercises that seem to be causing confusion. Criticisms of our actions are reported and discussed. If contentious issues have emerged we talk about how these can be negotiated so that everyone feels heard and respected. Quite often students write down comments expressing their dislike of something we insist they do. When this happens we know that we must take some time to reemphasize why we believe the activity is important and to make the best case we can about how it contributes to students' long-term interests. Even if we have spoken this case before, and written it in the syllabus, the critical incident responses alert us to the need to make our rationale explicit once again.

Using the CIQ doesn't mean that we constantly change everything we're doing because students tell us they don't like it. We both have nonnegotiable elements to our agendas that define who we are and what we stand for. To throw them away as a result of students' opinions would undercut our identities as teachers. For example, we won't give up our intention to get students to think critically, even if they all tell us that they want us to stop doing this. We will be as flexible as we can in negotiating how this agenda is realized, but we won't abandon it. We'll ask students to suggest different ways they might show us that they're thinking critically. We'll also vary the pace at which we introduce certain activities and exercises to take account of students' hostility, inexperience, or unfamiliarity with this process. But for us to abandon an activity that defines who we are as teachers would mean that we ceased to have the right to call ourselves teachers. So if students use their CIQ responses to express a strong opinion that challenges what you're trying to do, or how you're trying to do it, you owe it to them to acknowledge this criticism. But you don't owe it to them to abandon entirely your rationale for teaching. You need to make your own position known, justify it, and negotiate alternative ways of realizing your aims.

II. TREATING STUDENTS RESPECTFULLY

Theological teaching is more a matter of tone than it is of a commitment to certain approaches. For us, all pedagogic methods, techniques, and activities are potentially useful in the theological classroom—what makes them theological is the way they are used. The decision as to what is an appropriate use of any particular method is grounded in the kind of classroom research described in the previous section. Only if we know something of the diverse and conflicting emotional and cognitive rhythms present in a classroom can we judge which teaching approaches address these most productively. We contend that underlying good theological teaching is an attitude of respect for students' experiences that means we can never dismiss these as irrelevant. In a real sense each of us is the sum total of our experiences; not to recognize the importance of these experiences is not to recognize a person's value. Addressing this dynamic becomes particularly important when we broach with students' ideas and interpretations that seem to challenge faith, a process explored in chapters 2, 4, 5, 6, and 7. A respectful, and hence a theological, approach to teaching acknowledges the importance of experience and tries to place the analysis of such experience at the center of practice. In analyzing texts, for example, one of the most important questions we encourage students to ask is how the text exemplifies or contradicts their experiences, and the extent to which experiences that are pertinent to them are omitted from a text. In a sense, their own experiences of revelation and commitment become the text they study.

This is not to say that we view all experiences as being of equal value nor that we think it appropriate to celebrate uncritically all the experiences students bring to their studies. There is no basis for assuming that students' experiences always constitute a rich resource for learning that educators can build on as they construct curricula, develop teaching approaches, and arrange evaluative formats. In fact the converse is often the case. Students' past experiences can be distorted, self-fulfilling, unexamined, and constraining. Simply having experiences does not mean that they are reflected on, understood, or analyzed critically. Neither are experiences inherently enriching. Experience can be construed in a way that confirms habits of bigotry, stereotyping, and disregard for significant but inconvenient information. It can also be narrowing and constraining, causing us to evolve and transmit ideologies that skew irrevocably how we interpret the world. Sometimes learners' experiences convince them that there is only one way to view the world, that their perspective on things is the only legitimate one, and that anyone who disagrees with them is by definition idiotic, immoral, or dangerous. But we cannot teach theologically if we ignore learners' experiences, for in ignoring them we ignore who our students are.

How respect is recognized is, of course, differentially defined and perceived, a theme explored by Frieder Ludwig and others in chapter 8. What is a respectful acknowledgment of experience for one student can be experienced as patronizing by another. Faculty also have different notions of what constitutes respectful conduct. In team teaching is it disrespectful to interrupt a colleague whom you know unwittingly to be conveying false information or understandings, or is it disrespectful to allow them to dig themselves deeper into the hole of their own misconceptions? As Janet Ramsey explains in chapter 7, team teaching is one context in which students learn what respectful critique and conversation does, or does not, look like. Racially and culturally based notions of respect also come into play and complicate the picture considerably. For students from tribal or Asian cultures where reverence is accorded to teachers who are seen as both authoritative and wise, being respectful may mean writing down everything the teacher says and diligently following all the instructions she gives. A White European or Euro-American teacher may be completely unaware of how he represents colonial traditions in the eyes of African, Caribbean, or Asian students. For such a teacher to urge his students to critique the teacher's own ideas is to place those students in an exquisitely painful double bind. On the one hand the student wishes to earn the teacher's approval by following his instructions to the letter—in this case the instruction to find flaws, errors, omissions, and inconsistencies in the teacher's reasoning. On the other hand, engaging in this behavior feels inherently disrespectful, if not downright dangerous, and therefore must be avoided at all costs.

Practicing and modeling respect is essential in theological learning environments; yet, as Lawrence Lightfoot observes, respect is a term so widely employed that it has degenerated into a cliché.[16] What does it mean to show or practice respect in ways that deepen the concept and that do justice to its significance and magnitude? The root meaning of the word *respect* is "to regard," "to look at again," "to see discerningly." When we show respect for others, we work diligently at seeing them clearly for who they are, at trying to understand as much as we can the ways they have experienced the world, and the development of their own spirituality. In this sense, teaching respectfully has clear connections to Habermas's idea of communicative action.[17] Habermas says such action happens when people's attempts to communicate "are coordinated not through egocentric calculations of success but through acts of reaching understanding."[18] When we act communicatively we try to step out of our normal frames of reference to see the world as someone else sees it. We make this effort because we live in a world full of different cultures, agendas, and ideologies. In a sense living with others continually forces perspective-taking upon us. Life presents situations to us in which we need to understand others' desires and reach compromises with them. Sometimes we also need to live with the realization that compromise is impossible. The communicative action such compromises and containments call for requires a good faith effort to try and understand another's point of view. Interfaith dialogue and ecumenical teaching in particular call for the kind of communicative action envisaged by Habermas as the chief learning project of adulthood, and David Lose in chapter 2 explores this in more detail.

Of course one of the hardest contradictions to resolve in theological teaching is to know when it is legitimate and respectful to force students to engage with ideas and practices they would rather avoid but that we know are necessary for them to confront. How can we practice respectfully what Baptiste calls an ethically justified pedagogy of coercion?[19] After all, the ways we come to reinterpret old experiences and create new meanings from them often depend on being forced to review them through radically new lenses—lenses, moreover, that we either chose to ignore or were previously unknown to us. One can argue that a respectful treatment of students as people with potential for growth and development involves presenting them with activities and materials that will animate this progress even when they are reluctant to engage them.

Formation implies a constant movement forward and the catalysts producing such movement are often perceived as uncomfortable and unsettling by the learners concerned. This is a perennial dilemma faced by teachers who regard the encouragement of critical thinking as an important educational project. It often takes what Mezirow calls a disorienting dilemma—a discrepancy, anomaly, or disjunction between how one thinks the world should work and how it is actually working—to prompt the analysis of assumptions one has taken for granted as explaining the world adequately.[20] Presenting such discomforting dilemmas to students is therefore a justifiable educational intervention and one that often needs to be followed up by an insistence that students consider how the resolution of these dilemmas opens up new perspectives on familiar situations. The difficulties of doing this are explored, from different viewpoints, in all the chapters in this book.

III. MODELING A PUBLIC ENGAGEMENT IN LEARNING

Students sometimes assume that we are fully formed spiritual beings with an unbreakable faith, a fully realized vocational calling, and an ability to strike a healthy balance between professional, familial, and spiritual aspects of our lives. One of the most important teaching services we can provide for them—and one of the processes explored in most of the chapters in the present volume—is demonstrating the ways we are in constant formation, particularly how we are continually forced to question and rethink beliefs and actions with which we have grown comfortable. We maintain that if we are to ask students to contemplate biblical interpretations or pastoral practices that challenge their taken-for-granted notions of ministry, then we need to be able to show them how we also grapple with ideas and activities that cause us to question who we are and how we work. Our contention is that before asking students to engage in any learning process that involves risk, discomfort, or challenge (things that always accompany thinking critically about faith, for example) we need to model in front of them our own engagement with similar learning tasks. Our responsibility is to show them that we regard opening ourselves up to different perspectives and new ideas to be part of what it means to be a questing, spiritual being. Consequently, if we are trying to encourage students to recognize and challenge some of their most cherished assumptions we must first find a way to show them how we are also laying bare our own assumptions for critical analysis.

One of the things students tell us they appreciate the most in our teaching is when we speak aloud the internal decision-making processes that inform our choices and actions in the classroom. Students say that it inspires confidence when they see that we clearly have a plan, a set of reasons, for doing what we do. Explaining why you are introducing a particular classroom activity, changing learning modalities, choosing certain readings, demonstrating skills in a particular way, putting students in certain groups, or moving into a mini-lecture—these conversations with yourself that happen in front of students demonstrate to them that you are a thoughtful teacher. Knowing that they are in the hands of such a teacher builds students' confidence. No one likes to think that the person leading them in an activity is making it up as she goes along with no forethought, reasoning, or previous experience. This is particularly the case when the teacher is asking students to engage in a risky learning activity (as would be the case with learning critical thinking or reappraising one's processes of faith development) and in different ways all the chapters in this book explore this dynamic.

Thus an important element in building credibility in the

eyes of students is for teachers to make explicit the implicit assumptions about teaching and learning that guide their actions. A teacher should try to create a window into her head so students can see the reasoning behind her decisions. When students can see our thought processes they are often reassured that our decisions are not mindless but grounded in previous experience and researched assumptions. We would venture that it is almost impossible to be too transparent in this regard, to talk out loud too much. In hundreds of CIQs collected over the years students' appreciation of this behavior is an amazingly consistent theme. Comments are made concerning how learners really appreciate knowing why the teacher is doing what she is doing. They say that not only does this help them learn what is being taught, but that it also gives them the sense that they are in the hands of a trusted guide. To know why doctors wish us to take particular medications is an important element in our trusting that the doctor has our best interests at heart and that she knows what she is doing. To know the reasons why an auto-mechanic is suggesting that a certain part needs to be replaced is crucial to our trusting that we are not being conned. The same holds true for teachers. If students are to have confidence in our abilities they need to know, and trust, that there is a rationale behind our actions and choices.

Modeling a public engagement in learning must be done in an authentic way. The challenges we face and the risks we embrace must be real ones involving genuine struggle and discomfort on our part. In a theological context that stresses formation as an important dimension of learning, it is especially important that teachers be perceived as authentic, as engaged in what Cranton describes as "the expression of one's genuine Self in the community and society."[21] Palmer is typical of theologically grounded teachers when he declares "teaching holds a mirror to my soul" so that "the entanglements I experience in the classroom are often no more or less than the convolutions of my inner life."[22] In an authentic pedagogy this mirror is one that students as well as the teacher can peer into so that the connections between the teacher's inner ruminations and her external actions are made public knowledge. Students recognize teachers as authentic when those teachers are perceived to be allies in learning who are seen as trustworthy, open, and honest in their dealings with students. Colloquially students often say that such teachers "walk the talk," "practice what they preach," have no "hidden agendas" and that with such teachers "what you see is what you get."

Of paramount importance to students when judging a teacher's authenticity is the perceived congruence between words and actions, between what a teacher says she will do and what she actually does. Nothing destroys students' trust in teachers more quickly than seeing teachers espouse one set of commitments—for example, to democracy, active, participatory learning, critical thinking, or responsiveness to students' concerns—and then behave in ways that contradict these. Students usually come to know pretty quickly when they are being manipulated.

Students commonly mention how breaking espoused commitments such as the four mentioned above indicate that the teacher is acting in bad faith. Spuriously democratic teachers tell students that the curriculum, methods, and evaluative criteria are up for genuine negotiation and in large measure are in students' hands. As the course proceeds, however, it becomes clear that the supposedly democratically negotiated curricula to be studied, methods to be used, and evaluative criteria to be applied just happen to match the teacher's own preferences. Falsely participatory teachers tell students that they don't want to lecture too much, that they value students' contributions, and that they will use a mixture of teaching approaches (role plays, case studies, simulations, small group discussions, peer-learning triads) that require students' active participation. They then proceed to lecture most of the time, each week protesting that this is a temporary necessity because the class is falling behind. They also disallow time for questions or avoid answering those questions that are raised, as well as prematurely closing case studies or small group discussions because of pressures of time.

Teachers who are counterfeit critical thinkers say they welcome a questioning of all viewpoints and assertions, but then bristle when critique is applied to the teacher's own ideas. Such teachers also make it clear that certain viewpoints (often those the teacher dislikes) are out of bounds. Practicing phony responsiveness happens when teachers collect CIQs and then either edit out inconveniently critical comments or refuse to negotiate around any concerns students raise. In all these instances students quickly conclude that your word is worthless, that any promise you make cannot be taken seriously, and that you are not to be trusted. They may still think they can learn something from you, but it will not happen in a congenial environment.

The problem is that we may not realize how incongruent our words and actions appear to students. We may genuinely believe we are living out commitments we made earlier in the course and, in the absence of vocal student criticisms, be completely unaware of how much we're shooting ourselves in the foot. But, realistically speaking, few students will have the nerve to call you out on your lack of authenticity. Mostly they'll decide it's simpler not to risk offending you and safer to keep their head down and not make a fuss. So we may be entirely unaware of the impression we're creating.

How can teachers avoid unwittingly falling foul of the "do as I say not as I do" trap? Two responses suggest themselves. The first is to use the CIQ data to check for perceived inconsistencies in your words and actions. Our experience is that these are mentioned widely as soon as they are perceived to occur. We have sometimes made off-the-cuff statements that were expressions of mild preference that were then taken by students as ironclad declarations of classroom policy. As soon as we are seen to be contradicting these promises, students bring this to our attention using a route in which their anonymity is guaranteed—the CIQ. We can then address this apparent inconsistency in class. The second response is to be explicit about your commitments and convictions in the course syllabus, and find some way of assessing once or twice a semester how consistently you are living these out. For example, every now and again one of the muddiest point papers, or one-minute papers, might be devoted to this theme.

Modeling our own engagement in learning conveys to students that we are spiritual beings with lives and identities outside the classroom. Students recognize this when we move out from behind our formal identities and role descriptions to allow aspects of ourselves to be revealed in the classroom. Instead of being thought of as relatively faceless institutional functionaries or fully formed omniscient authorities, teachers are now seen as individuals moved by a quest for faith and a struggle with doubt. This is not to say that teachers should indiscriminately turn their classrooms into zones of personal confession in which their own spiritual crises are discussed in highly revealing ways. Authentic personhood is more appropriately evident in theological contexts when teachers use autobiographical examples to illustrate concepts and theories they are trying to explain, when they talk about ways they apply specific skills and insights taught in the classroom to their work outside, and when they share stories of how they dealt with the same fears and struggles that their students are currently facing as they struggle with new learning.

NOTES

1. V. M. Miller and M. M. Ryan, eds., *Transforming Campus Life: Reflections on Spirituality and Religious Pluralism* (New York: Lang, 2001).
2. M. A. Jablonski, ed., *The Implications of Student Spirituality for Student Affairs Practices* (San Francisco: Jossey-Bass, 2001).
3. L. English and M. Gillen, *Addressing the Spiritual Dimensions of Adult Learning* (San Francisco: Jossey-Bass, 2000); and E. J. Tisdell, *Exploring Spirituality and Culture in Adult and Higher Education* (San Francisco: Jossey-Bass, 2003).
4. S. L. Hoppe and B. W. Speck, eds., *Spirituality in Higher Education* (San Francisco: Jossey-Bass, 2005).
5. P. Palmer, *The Courage to Teach: Exploring the Inner Dimensions of a Teacher's Life* (San Francisco: Jossey-Bass, 1998).
6. J. Apps, *Teaching From the Heart* (Malabar, FL: Krieger, 1996).
7. P. Cranton, *Becoming an Authentic Teacher in Higher Education* (Malabar, FL: Krieger, 2001).
8. T. A. Angelo, ed. *Classroom Assessment and Research: An Up-*

date on Uses, Approaches, and Research Findings. New Directions for Teaching and Learning, no. 75. (San Francisco: Jossey-Bass, 1998). S. M. Brookhart, *The Art and Science of Classroom Assessment: The Missing Part of Pedagogy.* ASHE-ERIC Higher Education Report Series, Vol. 27, No. 1. (San Francisco: Jossey-Bass, 2000). L. W. Anderson, *Classroom Assessment: Enhancing the Quality of Teacher Decision Making* (Mahwah, NJ: Earlbaum, 2002). S. M. Butler and N. D. McMunn, *A Teacher's Guide to Classroom Assessment* (San Francisco: Jossey-Bass, 2006).

9. M. L. Warford, "Introduction." In M. L. Warford, ed., *Practical Wisdom: On Theological Teaching and Learning* (New York: Lang, 2004), 1.
10. R. Brady Williams, "The Vocation of Teaching: Beyond the Conspiracy of Mediocrity." In, M. L. Warford, ed., *Practical Wisdom: On Theological Teaching and Learning* (New York: Lang, 2004), 21.
11. M. Winkelmes, "Formative Learning in the Classroom." In, M. L. Warford, ed., *Practical Wisdom: On Theological Teaching and Learning* (New York: Lang, 2004), 163.
12. W. M. Sullivan, "Introduction." In C. R. Foster, L. E. Dahill, L. A. Golemon, and B. Wang Tolentino, *Educating Clergy: Teaching Practices and Pastoral Imagination* (San Francisco: Jossey-Bass, 2006), 6.
13. Ibid., 10.
14. Ibid., 100.
15. Ibid., 125.
16. Sara Lawrence Lightfoot, *Respect: An Exploration* (New York: Perseus Books Group, 2000).
17. J. Habermas, *The Theory of Communicative Action, Volume One, Reason and the Rationalization of Society* (Boston: Beacon Press, 1984). And J. Habermas, *The Theory of Communicative Action: Volume Two, Lifeworld and System—A Critique of Functionalist Reason* (Boston: Beacon Press, 1987).
18. Habermas, *Communicative Action*, 286.
19. I. Baptiste, "Beyond Reason and Personal Integrity: Toward a Pedagogy of Coercive Restraint," *Canadian Journal for the Study of Adult Education*, (2000): 14/1, 27–50.
20. Jack Mezirow, *Transformative Dimensions of Adult Learning* (San Francisco: Jossey-Bass, 1991).
21. Cranton, *Authentic Teacher*, vii.
22. Palmer, *Courage to Teach*, 2.

CHAPTER 2

"How Do We Make Space for Students to Seek Truth?" Teaching with Conviction

David J. Lose

The scene is familiar: You've just covered a complicated and contested issue, artfully presenting the contrasting sides with an even-handedness that even *Consumer Reports* would admire. Having set the stage for a rousing discussion, you settle back, confident that you haven't betrayed your hand in the least, the barest smile of satisfaction playing across your face. Until suddenly a student asks where you stand on the matter, placing you in an unavoidable quandary: Do you demur for the sake of the neutral space you have so carefully constructed and encourage the students to take responsibility for their own conclusions? Do you hedge, restating the significant pros and cons of one or more of the positions to model critical engagement yet refuse to divulge your stance? Or do you comply, favoring candor over neutrality and hoping that students will not be deterred from offering their own opinions out of an undue deference to your own?

This scene is, of course, not only familiar, but also unsettling, as it accentuates the ambiguous and ambivalent relationship that exists between public, and therefore presumably objective, knowledge and personal conviction. With the intent of untangling, or at least clarifying, this complex relationship, this chapter takes shape around a hunch, a set of assertions, and a proposition. The hunch: nascent inside most classroom teachers is the nagging suspicion that we ought to suppress our deepest convictions in order to present our material objectively. Whatever else we may believe, most of us trust that we ought *not* to influence our students' emerging and developing critical opinions of the material we cover but rather create the space in which they can freely cultivate their own positions and conclusions.

The assertions are three in number. First, teaching is about *penultimate transformation.* That is, through our teaching we invite students into a process of growth, development, and transformation of their beliefs and practices. At the same time, even as our students—and, indeed, we ourselves—may be experiencing significant change, our fundamental nature and condition remains unchanged; hence teaching is about penultimate transformation. Second, teaching prompts such transformation by drawing students into a pursuit of, and eventual encounter with, truth. We teach what we believe is true, and the power of our teaching rests in our obedience to that truth. Third, and for this reason, our convictions are an unavoidable part of who we are as teachers and consequently of what we teach. Therefore, not only is it impossible for us to suppress these convictions, but we should not even try, as our passions, convictions, and even biases give us a unique entrée into the truth of the subject we teach and can similarly provide our students the means by which to engage and appropriate critically the material and claims at hand.

The proposition: the act and stance of confessing, rather than proving, truth enables us to protect the space in which our students can form and express their opinions and simultaneously to honor, and even articulate, our own convictions. In fact, articulating one's convictions in this way can aid students to articulate and actualize their own beliefs and opinions, but doing so effectively requires equal measures of pedagogical discernment and discipline.

After exploring briefly the hunch and assertions that animate this chapter, I will develop a constructive proposal suggesting how and when teachers may usefully introduce their convictions, closing with several illustrations from the classroom.

I. CONVICTION AND CONVERSATION

While most of us admit that teaching material in a completely objective manner is not possible, we nevertheless strive toward this goal. Why? We believe that authentic teaching must offer a noncoercive environment in which students can discuss, wrestle with, evaluate, and ultimately come to their own conclusions about the material at hand. In this we are drawing, with Thomas Green, a distinction between instruction and indoctrination, activities with two very different ends. As Green relates, with instruction we hope to transmit to students sufficient information by which they can reach a conclusion based on the evidence at hand, helping them arrive at an answer for the right reasons. With indoctrination, however, we intend to lead students to a particular conclusion irrespective of the evidence, leading them to the right answer, as it were, whatever the reasons.[1] The space that separates instruction from indoctrination is that very same space we seek to create and preserve by fencing our convictions behind objective treatment of our material for fear of encroaching upon our student's freedom of inquiry.

But what if objectivity is not simply impossible, but not desirable? That is, what if the quest for objectivity itself impedes the learning process because it obscures deeper subjective and assertive claims? While this may sound like a radically postmodern stance to advocate, a view much like it was articulated by Rudolf Bultmann, the German New Testament critic, in the first quarter of the last century. Writing in 1926, Bultmann challenges the notion that it is possible to offer an objective view of New Testament history:

> There is an approach to history which seeks by its *method* to achieve objectivity; that is, it sees history only in a perspective determined by the particular epoch or school to which the student brings. It succeeds, at its best, in escaping the subjectivity of the individual investigator, but still remains completely bound by the subjectivity of the method and is thus highly relative.[2]

For Bultmann, the stab toward objectivity is not only impossible but actually perilous as the interpreter, beguiled by the illusion of neutrality, easily falls prey to the inherent biases of whatever methodology she or he employs. Worse, according to Bultmann, such an approach misses the basic import of history, that is, to come to some sense of the relationship between a past event and one's present circumstances.[3] The best route for the historian, therefore, is to enter into a constant dialogue, first with the historical matter at hand and, second, with the historian's audience. For this reason, Bultmann offers historical study not as an objective presentation of the facts, but rather as an invitation to a living encounter:

> Thus I would lead the reader not to any "*view*" of history, but to a highly personal *encounter* with history. But because the book cannot in itself be for the reader *his* encounter with history, but only information about *my* encounter with history, it does of course as a whole appear to him as a *view*, and I must define for him my point of observation. Whether he afterward remains a mere spectator is his affair.[4]

According to Bultmann, this type of personal encounter, because it necessitates taking a position within history and making an existential commitment, lends itself to greater objectivity because it refrains from setting up criteria established beyond history to pronounce value judgments.[5]

Admittedly, Bultmann is discussing history broadly and New Testament interpretation more particularly. Nevertheless, I would suggest that any field in which competing views exist—including contrasting theories about a particular phenomenon within the natural sciences—may be approached in similar terms precisely because we are not merely presenting students with information but inviting them into critical engagement with, and eventual ownership of, a particular interpretation of the evidence available. That is, whenever we are seeking to discern which of several claims or interpretation is "true," then we seek to draw our students into a living encounter with the truth we pursue.

A half century later, Parker Palmer echoes Bultmann's desire to bring his reader into a "highly personal" encounter with the subject matter at hand because, according to Palmer, all truth is personal. This is not the same, Palmer is clear, as saying that all truth is subjective or relative, but it is to argue against the notion that truth is objective. Truth, according to Palmer, exists neither "out there" as an entirely objective set of facts nor "in here" as entirely subjective opinions and passions. Rather, truth is both in us and simultaneously beyond us, and we discover it as we enter into a dialogue between ourselves and our subject matter. In the classroom shaped by these convictions, as Palmer writes:

> Students and subject would meet in ways that allow our passions to be tempered by facts and the facts to be warmed up, made fit for human habitation, by passions. In this kind of education we would not merely know the world. We ourselves, our inner secrets, would become known; we would be brought into the community of mutual knowing called truth.[6]

For this reason, when we eschew our own beliefs and opinions, we not only perpetuate an illusion of objectivity that is misleading, but actually keep our students at a distance from the truth they might discover. By denying our students the opportunity to apprehend the ways in which we have personalized knowledge we deprive them of an example by which to do the same. The goal, again, is not to lead them to a particular destination, but to equip them for such a journey. The challenge for teachers, therefore, is not to bracket out their convictions but rather to employ those convictions in a manner that creates, rather than narrows, the space in which students can articulate and appropriate their own.

As Palmer admits, "space" may seem like a somewhat vague term to use to describe the intellectual freedom we covet for our students, but most of us will recognize the experience of living in such space when we are granted it. As he writes:

> to study with a teacher who not only speaks but listens, who not only gives answers but asks questions and welcomes our insights, who provides information and theories that do not close doors but open new ones, who encourages students to help each other learn—to study with such a teacher is to know the power of a learning space.[7]

Such space, as Palmer goes on, is essential if students are to move beyond the pattern of reception and regurgitation that mars so many learning settings toward the genuine appropriation of the material that we desire for our students. Because the goal is actual appropriation of—that is, to come to some reasoned, personal convictions about—the material, the starting place to create such space is in offering our own convictions. As Palmer writes, the "space on which teaching depends is that created by the claims of truth on our lives." When such space is created, he continues, it "draws students, teacher, and subject alike into truth's own drama."[8]

Philosopher Paul Ricoeur suggests a similar dynamic when he describes the process of participation and distanciation that leads to genuine appropriation. Eschewing the modernist, even Romantic, distinction between neutral observation and objective evaluation, Ricoeur proposes that one needs both an immersion into the existential import of the topic (participation) as well as the critical space in which to question, wonder about, even reject the conclusions offered (distanciation) in order genuinely to actualize and internalize the truths offered (appropriation).[9] This movement from participation and distanciation to appropriation is the repeating dynamic in what has many analogues to an ongoing dialogue about truth between teachers, students, and the subject matter. In such a formulation, teachers cannot refrain from speaking their convictions but instead may learn how to speak in a way that continues, rather than frustrates, the conversation. It is to isolating the particular kind of speech that will facilitate such a conversation that we next turn.

II. CONVICTION AND CONFESSION

Jurgen Habermas, David Tracy, Richard Rorty, and others have advocated a dialogical approach to the pursuit of truth. Each has sought to outline the necessary conditions within which such a conversation may take place. Tracy, for instance, summarizing Habermas, suggests the following hard rules for authentic conversation:

> Say only what you mean; say it as accurately as you can; listen to and respect what the other says, however different or other; be willing to correct or defend your opinion if challenged by the conversation partner; be willing to argue if necessary, to confront if demanded, to endure the necessary conflict, to change your mind if the evidence suggests it.[10]

Beyond the conditions necessary for conversations about truth, however, we may ask whether there is a particular kind of speech that lends itself to fostering this kind of conversation. In this section I suggest that there is, proposing that the Christian understanding of "confessing" truth serves as an appropriate model of teachers.

In brief, I define *confession* as "the act of asserting one's deepest convictions (and at times the warrants for those convictions) without offering or insisting upon final proof of those convictions."[11] Understood in this way, confession commends itself to us on at least four levels as a salutary practice, or perhaps more accurately stance, to employ in the classroom. First, confession deals with ultimate issues. This is important to underscore in order to avoid the mistaken notion that when we speak of fostering safe space in the classroom we are advocating a tentative, even milquetoast, approach to teaching. Far from it—confession deals always and only with things that matter. In fact, in its use in the New Testament as a noun, confession always implies a summation of the essential message of the early church, naming those central matters around which the community of faith gathers and apart from which it can have no meaningful life. Confession is about asserting the truth.

Second, confession is inherently responsive in character, attending not simply to the convictions of the confessor but to the needs of the audience. As Douglas John Hall, one of the foremost theologians advocating the Christian practice of confession, writes, "If anything is to be regarded as confessional, it is not only the internal condition of the confessor that must be considered (for example, the question of sincerity), but also the external circumstances in which the act is undertaken."[12] Confessing, he continues, "does not mean saying *everything*. It means saying—whether with words or deeds or sighs too deep for either—the one thing that *needs* to be said, then and there."[13] Again, the New Testament use of the word is instructive, as confessing, when used as a verb, describes offering an articulation of the faith in response to the perceived need of the community. Confession, therefore, draws teacher and student into a relationship governed equally by conviction and hospitality, responding to the perceived need of the audience and, indeed, the larger conversation one has joined.

Third, confession is assertive, and therefore provocative, speech about truth. That is, according to the speech-act theory of J. L. Austin and John Searle, confessing anticipates, invites, even provokes a response.[14] It is inherently dialogical, even relational, and seeks to draw its recipient into the conversation.

Fourth, and perhaps most important, although confession is provocative speech, it also makes transparent the larger commitment of the speaker to the very act of the conversation and thereby also to its intended audience. In this way confession avoids the competitive, even destructive, elements of typical rhetorical argumentation. In their article "Beyond Persuasion: A Proposal for an Invitational Rhetoric," Sonja K. Foss and Cindy L. Griffin suggest that much of the coercive element of traditional rhetoric—which in turn has historically influenced pedagogical theory—is the explicit goal of the speaker to change his or her audience through persuasion. In response, Foss and Griffin advocate a rhetoric of invitation that creates the necessary space in which self-directed change may occur. At the heart of their proposal rests the conviction that in order to avoid the coercive elements of traditional rhetoric, the speaker must guarantee from the outset his or her unconditional regard for the audience.[15] Only under such circumstances, they contend, can a speaker safeguard the space necessary for Ricoeur's distanciation to occur.

Confession enables the speaker to guarantee regard for the hearer because it does not seek its validation from its reception but rather is validated by the integrity with which it is offered. When one confesses love, for instance, although the confessor is deeply invested in the response of the beloved, the integrity of the confession is nevertheless not dependent on that response. Whether the beloved responds, "I love you too!" or "I'm sorry, but while I am flattered by your feelings I do not love you," the integrity of the confession of love remains valid. This is most certainly not the case when one attempts to prove truth, where rejection of the assertion turns one naturally into an adversary. Confessing our convictions in the classroom, therefore, not only prompts an encounter between students and the subject matter (participation), but it also protects the space of the hearer to engage, wonder about, consider, even reject the material at hand (distanciation), thereby creating the possibility of penultimate transformation (appropriation).

III. CONFESSION AND DISCERNMENT

From the discussion thus far, it may appear that I think every statement that flows from the mouth of the teacher should be confessional in nature. This is hardly the case. The great majority of our teaching is descriptive rather than confessional, as we regularly offer information, background, and context as the backdrop to the significant truth claims at hand. But beneath all description ultimately lies confession (as even mathematical proofs rest upon those unproved assumptions we call axioms). And when we get to those significant moments of offering truth claims so as to provoke and invite our students into their own pursuit of truth, then making those confessions explicit can be helpful. You will know when you are there, standing on the edge between description and confession, because at those moments your pulse quickens and you seem to command a greater than average level of attention as those who listen sense you are about to get to the heart of the matter.

But one does not confess, or even confess in the same way, each time this moment arises. Rather, one offers a particular confession—or not—in relation to the immediate context, including the distinct need of the hearer and the particular aim of the instructor. While the various permutations and manifestations of confession are endless, two concrete examples and a third more general one may help get at the kind of discernment I am advocating.

The first example takes shape in a senior-required class

on biblical interpretation and congregational leadership. Called "Exercises in Biblical Theology," this class at its best serves as a capstone course for students seeking to extend their interpretation of Scripture into their practice as congregational leaders. At its worst it leaves students and instructors sorely frustrated, as indicated by the nickname some have given it: "Exercises in Biblical Futility." Both the highs and the lows surrounding this course arise, I think, because it consistently draws students into exercises and examples of biblical interpretation in the service of congregational mission that are as indeterminate as they are concrete. In one such exercise students are engaged in a mock debate on the practice of slavery on the basis of biblical exegesis. While students often approach this exercise with low expectations—after all, everyone knows that slavery is evil—they are often deeply affected by the discovery that it is quite difficult to argue against slavery on the basis of Scripture.

In this case, while I intimate that the exercise is an important one to the course and, therefore, that their preparation work is worth the effort, I save my confession regarding my own first experience with this exercise and the further reflection on the nature of biblical interpretation and critical hermeneutics until near the end of the class discussion, as the exercise itself is powerful enough to draw students into serious and at times difficult engagement with their own presuppositions about the nature of Scripture. My confession, in this case, serves to affirm their own struggles as well as to extend to them an example of how one person (namely, me) moved through the interpretive dilemma toward some sense of deeper conviction about critical biblical interpretation.

In the plenary presentation of another course I state my convictions about the subject matter right up front. It is an introductory preaching course, and the subject is "law and gospel," the central Lutheran hermeneutic for interpreting God's activity in the world and Scripture. Because of the importance of this hermeneutic to Lutherans (it is a central topic in several courses in the curriculum), and because there is some significant debate among Lutherans about its nature and application, the topic often proves challenging to Lutheran students (they feel pressure to get this one right) and frustrating to students of other traditions (they are by this time in the curriculum often fed up with what feels like a Lutheran obsession). For these reasons, at the outset of my presentation I describe what will follow as a "proposal," the Lutheran wager about how to make sense of God's activity in the world. I then go on to describe several similar proposals from other traditions—sin and grace, fall and redemption, the human condition and God's response, cross and resurrection—which attempt to get at some of the same issues. I then suggest that the students receive the presentation as an invitation into a particular worldview, suggesting that Lutheran students can gain practice at identifying how this hermeneutical dynamic might play out in Scripture, that non-Lutheran students will also need to fashion some explicit hermeneutic, and that the law-gospel one, even if it does not prove convincing to them, may yet sharpen their own proposals. In this case, naming my convictions about this topic at the outset functions—I hope!—both to relieve some of the tension around the topic (almost inviting a "willing suspension of disbelief"), to set some of the boundaries (this is my confession, not a rule of faith), and to get the pedagogical aim out front (to challenge them with one particular proposal of how we experience God's work in the world).

For a third example I want to return to the theoretical yet common experience named at the outset of this chapter—the question from a student regarding our stance on a complicated and debated issue. At our place much further along in the discussion about the relationship between conviction and pedagogy, we may now venture that any of the three possible responses—demurring, hedging, or complying—might be the most salutary depending upon the particular aim of the instructor and need(s) of the student. At that particular moment in that particular course and with that particular body of students, it might be, that is, a time to share one's position, or model how one critically evaluates one of the positions, or holds one's convictions back to prod students to engage the subject matter for themselves first. This is where it is important to appreciate confession not simply as an act but also as a position or an attitude toward life and teaching. Those students who have experienced the candor of a teacher regarding convictions about the truth will be likely to go along with the instructor in any given moment, trusting that his or her response is governed by a concern for the journey of the student.

In such a scenario, the teacher is not so much the expert but an experienced guide and cotraveler. Sometimes the image that comes to mind for me is of a rafting guide who takes students through both the placid waters and the rapids, neither doing the work for them nor abandoning them to the white water, but using his or her experience on the river to guide, prompt, challenge, and coach them to draw from themselves more than they had previously imagined they could do as they navigate their way downstream.

One can only play such a role, of course, if one is willing to get wet, not only talking with others about the raft trip but jumping into the boat to be a participant in the journey. For teachers, this means abandoning an understanding of teaching as the transmission of knowledge and embracing, instead, the notion that teaching is about active participation, struggle, and confession, with all the ambiguities and vulnerabilities of such a pedagogy intact. This may take some time to get used to; leaving the comfortable confines of objective truth is surely risky. But then the pursuit of truth has never been for the faint of heart.

NOTES

1. Thomas F. Green, *The Activities of Teaching* (Troy, NY: Educator's International Press, 1998 [1971]), 31.
2. Rudolf Bultmann, *Jesus and the Word*, trans. from the German (*Jesus*, 1926), by L. P. Smith, E. H. Lantero (New York: Scribner's, 1934 [1962]), 5.
3. "The examination of history is no neutral orientation about objectively determined past events, but is motivated by the question how we ourselves, standing in the current of history, can succeed in comprehending our own existence, can gain clear insight

into the contingencies and necessities of our own life purpose" (Ibid., 10).

4. Ibid, 6–7.
5. Bultmann develops these convictions more fully in his essay "Is Exegesis Without Presuppositions Possible?" in *Existence and Faith: Shorter Writings of Rudolf Bultmann*. Translated by Schubert M. Ogden (Cleveland, OH: World Publishing, 1960), 289–298. Here he argues both that exegesis without presuppositions is not possible and that one approaches greater, though never complete, objectivity by admitting one's presuppositions so as to bring them to light for critical engagement and dialogue.
6. Parker Palmer, *To Know as We Are Known: Education as Spiritual Journey* (San Francisco: HarperCollins, 1993 [1983]), 36.
7. Ibid, 70.
8. Ibid, 79.
9. See Paul Ricoeur, "Appropriation," in *Paul Ricoeur: Hermeneutics and the Social Sciences: Essays on Language, Action and Interpretation*, edited, translated, and introduced by John B. Thompson (Cambridge: Cambridge University Press, 1981), 182–195.
10. David Tracy, *Plurality and Ambiguity: Hermeneutics, Religion, Hope* (San Francisco: Harper & Row, 1987), 19. For additional resources related to nurturing conversation, see Katie Day's *Difficult Conversation: Taking Risks, Acting with Integrity* (Alban Institue, 2001); though addressed primarily to congregational issues, her insights into the nature of tending conversation on difficult topics is easily transferable to a variety of settings, including the classroom.
11. I explore the biblical, theological, and linguistic dimensions of confession in much greater depth in *Confessing Jesus Christ: Preaching in a Postmodern World* (Grand Rapids, MI: Eerdmans, 2003).
12. Douglas John Hall, *Confessing the Faith: Christian Theology in a North American Context* (Minneapolis, MN: Fortress Press, 1996), 9.
13. Ibid., 11.
14. John R. Searle, *Expression and Meaning: Studies in the Theory of Speech Acts* (London: Cambridge University Press, 1979), 12-20.
15. Sonja K. Foss and Cindy L. Griffin, "Beyond Persuasion: A Proposal for an Invitational Rhetoric." *Communication Monographs*, 62 (1995): 1–18.

CHAPTER 3

How Do We Invite Students into Conversation? Teaching Dialogically

Stephen D. Brookfield

Of all the methods used by seminary teachers to develop critical thinking by students on matters of faith and pastoral practice, it is discussion that is touted as the most appropriate. Discussion-based classrooms appear to equalize student-teacher power relationships, to affirm the validity of students' opinions, to get learners used to grappling with diverse (and sometimes contradictory) perspectives, and to encourage students to take responsibility for the development of their own judgments. For some of its advocates classroom discussion has an even wider political resonance as constituting a democratic learning laboratory. Social philosophers such as Jurgen Habermas believe that the same basic rules of full, free, and equal discourse that govern good classroom discussion constitute an ideal speech situation that can also be applied to judging whether or not the wider community is reaching its economic, social, and political decisions in a fair and morally defensible way.[1] For him, good discussion, and therefore good democratic process, depends on everyone contributing, on everyone having the fullest possible knowledge of different perspectives, and on everyone being ready to give up their position if a better argument is presented to them.

A much darker perspective on discussion is provided by the late French critic, Michel Foucault, who analyzes the microdynamics of power. Foucault argues that in modern society people learn to internalize norms (including norms governing discussion participation) that serve to keep existing unequal structures intact.[2] In higher education the norm of good discussion equates participation with extroversion and intelligence with an articulate command of academic jargon. It holds that good discussion is distinguished by garrulous and confident speakers who talk cogently about ideas and concepts covered in lectures and assigned reading, and who then explain how these illustrate central themes of the content studied. If this norm is unchallenged by teachers it quickly establishes an unequal pecking order of contributions in the group and a negative conversational dynamic. Students who want a good grade will do their best to exemplify this norm by taking up as much of the available airtime as they can. They will monitor themselves and others to gauge how they are doing in the discussion performance stakes, turning the conversation into a competitive intellectual game. In effect, they will exercise what Foucault calls disciplinary power on themselves; that is, they will watch themselves to make sure they are behaving in the way they feel the discussion leader (the judge of what constitutes good participation) desires.

For discussion to contribute to students' formation it must strive to exhibit certain features. Theological teaching may wish to invite students to contemplate the mysteries of faith, God's work, the Holy Spirit, and existence but there is little that is mysterious about the qualities of good discussion. Far too often teachers believe that whether or not discussion takes off is down to the chemistry of a particular group; either it's there or it isn't. In reality, the success of discussion as a learning tool—as something that helps students think on their feet, become aware of diverse perspectives, develop understanding of and even empathy for supposedly oppositional views, and be able to tolerate higher degrees of ambiguity—depends to a large extent on the degree to which the teacher structures discussion participation. A good discussion leader is not someone who shows up relying on his ability to improvise depending on what points students bring up, but one who focuses deliberately on naming and encouraging behaviors that diverge from the "discussion as intellectual showing off" model that is the default model people revert to unless it is challenged early on.

Of prime importance in the seminary classroom is the early

establishment of criteria for discussion participation that stress active listening, showing appreciation for others' contributions, and making connecting or synthesizing comments. Students need to realize early on that developing the qualities of empathy, understanding, and compassion so crucial for ministry work depends partly on understanding others' viewpoints, and the reasons these views are held, even when the views are ones that the student strongly disagrees with. Developing these capacities is something that discussion is uniquely suited to, stressing as it does the need to attend carefully to the words of others and the ability to hold several different, even antithetical, ideas in one's head while formulating one's own response.

Establishing clear criteria for effective participation is crucial if students are to take discussion seriously. They need to understand that participating effectively in discussion does not necessarily mean talking a lot or showing everyone else how much they know or have studied. Good discussion participation involves people trying to build on, and synthesize, comments from others and on showing appreciation for others' contributions. It also involves inviting others to say more about what they are thinking. Some of the most helpful things students can do that improve the quality of discussion have very little to do with making original contributions. For example, calling for a quiet interlude so that people can mull over provocative points that have been raised, bringing a new resource to the classroom, or posting an observation about that week's class discussion online are excellent behaviors that will improve the quality of conversation; yet none of these involves talking very much (if at all) or displaying one's knowledge. There are multiple ways quieter learners can participate in discussion.

I. GETTING DISCUSSION STARTED

The opening moments of a discussion are often problematic, particularly if students don't know each other or the teacher very well. Asking generalized, vague questions such as "what did you think of the assigned reading?" or "would someone like to start us off by telling us what they think about the topic today?" can quickly kill any nascent energy in the room. Early on in the life of a group, therefore, it can be helpful to begin the conversation with one of the three exercises described in this section.

A. Sentence Completion Exercise

One way to focus students on the topic at hand and to ensure that what gets talked about is in some way connected to their own concerns, is to start the discussion session with a sentence completion exercise. Students are asked to complete on their own whichever of the following sentences seem appropriate:

- What most struck me about the text we read to prepare for the discussion today is . . .
- The question that I'd most like to ask the author(s) of the text is . . .
- The idea I most take issue with in the text is . . .
- The most crucial point in last week's lecture was . . .
- The part of the lecture/text that I felt made most sense to me was . . .
- The part of the lecture/text that I felt was most confusing was . . .

Students then form into small groups and read out the full sentences to each other. As students hear each other's responses they jot down whichever of their colleagues' responses they would like to hear more about. After everyone has read out all their responses students can ask other students why they wrote what they did. Finally, the small group members choose one or two responses to report to the whole class when the teacher calls the small groups back together.

B. Generating Truth Statements

One task that Frederick and Van Ments suggest for the start of a discussion is to ask students to generate what they call "truth statements"[3] or "statements worth making"[4] based on their preparatory reading. Students are split into small groups and each group is asked to generate three or four statements that they believe to be true on the basis of their reading. The point of this exercise is not so much to produce undeniable facts or theories but to generate, and then prioritize, questions and issues around which further discussion and research is undertaken. The exercise helps participants develop an agenda of items for discussion and suggests directions for future research they need to conduct if they are to be informed discussants.

C. Respond to Contentious Opening Statements

Sometimes a strongly worded statement—spoken or written—is a good way to get the blood flowing and conversation going. This statement can be one that's already in the public domain or one that a teacher writes for this purpose. The statement should be one that's deliberately provocative, even inflammatory, and one that will likely produce strong emotional responses in students. Certainly it should be one that challenges at a fundamental level some of the assumptions that students take for granted or hold on to most fiercely. It's important to state in this exercise that no one assumes that the teacher agrees with the statement's contentious sentiments. The teacher bringing the contentious statement to the group is doing so only to generate conversation.

After the statement has been made, the conversation opens with group members trying to understand the reasoning and circumstances that frame such a statement. Why would someone hold these views? What in the author's experience led her to write or utter such ideas? What possible grounds could we advance to support the making of such an argument? Students are asked to be devil's advocates, coming up with evidence and rationales that are completely outside their usual frames of reference. This kind of perspective taking is a cognitive warm-up. It serves the same function in discussion as stretching does at the start of an aerobic workout. By examining the grounds for a view that is contrary to their own, students engage in a form of intellectual muscle flexing. Moreover, being forced to take seriously opinions that they strongly disagree with helps draw students into the discussion at an emotional level.

D. Scaffolding Discussion Participation through Structured Conversation

Early on in a discussion-based course it is a good idea to introduce students to a number of exercises designed to equalize participation and to teach students that listening, appreciating, and synthesizing are just as crucial to good discussion as is making brilliant original contributions. For students unused to discussion, or for those introverts who find talking in public an excruciating ordeal, an orientation or induction period is particularly appreciated. Such a period comprises a scaffolding experience, a time when students learn a series of protocols where the ground rules for participation are clear and the intimidating need to come up with impromptu contributions is removed.

E. Circle of Voices

The circle of voices is a protocol that students can learn on the first day of class. Participants form into circles of about five people to discuss a topic assigned by the teacher. They are allowed a minute or so of silent time to think about what they want to say on the topic of discussion once the circle of voices begins. After this silent period the discussion opens with each person having a period of uninterrupted airtime of no more than a minute. During this time each speaker can say whatever she wishes about the topic at hand. While each person is speaking no one else is allowed to interrupt. People take their turns to speak by going round the circle in order, which removes from participants the stress of having to decide whether or not they will try and jump in after another student has finished speaking.

After the initial circle of voices has been completed and everyone has had the uninterrupted chance to make their opening comments, the discussion opens out into a more free-flowing format. As this happens a second ground rule comes into effect. Participants are only allowed to talk about another person's ideas that have already been shared in the opening circle of voices. Participants cannot jump into the conversation by expanding on their own ideas; they can only talk about their reactions to what someone else has said in the opening round. The only exception to this ground rule is if someone asks a group member directly to expand on her ideas. This second ground rule prevents the tendency toward grandstanding that sometimes afflicts a few articulate, confident individuals.

F. Circular Response

The circular response exercise is a way to democratize discussion participation, to promote continuity of conversation, and to give people some experience of the effort required in respectful listening. It was developed by Eduard Lindeman as part of his efforts to democratize conversation amongst living room learning groups and to help community groups focus on two or three shared concerns instead of trying to pursue multiple agendas.[5]

As with the circle of voices the exercise begins with participants having a minute or so to think about their response to a discussion question or topic assigned to them. Participants form into circles of six to eight people and the conversation begins with a volunteer who takes up to a minute to say whatever she thinks about the topic concerned. After the minute is over, the first discussant yields the floor, and the person sitting to the discussant's left speaks for a minute or so. The second speaker is not free, however, to say anything she wants. She must incorporate into her remarks some reference to the preceding speaker's message and then use this as a springboard for her own comments. This doesn't have to be an agreement—it can be an expression of dissent from the previous opinion. It can also be an expression of confusion where the second discussant identifies some aspect of the first speaker's remarks that she finds difficult to understand. For example, the second speaker may talk about her puzzlement at the first speaker's interpretation of a well-known biblical passage.

After a minute or so, the second discussant stops speaking, and the person to her left becomes the third discussant who follows the same ground rule to refer to some aspect of the second speaker's message as the springboard for her own comments. Following this pattern the discussion moves all the way around the circle. Each discussant must ground her comments in reference to something the previous speaker has said. After everyone has had a turn to speak, the floor is opened for general conversation, and the previous ground rules are no longer in force.

The interesting thing about this exercise is that the seventh or eighth person to speak has no inherent advantage over the first or second contributor. This is because the eighth person cannot sit in reflective luxury rehearsing a perfect contribution, because she has no idea what the seventh person is going to say until that person speaks. Indeed, the first person to speak has the easiest task of all in circular response because she does not have to use a previous speaker's comments as the springboard for her remarks.

G. Conversational Roles

Students often tell us that they find it helpful to know at the outset of a discussion the sort of conversational role they are required to play. Knowing that they have a particular task to fulfill seems to remove some of the performance anxiety created by the invisible norm of good participation. Practice in playing different conversational roles helps create opportunities for the more tentative students to speak, thereby building their confidence. Any roles assigned must, of course, be alternated so that everyone takes a turn. It is tempting but abusive to assign the quietest role to the most vociferous student each week. A number of commonly used conversational roles are given below.

Problem, Dilemma, or Theme Poser

This participant has the task of introducing the topic of conversation and draws on personal ideas and experiences as a way of helping others into conversation about the theme.

Reflective Analyst

This member keeps a record of the conversation's development and every 20 minutes or so gives a summary that focuses on shared concerns, issues skirted, and emerging common themes.

Scrounger

The scrounger listens for and records helpful resources, suggestions, and tips that participants have voiced as they discuss how to work through a problem or situation. The record of these ideas is read aloud before the session ends.

Devil's Advocate

This person listens carefully for any emerging consensus and then formulates and expresses a contrary view. This keeps groupthink in check and helps participants explore a range of alternative interpretations.

Detective

The detective listens carefully for unacknowledged, unchecked, and unchallenged biases that seem to be emerging in the conversation and brings them to the group's attention. This person assumes particular responsibility for alerting group members to concerns of race, class, and gender by listening for cultural blindness, gender insensitivity, and comments that ignore variables of power and class.

Theme Spotter

This participant identifies themes that arise during the discussion that are left unexplored and that might form a focus for the next session.

Umpire

This person listens for judgmental comments that sound offensive, insulting, and demeaning and that contradict ground rules for discussion generated by group members.

Textual Focuser

Whenever assertions are made about a text that seem unsupported or unconnected to the actual text being discussed, this person asks the speaker to let the group know where in the text the point being made occurs.

Evidential Assessor

This student asks speakers to give the evidence for empirical generalizations that are stated as self-evident fact but that seem more like opinion.

Synthesizer

This person attempts to underscore links between different contributions.

H. Conversational Moves

An alternative to assigning conversational roles is to use the conversational moves exercise. Here the teacher pastes a number of conversational moves (speaking directions) on 3x5 cards and randomly distributes these among participants at the beginning of a discussion session. These moves should roughly parallel the criteria for good discussion participation published in the course syllabus.

Students read the move on their card and are asked to practice their move at some point during the discussion that follows. When the discussion is over the entire list of moves is distributed so people can see the wide variety of ways that discussion participation can be recognized. If they wish to, participants can recap how they tried to make the moves they were allocated.

Specific Moves

- Ask a question or make a comment that shows you are interested in what another person says.
- Ask a question or make a comment that encourages another person to elaborate on something they have already said.
- Make a comment that underscores the link between two people's contributions.
- Use body language to show interest in what different speakers are saying.
- Make a specific comment indicating how you found another person's ideas interesting/useful.
- Contribute something that builds on, or springs from, what someone else has said. Be explicit about the way you are building on the other person's thoughts.
- Make a comment that at least partly paraphrases a point someone has already made.
- Make a summary observation that takes into account several people's contributions and that touches on a recurring theme in the discussion.
- Ask a cause-and-effect question—for example, "Can you explain why you think it's true that if these things are in place such and such a thing will occur?"
- When you think it's appropriate, ask the group for a moment's silence to slow the pace of conversation and give you, and others, time to think.
- Find a way to express appreciation for the enlightenment you

have gained from the discussion. Be specific about what it was that helped you understand something better.

- Disagree with someone in a respectful and constructive way.
- Create space for someone who has not yet spoken to contribute to the conversation.

I. Quotes to Affirm and Challenge

This exercise is designed to make it easier to begin discussions that are grounded in students' prereading of an assigned text. Students are asked to bring to class two quotes they have chosen from a text they have read to prepare for the class. One quote is chosen because the student wishes to affirm it. The other is one the student wishes to challenge. Students form small groups and each member takes a turn to propose the quote they wish to affirm and the reasons for doing so. The quote does not have to be defended as empirically true. Sometimes a participant will propose a quote because it confirms a point of view she holds or supports what her intuition or experience tells her is accurate. Sometimes she feels the quote states the most important point in the text, or it is chosen because it contains a crucial new piece of information or different perspective. At other times the quote is affirmed because it is rhetorically rousing or lyrically expresses an idea. When everyone in the small group has proposed a quote to affirm, the group chooses one to report to the larger class. During this whole class discussion each group explains why it was that they chose the particular quote they did.

The "quote to challenge" activity follows the same procedure, only this time students choose a quote that they disagree with, find contradictory, believe to be inaccurate, or consider reprehensible and immoral. The quote to challenge is then reported back to the class along with the rationale for its choice.

J. Snowballing

Students uncomfortable with even small group participation can be drawn into individual voice, and then into whole class discussion, through the process known as "snowballing". This protocol begins with individual solitary reflection and proceeds gradually and incrementally (if numbers allow) until the discussion involves the whole class. The process begins by students individually and silently spending a couple of minutes jotting down their thoughts about an assigned discussion question. After this reflective beginning students then form into pairs and spend about five minutes discussing each other's ideas. When the five minutes are up each pair then joins another pair to form a quartet. The quartet conversation opens with each pair sharing a question they raised, a difference they noted in their conversation, or a new insight that suggested itself. After 10 minutes each quartet joins another quartet to form octets. Again, the octets begin their conversation with each quartet sharing a question they raised, a difference they noted, or an insight that suggested itself in their conversation. After 20 minutes the octets join other octets to form groups of 16 and, again, share one of the three conversational themes mentioned. In a class of around 32 the class ends by each group of 16 joining the other for a final conversation. Through snowballing a class of 32 students that began with individual, private, and silent reflection ends up in whole class discussion.

II. GUIDED DISCUSSION

I have often heard teachers say that they run guided discussions, and I am always made uncomfortable by that term. If the phrase is used to describe the way a teacher leads the discussion towards a predefined end point then it is, in my view, an oxymoron. Discussion is, by definition, a free and open conversation in which no end point is specified in advance. It entails new and unpredictable avenues of inquiry that constantly emerge and people changing their minds as they consider new evidence or alternative interpretations of existing evidence. At the heart of discussion is the open and unpredictable creation of meanings through collaborative inquiry. It is intellectually dishonest for a discussion leader to have decided in advance what these meanings should be and to call the resulting conversation a discussion.

This does not mean that the deliberate initiation of students into previously determined meanings or understandings through a Socratic dialogue is somehow invalid. On the contrary, it is a crucial element in introducing students to new concepts, bodies of knowledge, or areas of inquiry and is a strategy I use myself. In teaching critical theory I take full responsibility for introducing difficult concepts such as ideology, hegemony, liberation, and praxis in as clear a way as I can by talking with students about the different ways they understand those terms. But when I do this I am *not* teaching through discussion. I have a clear purpose in mind which is to make sure learners are inside the concept. To use a term borrowed from R. S. Peters, I want to be sure that students command the "grammar" of the subject; that is, that they understand fully the criteria by which good and bad examples of intellectual work in the subject are determined and that they grasp correctly the essential conceptual building blocks of a particular body of knowledge.[6]

Just because teachers and students are talking does not mean they are engaged in discussion. The intent and manner of the talk are crucial. For example, if I question students to make sure they have understood Marcuse's concept of repressive tolerance in the way he intended it to be understood, I do use classroom talk, but I am definitely *not* using discussion.[7] My approach is more like a structured Socratic dialogue. However, when I ask the group to talk about the meaning this concept has for students' own experiences, the extent to which it explains things they have seen in their lives, the degree to which it raises the specter of censorship for them or contains an implicit arrogance, then I *am* using discussion. I have no idea where the conversation will turn and no predetermined objectives that must be met before the day's class has finished.

A guided discussion is not only a contradiction in terms, it is also a profoundly inauthentic process. If you are asking students to enter into a collaborative inquiry to explore and create multiple meanings it is dishonest to have worked out in advance what those meanings will be. In a classic article, Paterson describes such conversations as counterfeit discussions led by a teacher "who unobtrusively and skillfully synthesizes the various discussion contributions of his students, by judicious selection and emphasis, into a neatly structured and rounded proposition or body of propositions, which are then presented as the 'conclusions' of the 'class discussion'."[8] In my experience I know very quickly when I'm in a counterfeit discussion, and my immediate impulse is to get out of it as soon as possible.

I have often found myself a participant in a discussion where the leader is nudging the conversation along to a predetermined conclusion with which he agrees. I see this happen when the leader ignores questions or ideas raised by students that are inconvenient or awkward for his position. It also occurs when a teacher reframes what a student has said in a way that distorts the student's meaning to support the leader's views. If something is forcing me to stay in the room during such a discussion, then I mount a consciousness strike. I withdraw my mental labor and start turning over in my mind some work or research problems that have no connection to what we're talking about. In my view guided discussion is a self-negating concept if it means guiding talk towards a particular position or point of consensus. Whenever this happens it means that certain perspectives and information have been excluded at the outset.

It does make sense, however, to describe a discussion as guided if what is being guided are the processes by which students are helped to listen respectfully, seek clarification and understanding of each others' ideas, and create opportunities for all voices to be heard. In guided discussions we can guide students in learning the habits of democratic discourse but not in learning predetermined conclusions or prechosen meanings. Guiding the process of discussion makes sure everyone gets a chance to participate, no one person dominates unfairly, and individuals cannot hijack the topic for their own ideological conversion of other participants without themselves being open to listening to others' points of view. Indeed, unless the teacher deliberately intervenes to guide the process of discussion to prevent these things happening, the patterns of conversational dominance that exist outside the classroom will immediately reproduce themselves inside. Those learners with intellectual capital, cultural prestige, and command of the dominant linguistic discourse will be listened to seriously, while those who are quiet, marginalized, unconfident, or whose first language is not English, will remain on the conversational periphery.

NOTES

1. J. Habermas, *Autonomy and Solidarity: Interviews with Jurgen Habermas* (London: Verso, 1992 (revised)).
2. M. Foucault, *Power/Knowledge: Selected Interviews and Other Writings, 1972–1977* (New York: Pantheon Books, 1980).
3. P. Frederick, "The Dreaded Discussion: Ten Ways to Start" In D. Bligh (ed.), *Teach Thinking By Discussion* (Guildford, England: Society for Research into Higher Education/NFER-Nelson, 1986): 144.
4. M. Van Ments, *Active Talk: The Effective Use of Discussion in Learning* (New York: St. Martin's Press, 1990), 38.
5. S. D. Brookfield, ed., *Learning Democracy: Eduard Lindeman on Adult Education and Social Change* (New York: Routledge, 1988).
6. R. S. Peters, ed., *The Concept of Education* (Boston: Routledge, Kegan and Paul, 1967).
7. H. Marcuse, "Repressive Tolerance." In R. P. Wolff, B. Moore, and H. Marcuse, *A Critique of Pure Tolerance* (Boston: Beacon Press, 1965).
8. R. W. K. Paterson, "The Concept of Discussion: A Philosophical Approach," *Studies in Adult Education* (1970, 1 [2]): 47.

CHAPTER 4

"How Do We Meet Students Where They Are, While Challenging Them Further?" Teaching Developmentally

Mary E. Hess

Every year in my introduction to Christian education, I do an exercise in which I ask groups of students to read a children's book together. These books raise questions and provoke curiosity about themes that have Christian connections. They demonstrate a great way to invite students into a practice that more and more families are sharing (the reading of bedtime stories) in a way that highlights that practice's potential for faith formation and that invites adults to ask questions they might otherwise not voice.

One of the books I frequently use is *Becoming Me,* a picture book about creation written by Martin Boroson and Christopher Gilvan-Cartwright, that is told from the point of view of God. It's a brief story, accompanied by vivid, modernist images, that most of my students encounter for the first time with delight. Yet one year I was startled to discover, when the students returned to the plenary gathering of the class, that some of the students in the small group reading that book had interpreted it as both heretical and blasphemous, too dangerous to give to adults let alone share with young children. The emotions of these students were pitched so high that two of them had flushed faces, and the body language of several other students suggested that the small group discussion had been heated.

I was not prepared for such a response and uncertain how

to handle it. Inwardly I was immediately defensive. How could they interpret the book that way? Why were they so hostile? Outwardly I tried to make my expression look calm, and I encouraged the group to share their experience with the book. The two students who had had the strongest reaction began to speak rapidly, with loud voices, almost belligerently, about the theological implications of the book. The rest of their small group, and increasingly the rest of the room, shrank back into silence and looked increasingly uncomfortable.

Usually I trust a class to respond well to small group feedback, but this group's response clearly demanded something more. I found myself moving forward toward them, talking across their complaints, and voicing my surprise at their reaction. Internally I was angry at what felt to me like their petty refusal to take the book seriously enough and confused about what could be the "right" thing for me to do in response.

It is moments like this that come back to me when I think about surprise in the classroom. Rarely have the surprises felt good—at least initially—and rarely have I had any idea how to respond to them at the moment they occur. In this case so much was at stake: my own authority and credibility as the teacher in the room and my students' sense of trust that I could structure and sustain an atmosphere of open and respectful inquiry. The emotional intensity of the two argumentative students suggested that they, too, had something at stake. What to do?

I don't know what the "right" answer is in these cases, and that evening I stumbled through my own internal chaos barely well enough to shape the rest of the evening's class. But I do know that the moment brought vividly to mind for me a biblical passage that I often ponder. Paul writes, in the first letter to the Corinthians:

> When I came to you, brothers and sisters, proclaiming the mystery of God, I did not come with sublimity of words or of wisdom. For I resolved to know nothing while I was with you except Jesus Christ, and him crucified. I came to you in weakness and fear and much trembling, and my message and my proclamation were not with persuasive words of wisdom, but with a demon-

> stration of spirit and power, so that your faith might rest not on human wisdom but on the power of God. (I Cor 2:1–5)

What does it mean to "know nothing except Jesus Christ, and him crucified"? And what possible connection does this passage have with teaching? As professors we spend long years toiling away at study that aims to prepare us for sharing "sublimity of words and wisdom"—not its opposite. Certainly walking into a classroom full of students demands a kind of authority and credibility that seems at odds with "weakness and fear and trembling." Yet I return to this passage again and again, because it holds a resonance that strikes a deep chord within me.

Moving into a classroom surprise such as the one detailed above is an experience of deep clarity. These are the moments when I realize that no matter what I do, what is learned isn't up to me. The energy and the passion of curiosity, the fears and the threat of "not knowing," any catalyst for learning that emerges in a classroom—these are gifts of a power greater than I, and any learning that emerges from them is also a gift of that Teacher. This experience is perhaps the closest I have come in my own life to knowing something of what is meant by the Greek term *kenosis* (Phillipians 2:7), a term that has shifted meaning depending on the context in which it is engaged, but for me, is a mark of the self-emptying that is possible in deeply relational, respectful interaction.[1]

Given that reality, what does it mean to teach in a way that comes bearing Christ? For me the answers to this question have come most directly out of the educational literatures. They have emerged from descriptions of teaching and learning that privilege collaboration and openness, that conceive of teaching and learning in deeply relational ways. These descriptions evoke, almost inevitably, theological themes.

I. MODELS FOR LEARNING AND TEACHING

Consider for a moment Parker Palmer's images for various processes of teaching and learning shown in Figures 4.1 and 4.2.

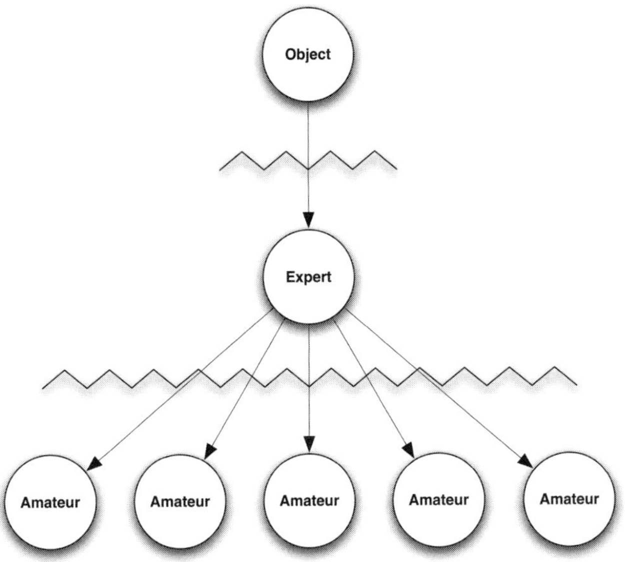

Figure 4.1 "The objectivist myth of knowing"

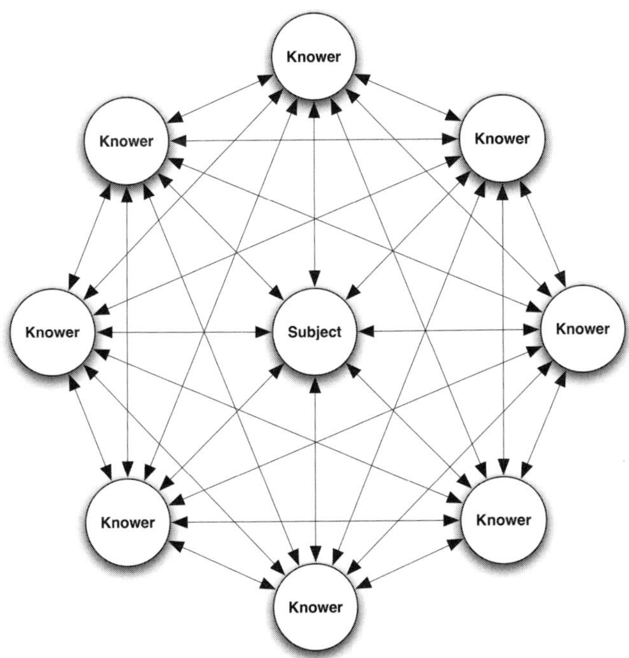

Figure 4.2 "The community of truth"

His first image depicts a process in which the responsibility for learning is clear—the expert transfers information to amateurs who passively receive it. This is an image of teaching and learning that promotes what Paulo Freire once termed "banking education," in which learning is "deposited" into the previously blank minds of passive recipients.[3] The benefits to such a process are obvious: teacher and student roles are clearly delineated, the nature of authority is directly linked to the expert's connection to the topic, it is relatively easy to measure the effectiveness of the teacher (did the information indeed get transferred?), the one-way nature of the process avoids the potential dilemma of situational or contextual factors contradicting the teacher, and so on. This is not a process, however, that permits much by way of "relationality"—particularly if relationality demands two-way communication.

Parker Palmer's second image, on the other hand, something he has labeled "the community of truth," provides a rich and complex model for the process of learning that evokes multiple paths of interrelationship. It is critical to understand that Palmer's notion here is not of relativism but rather of relationality:

> . . . by Christian understanding we must go one step further—and it is a critical step. Not only do I invest my own personhood in truth and the quest for truth, but truth invests itself personally in me and the quest for me. "Truth in person" means not only that the knower's person becomes part of the equation, but that the personhood of the known enters the relation as well.[4]

You can see this understanding at work in the ways in which Jesus taught. Over and over again he drew on notions of relationship to carry meaning—siblings, parents, communities, and so on. He is most often depicted as teaching in the midst of communities, relationally, not in didactic, transmissive patterns of practice.

Trinitarian theology suggests many other themes that do not map easily onto the transfer of information process, while they do map more directly onto a "community of truth" paradigm. God created the world, and in doing so created it *whole*, and thus organically in connection, one to another. Palmer's image of the community of truth makes those connections visible and points to a reliance upon connectivity that makes learning possible. As Malcolm Warford writes, "teaching is often viewed as a solitary venture of self and subject, but on another level we know that both teaching and learning are a matter of relationships significantly shaped by the community in which they occur."[5]

God gave God's only Son that "all might have life and life eternal"—a self-giving that is the very definition of *kenosis*—of "pouring oneself out"—a form of teaching that points *not* to the expertise of the teacher, but rather to the truth of the "great thing" around which we gather (to use another of Palmer's terms).[6] While in Palmer's first image it is easy to point to the role of the teacher—the expert—and to make specific claims about the authority of such a teacher, it is also easy to miss the way in which the learners have no direct connection to the thing about which they desire to learn. They have no relationship with the subject except as mediated through the teacher. While it is clearly appropriate to understand that Jesus is our mediator, that conviction does not make the theological educator the only mediator "through which" one encounters truth.

Indeed, the kenotic nature of the salvific event of Christ's entry into our lives is fruitfully kept at the heart of our learning and teaching as educators in Christian communities. As Paul writes, "I came resolved to know nothing while I was with you except Jesus Christ, and him crucified." Palmer's second image provides a map for doing so if one puts that saving event at the heart of the map as the "great thing" around which we gather as we seek to know and to learn. There is no obvious role for a teacher in this map but that does not mean that teachers are not present. It simply points to the reality in Palmer's vision that *all* are teachers in some way, just as *all* are learners—we *all* "know as we are known." Indeed, the fundamental task of a teacher in this kind of process is to get out of the way sufficiently to allow learners to engage the central topic; to create an environment in which direct relationship and direct engagement with the subject is possible. It is fundamentally a kenotic posture for a teacher, rather than an "expert" role. As Paul writes, "I came resolved to know nothing while I was with you except Jesus Christ, and him crucified"—a knowing that freed Paul to engage widely diverse cultures as contexts in which to share and learn the Good News.

It should go without saying, but nevertheless needs to be noted, that *kenosis* flows from a fundamental self giving, and that one must first "have a self" to "give a self." In other words, this description is not a recipe for teachers simply to tell students whatever they want to hear or for people with varying amounts of ignorance to share that ignorance with each other, but rather, for teachers to create learning environments in which differing knowledges can be tested, brought into relationship, and affirmed or discarded.[7] In this kind of process teachers must be so deeply attentive to the subject they are teaching that they are able to be at once clearly loyal to a specific interpretation and yet demonstrably open to new insights. As Victor Klimoski points out:

> Being attentive is important in all aspects of a person's growth and development. First and foremost, it means being attentive to the movement of God in one's life, through the Word, and in the tradition one bears. When we are advised to listen for God's voice, it means we need to be still. We need *the ability to let go of our conclusions* long enough to grasp the sort of questions that should dog our steps.[8]

II. DEVELOPMENTAL CHALLENGES: SELFHOOD AND LEARNING

Yet this stance, this fundamental ability to let go of conclusions is not an easy one. What does it mean to "have a self" in order to "give a self" in the context of teaching? Robert Kegan identifies some of the dilemmas in this kind of teaching as stemming from the developmental challenge of moving from third-order to fourth-order knowing.[9] Kegan defines a key distinction between people making meaning in third order frameworks, and those doing so in fourth order frames, as the ability to differentiate oneself from the surround in which one is embedded.

I frequently have students, for instance, who feel personally challenged on some fundamental level of their identity if you disagree with them. Perhaps the furthest they will go is to suggest that everyone has a belief about a question, and so be it. In other words, you can believe that, and I will believe this, and there's no way to finally arbitrate between the two positions. Alternatively, students will argue that there is only one way of viewing a question—the authority of scripture, for instance—and any other way is and must be seen as demonstrably false. In both of these cases students feel personally threatened by acknowledging that there are multiple and valid lenses through which to consider a particular question and come to a decision. In the first case a student might recognize the multiplicity of beliefs but see them as carrying equal weight. In the second case, a student might recognize the multiplicity, but solves the dilemma it poses by claiming a personal stance as the only authoritative position. In the example I described at the beginning of this chapter, I believe the students who were so visibly upset felt challenged to the core of their identity—both by a professor using a children's book to invite broader meaning-making and by colleagues who refused to confirm their intrepretation of the book. They had no place in which to embed themselves, no group with which to align, and thus experienced a deep and personal threat.

This way of constructing meaning makes it virtually impossible to welcome such students into the kind of critical discourse at the heart of much theological study, where differing nuances of interpretation are understood as legitimate and valid and where one's interpretive stance defines one's position, but not necessarily the whole of the field. In the context of seminary education, our students face the particular challenge of desiring and even needing to proclaim the authoritative nature of Christian truth claims, but also needing to find ways to do so that are deeply contextualized, deeply situated, founded on and funded by a specific space within a specific community. As Palmer's second image makes so strikingly visible, truth lies at the heart of the community, and each of us has singular knowledge of it—but each of us also only holds parts of the puzzle.

In explaining how to support this kind of learning, Palmer writes:

> We invite *diversity* into our community not because it is politically correct but because diverse viewpoints are demanded by the manifold mysteries of great things.
>
> We embrace *ambiguity* not because we are confused or indecisive but because we understand the inadequacy of our concepts to embrace the vastness of great things.
>
> We welcome *creative conflict* not because we are angry or hostile but because conflict is required to correct our biases and prejudices about the nature of great things.
>
> We practice *honesty* not only because we owe it to one another but because to lie about what we have seen would be to betray the truth of great things.
>
> We experience *humility* not because we have fought and lost but because humility is the only lens through which great things can be seen—and once we have seen them, humility is the only posture possible.
>
> We become *free men and women* through education not because we have privileged information but because tyranny in any form can only be overcome by invoking the grace of great things.[10]

Developmentally, however, this attention to "the grace of great things" is not an easy position to inhabit, nor is it a simple one into which to grow. The challenges are difficult enough in the context of typical higher education where students often displace the "threats" onto cognitive dissonance and remain unengaged.[11] In theological contexts, with the high emphasis placed on normativity, and in the seminary context, where students are studying to lead communities, these challenges can become identity threatening and fundamentally undermine the "great things" we all seek to engage.

This intersection is the point at which Kegan's work becomes so interesting in a seminary context, because it provides a concrete—and surprisingly friendly to Christian faith—process for walking with students through these developmental shifts.[12] At the heart of the strategy he and Lisa Lahey have developed is the metaphor of "mental machinery."[13] While on the one hand such a metaphor might seem like a capitulation to the instrumentality I objected to earlier, it is in fact a bridge metaphor—a way of seeing that prompts the development of certain practices of language, of certain habits of reflection—and in doing so it opens up the relationality of knowing described in Palmer's images.

At the center of the mental machinery are seven languages, seven ways of describing and entering into reality that build a habit of mind and practice that moves from third-order knowing (embedded in a surround where identity is held by the culture) to fourth-order knowing (where the surround is now held, rather than holding, empowering a person to self-differentiate sufficiently). Kegan and Lahey describe four personal, or internal, languages and three social languages. Working together, the seven languages create an agile and adept stance for learning—particularly the kind of learning that theological educators desire so strongly to support.

These seven languages also map a pragmatic stance for teachers, giving us concrete strategies for living from within our identity as faithful Christians outward to supporting our students in their own rooted, yet open, identities. The first four, which Kegan and Lahey term "personal" languages, map specific moves from what might be indentified as third-order knowing, to a stance that allows for fourth-order frames. They are

- Moving from complaint to commitment;
- Moving from the language of blame to that of personal responsibility;
- Moving from the language of New Year's resolutions to competing commitments; and,
- Moving from big assumptions that hold us to assumptions that we hold.[14]

A. From Complaint to Commitment

Consider how these languages help us in our classrooms. Take the first one—moving from the language of complaint to the language of commitment. Kegan and Lahey's assertion is that deep within our complaints lie corresponding commitments that give rise to the complaint. Seeking to understand the commitment brings a different and more constructive energy to the situation. When students complain to me about the amount of required reading I've assigned, I explore with them where that complaint arises from. Is it a commitment to another course that is taking priority over their comitment to this one? Is it a desire to read deeply and integrate and the corresponding fear that with this much reading they won't be able to do so? Is it that they don't yet know how to read in different ways (skim for crucial points, read deeply with their questions, and so on) and so can't imagine spending the time they think it will require? The answers to those questions shape my responses and suggest differing ways of moving forward.

Over the years I have moved several books from "required" to "recommended" on my syllabi due to sustained exploration with my students of their complaints. In the process, I've discovered that my entirely reasonable fears of not covering the ground sufficiently are more than outweighed by the positive and even transformative learning that comes from the deep engagement which is possible when students' strong commitments are respected.

The language of complaint is pointed at my learning as a teacher, as well. Many of the complaints I find myself voicing have at their heart a deeper commitment. Forcing myself to state the issue as a positive commitment, rather than a negative whine, both affirms such a commitment and frames it in a way that empowers me.[15] When I complain that my colleagues refuse to talk about their teaching, for instance, I need to recognize that what I am committed to is finding ways to open up dialogical space for reflecting on teaching, particularly my own. Looked at it in this way, I am forced to acknowledge that my complaint might hold the seeds of its own resolution. This language leads naturally to Kegan and Lahey's second language, that of moving from a language of blame to one of personal responsibility.

B. From Blame to Personal Responsibility

One way in which Kegan and Lahey speak of this language is to suggest asking this question: "What are you doing, or not doing, that is keeping your commitment from being more fully realized?" In the contexts in which I teach, one frequent complaint that is often heard has to do with the ways in which students dismiss classical theological disciplines as not being relevant to contemporary ministry. Why can't our students trust us that learning hermeneutics matters? Or, why can't they see that systematic theology holds important keys to providing coherence and congruence? Most of the time these complaints are framed as problems from the students' standpoint. The students, that is, just don't "get it."

I begin with my own underlying assumption that study of classical disciplines is crucial to engagement in contemporary ministry. When I ask myself what I am doing, or not doing, to keep this commitment from being realized, I begin to consider my complaint from a different angle. Why don't my students understand that their epistemological commitments shape how they lead learning? Perhaps because I haven't helped that understanding come alive for them. Given the cultural contexts we inhabit, a postmodern turn of mind rarely accepts assertions—particularly from institutional authorities—as *a priori* correct. Just because I've told my students that an underlying epistemology matters doesn't mean they understand that is the case, or why, even if they understand the terminology—and many of them don't. So how can I help them "sympathetically identify" with such an understanding? How can I engage them, provide enough routes into the material and enough immediate connecting points, that they begin to see, in their own imagination, in their own experiences, how what one believes about knowing shapes how one teaches? Is it possible that my own teaching has not been effective? Do I even know how to go about inviting them effectively into the material I wish to share? And if I don't, does that mean I am unqualified for my current post?

Such doubts emerge all too often in the work of teaching, and all too often there are few places to voice, let alone explore, such self doubt.

Part of the response to such dilemmas, I've found, is to recognize that it's not enough to work with these challenges on only the cognitive level because the affective and the psychomotor levels carry at least as much power in shaping student understanding. That is, it's not enough to simply work with intellectual concepts: I have to engage student feelings and shape experiences in which they can practice, or embody, what we're learning together. The very way in which I approach their concerns teaches something about whether or not their concerns matter, which in turn teaches them something about the integrity of the classroom.[16] The same is true about my own doubts. Do I simply push them down, ignore them, all too often take that internal energy and blame the student for her problem? Or do I ask myself the questions that bring me beyond my own limited nature and break open room for the Spirit to move?

Recognizing that I bear some personal responsibility in the situation is not, of course, to assume that I carry all of it and the student bears none. As I noted earlier in this essay, a kenotic teaching posture demands an engagement with the truth at the heart of the circle of knowing, it demands that there be a *there* around which we gather. I bear responsibility, the student bears responsibility, and together we meet in a specific context and around a specific topic that carries its own substance and context.

C. From New Year's Resolutions to Competing Commitments

Recognizing the larger context in which we are embedded moves us to Kegan and Lahey's third language, that of moving from New Year's resolutions to competing commitments. Most of us are familiar with New Year's resolutions—those bright and cheery resolutions to begin the New Year afresh—to lose 10 pounds, to grade papers within one week of submission, to write regularly, and so on and on and on. Kegan and Lahey point out that one of the problems with such resolutions is that they don't take into account the reality that many commitments coexist and often conflict with each other. The language of resolutions also tends to put a negative spin on the task at hand, given all of the times I am not successful in keeping them.

I may be committed to grading papers within one week of receiving them, for instance, but I am also committed to preparing well for each of my classes. If I can't get papers back in time, then surely it's a failure on my part. Yet in a world of twenty-four-hour days, there may not be time to do both well. Facing the challenge of recognizing one's own limitations requires the ability to get outside of oneself enough to consider these competing commitments, along with the specific underlying assumptions that may be preventing us from effectively meeting them.

I know that, for myself, far too often I bring papers home and grade them late into the night, rather than admitting that I can't do all that is on my plate within the reasonable framework of a work week. Other of my colleagues skimp on their paper comments or pull out lectures they've given over and over again, all by way of managing the time pressures. But how often, if at all, do we sit down with each other and acknowledge that the pressure has become too much? Given the very real financial stresses that beset seminary education, it can feel downright dangerous and somehow disloyal to ask whether we are pushing too hard. Yet very similar pressures face our students once they enter their ministries. While our explicit curriculum may intend that they learn how to delegate effectively and share the burden of ministry, our implicit curriculum very often teaches them that individuals need to soldier on, finding ways to manage the stresses individually.

That implicit curriculum—and beneath it, the unvoiced null curriculum of "it's always been done this way, and if we don't continue to do it this way the whole church will fall apart"—holds powerful sway. Like the images shared early in this chapter drawn from Palmer's work, the "great things" at the heart of our engagement can demand more of us than we recognize and shape more of our teaching and learning than we are ready to admit that they do. Finding ways to name our conflicting and competing commitments often leads directly to recognizing the key assumptions at the heart of our practices. It is at this point that the final language of Kegan and Lahey's four personal languages, the foundation of their mental machinery model, becomes so important.

D. From Big Assumptions That Hold Us to Assumptions We Hold

Kegan and Lahey assert that we need to move from the language of big assumptions that hold us to the language of assumptions that we hold. This is a clear marking point in moving from one order of consciousness to another. In Kegan's terms what was once "subject"—what once held us to the point that we could not see it—becomes "object"—or something that we can now hold at arm's length and consider. One of the biggest such assumptions to pervade theological education is that of teaching authority, that of the difference between the objectivist myth of teaching and learning described in Palmer's first image, and the more relational, connected process of his second.

The objectivist, instrumental image of teaching assumes that the acknowledged authority or expert best mediates interaction with the topic under consideration. Indeed, it posits that such interaction is essentially unidirectional, proceeding at the invitation of the teacher and in the direction the teacher outlines. As long as we are held by this assumption, it is impossible to question it, to even begin to build a relationship to it, rather than being held by it. Perhaps it is true, but how can we know unless we consider other alternatives? How can we know unless we can imagine our way into a space in which it is not the case?

I am convinced that part of the challenge I face in my own teaching context at Luther Seminary in St. Paul, MN, comes from this unexamined assumption. So much flows outward from it! Not the least is an MDiv degree program structured so rigidly that in their first year our students have only one half-credit elective choice, in the second year only one full-credit elective choice, and it is only in their fourth year (our students spend their third year on internship) that they are allowed three electives. Such tight structuring assumes that the institution, and the faculty as its primary arbiters, knows what's best for students. Yet our students are an increasingly diverse group, coming from a variety of contexts, a vast array of different experiences, with a wide spectrum of abilities. Our curriculum assumes a "just in case" kind of focus—you need this learning just in case you come across this particular situation, rather than a "just in time" focus—here's the information you need at the point in time that you are ready to use it. We need to remember that as Paul writes to the Corinthians, "I did not come with sublimity of words or of wisdom. For I resolved to know nothing except Jesus Christ, and him crucified." This core conviction can be a key from which all else flows.

What does it mean to know nothing except Jesus Christ and him crucified? Surely not that we all should simply show up and wait passively for information to be showered upon us. But what kind of learning environment creates an active space of listening for such a revelation? What kind of design can structure the space to allow for the best opportunity for such engagement? This is the fulcrum of Kegan and Lahey's work as well, for the four languages just described build a foundation personally, an internal set of mechanisms, but they must be embedded in the three social languages that Kegan and Lahey delineate.

E. From Prizes and Praising to Ongoing Regard

The first of these social languages is the movement from the language of prizes and praising to that of ongoing regard.

One way to think about this shift is deeply theological: it is moving away from a space in which one's actions earn merit, to one in which one is gifted simply by being a child of God. In other words, it is the difference between a world of earned merit and one of overflowing, unmerited, and unearned but freely available *grace*.

Do our students entering our classrooms understand themselves as fully capable learners, gifted with unique gifts that must be shared to enable learning for everyone—the multiple focal points of Palmer's second, connected image—or do they instead enter our classrooms seeking to discover, in the shortest time possible, what the teacher wants and how to deliver it? Are our practices of evaluation—particularly within degree program structures where incentives defined as grades are still in place—focused on attributing certain traits to students and thus forming them, or are they focused on recognizing and noting our experience, either positive or negative, leaving the other informed (but not formed) by our words? For example, "Martin, your writing demonstrates your brilliance," versus, "Martin, I appreciate the way in which your writing caused me to think in new ways about what epistemology means." The first statement attributes a trait to the student; the second describes how the student had an impact on my own learning. The first awards a "prize" to the student on a particular assignment; the second suggests that the student has the ability to teach.

Kegan and Lahey note several characteristics of this kind of language use, among them that it:

> Distributes precious information that one's actions have significance; infuses energy *into* the system; Communicates appreciation or admiration directly to the person; Communicates *specific* information to the person about the speaker's personal experience of appreciation or admiration; *Non-attributive*, characterizes the speaker's experience, and not the person being appreciated; Sincere and authentic, more halting and freshly made; Transformational potential for both the speaker and the person being regarded . . .[17]

Providing a menu of assignments in a class that allows an individual student to contribute her best gifts to the classroom communicates something very differently from a single assignment that all students must complete. Providing opportunities for students to take the risk of trying something they're *not* good at, with deliberate incentives for trying something new and difficult rather than steep penalties for failing, contributes to an environment of ongoing regard.[18] Using critical incident reports, described elsewhere in this book, pointedly communicates that student experience of the learning event matters.[19]

As these are clearly social languages, their implementation must stretch beyond any individual classroom. Set within the often competing commitments of higher education, creating an environment of ongoing regard can be difficult. Yet there are ways of doing so, not the least being using the core theological categories at the heart of the curriculum as central organizing principles, rather than defaulting to those of higher ed.[20] Rather than organizing theological education in terms of prizes going to those most recognized by specific guilds or other organizations, it is possible to organize theological education in terms of matching people's God-given gifts to specific tasks and roles.

In my context it is clear that certain people are gifted as teachers, others as writers, still others as administrators. Providing room for each set of gifts to be identified and given room to flourish contributes to an overall atmosphere quite different from that in which higher education usually exists. It also inevitably creates constructive synergy that spreads energy, as opposed to stress-filled busyness that simply saps energy.

F. From Rules and Policies to Public Agreement

Deliberately moving in these directions, which tends to be moving against the grain of much of higher education, requires the next language that Kegan and Lahey have identified: that of public agreement (as distinguished from that kind of institutional language which resides in "rules" and "policies").

Most of us are quite familiar with what is meant by "rules and policies"—these are elements of institutions that exist within a complex web of governance (city, state, and federal laws, for instance, require most institutions to specify their rules and policies for dealing with specific issues). Rules and policies are almost universally developed from the top down of an organization and rarely provide constructive ground for engagement. You may first encounter a rule in the event of breaking it and encountering the resulting punishment. The language of rules and policies is observed most often in the specific, intermittant nature of its application to infraction than in ongoing, constructive modes for shaping engagement. You know you are not "supposed to do that," but you may not be as clear about what you *are* supposed to do. Students know, for instance, that they should not use exclusively male pronouns to refer to human beings in their papers, but they can often not articulate *why* that is the case, let alone suggest creative alternatives for referring to human beings.

The language of public agreement, by way of contrast, is a "vehicle for responsible people to collectively imagine a public life they simultaneously know they would prefer and know they will, at times, fall short of."[21] This is the language of *covenant* rather than contract. It is a language of relationship, of commitment to each other. It is the language that teachers often ask small groups to develop at the beginning of a collaborative process. "What will be our agreement about collaboration? How will we know if we are indeed living into it?" Such an agreement allows individual members of a group space in which to call the group into accountability. It is a language that demands as well as facilitates participation. Much of what we have described as the process of using CIQ forms seeks to embody this kind of group space. Similarly, the very ground rules we established for the teaching/learning reflection group out of which this book grew were a covenant for our participation.

I would go so far as to argue that Paul's rhetoric in the letters to the scattered churches of the first century was an attempt to articulate such a language, to provide a constructive and public agreement about what these communities were to be about. He argued that he came not with "sublimity of words and wisdom" but with a deep connection to a living God, one who had been broken on a cross that we might live into God's creating Word. Paul's witness was to scattered communities and attempted to build amongst them a shared openness and hospitality to engagement with "others." Can there be a better way to frame our own learning communities?

At the beginning of each course I teach, we spend some time exploring this notion of a language of public agreement. One obvious example involves walking with my students through the syllabus for the course. I try to design all of my courses with room for improvisation, and helping each other understand what that can mean begins in the first session of the class. I have found Stephen Brookfield's "course caveat" a good catalyst for this conversation because it names the limits of the negotiation, but also provides room for discussion.

What You Need to Know about This Course

As a student, I very much appreciate the chance to make informed decisions about the courses I take. I want to know who the educator is, what his or her assumptions are, and what he or she stands for before I make a commitment to spend my time, money, and energy attending the class. So let me tell you some things about me and how I work as an educator that will allow you to make an informed decision as to whether nor not you wish to be involved in this course.

I have framed this course on the following assumptions:

1. That participating in discussion brings with it the following benefits:
    - It helps students explore a diversity of perspectives.
    - It increases students' awareness of and tolerance for ambiguity and complexity.
    - It helps students recognize and investigate their assumptions.
    - It encourages attentive, respectful listening.

- It develops new appreciation for continuing differences.
- It increases intellectual agility.
- It helps students become connected to a topic.
- It shows respect for students' voices and experiences.
- It helps students learn the processes and habits of democratic discourse.
- It affirms students as cocreators of knowledge.
- It develops the capacity for the clear communication of ideas and meaning.
- It develops habits of collaborative learning.
- It increases breadth and makes students more empathic.
- It helps students develop skills of synthesis and integration.
- It leads to transformation.

2. That students attending will have experiences that they can reflect on and analyze in discussion.

3. That the course will focus on the analysis of students' experiences and ideas as much as on the analysis of academic theories.

4. That the chief regular class activity will be a small group discussion of experiences and ideas.

5. That I as teacher have a dual role as a catalyst for your critical conversation and as a model of democratic talk.

So please take note of the following "product warnings"!

If you don't feel comfortable talking with others about yourself and your experiences in small groups, *you should probably drop this course.*

If you don't feel comfortable with small group discussion and think it's a touchy-feely waste of valuable time, *you should probably drop this course.*

If you are not prepared to analyze your own and other people's experiences, *you should probably drop this course.*

From Stephen Brookfield and Stephen Preskill, *Discussion as a Way of Teaching: Tools and Techniques for Democratic Classrooms* (San Francisco: Jossey-Bass, 1999), 60–61.

G. From Constructive to Deconstructive Criticism

The final language that Kegan and Lahey describe is that which moves from the language of constructive criticism to that of deconstructive criticism. Given how most of us were trained to practice constructive criticism, it can be jarring to recognize the assumptions upon which it rests. For instance, constructive criticism:

> assumes the perspective of the feedback giver is right and correct . . . An accompanying assumption is that there is only one right answer . . . As long as we hold our view to be true—we have a vested interest in maintaining the truth. . . . Once we establish our meaning as the standard and norm against which we evaluate other people, we essentially hold them to our personal preferences.[22]

Criticizing constructive criticism is not an argument for the impossibility of normative truth. Rather, Kegan and Lahey point beyond notions of destructive and constructive criticism to what they have instead labelled "deconstructive criticism," which assumes that offering criticism is an opening for engagement in real dialogue that seeks to foster substantial learning. Such engagement rests on a series of "deconstructive propositions":

1. There is probable merit to my perspective.
2. My perspective may not be accurate.
3. There is some coherence, if not merit, to the other person's perspective.

4. There may be more than one legitimate interpretation.
5. The other person's view of my viewpoint is important information to my assessing whether I am right or identifying what merit there is to my view.
6. Our conflict may be the result of the separate commitments each of us hold, including commitments we are not always aware we hold.
7. Both of us have something to learn from the conversation.
8. We need to have two-way conversation to learn from each other.
9. If contradictions can be a source of our learning, then we can come to engage not only internal contradictions as a source of learning but interpersonal contradictions (i.e., "conflict") as well.
10. The goal of our conversation is for each of us to learn more about ourselves and the other as meaning makers.[23]

Note how these propositions shift learners and teachers from the mode of being the owners of truth to being seekers of truth. Quite visibly they move us from the instrumental process depicted in Palmer's first image at the beginning of this chapter to his second, more relational image of the "community of truth." In making this move, we rely on our faith that there is, indeed, truth to be discovered—but our very faith shapes the humility of our search for truth.[24]

These propositions are a basis by which to begin a true conversation. They are a clear foundation for the kind of learning involved in discipleship. As Paul notes, "I come not bearing wise words of wisdom, but only Christ, and him crucified." Paul knows something whereof he speaks, in having had his entire life turned upside down, quite literally struck from his previous authoritative stance into blindness, and turned to a new road.

It is important to recognize that:

> A language of deconstructive criticism is not a language of discounting one's own negative evaluation. Rather it's about holding two simultaneous realities together. And practicing a language for deconstructive conflict does not leave one in paralysis of analysis, unable to act, merely better understanding the conflict. Finally, language for deconstructive conflict is not practiced first of all for the purpose of making the conflict disappear or even reducing its intensity.[25]

Indeed, this kind of language can at times heighten awareness of the differences that exist in a given situation.

This language is an argument for the nuanced and complex notion of truth that Palmer identifies as *troth,* or the truth for which one gives one's life.[26] Such truth is neither easily derived nor simply specified. This is the kind of truth for which Jesus was crucified and on the basis of which we as sinful human beings are redeemed. This is also the truth—through pledging of troth—that most often poses the really painful dilemmas of growth for our students and ourselves. To return to the situation I described at the beginning of this chapter, my students who were so visibly outraged by their reading of a children's book and the differing responses their colleagues made to it, were caught on the horns of a dilemma for which they had no solution. They did not hold the "deconstructive propositions" listed above. And it is doubtful that had I simply listed these at the beginning of the class they would have been able to comprehend them. Almost anything I did at that point in the classroom probably was not going to enter their space and change their perceptions. However, my actions could—and most likely did—have an impact on many of the other students in the room.

From the perspective of hindsight, had I already had a "language of public agreement" in place with them, I could have found more constructive ways to bring them into dialogue. Indeed, many of the exercises that Stephen Brookfield describes in chapter 3 of this volume for learning through dialogue are carefully structured to create precisely that kind of space. For students who are not yet able to make the shift from third to fourth-order meaning-making, providing such carefully structured environments is critical. They function as a form of container, or "holding environment" in Kegan's terms, that provides space in which teachers can model and students can experiment with and explore differing perspectives.

Such exercises also begin to invite students into the kinds of practices that live in these other "languages" that Kegan and Lahey have defined and which shape so much of what we are attempting to do in sharing the texts of classical discliplines with them. In doing so we provide room for our students—and ourselves!—to practice the "mental machinery" of growth and development that may indeed allow us to embody Paul's words:

> When I came to you, brothers and sisters, proclaiming the mystery of God, I did not come with sublimity of words or of wisdom. For I resolved to know nothing while I was with you except Jesus Christ, and him crucified. I came to you in weakness and fear and much trembling, and my message and my proclamation were not with persuasive words of wisdom, but with a demonstration of spirit and power, so that your faith might rest not on human wisdom but on the power of God. (I Cor 2:1–5)

NOTES

1. Sarah Coakley explores a number of ways of thinking about *kenosis* in her chapter "Kenosis: Theological meanings and gender connotations," in a text edited by John Polkinghorne, *The Work of Love: Creation as Kenosis* (Grand Rapids, MI: Eerdmans, 2001). One of my MA students at Luther Seminary, Claire Bischoff, also wrote an excellent thesis on this topic, which is available through our library: "Truth-centered Communities: Taking the Trinity Seriously in Religious Education." MA thesis, Luther Seminary, 2004.
2. These images are drawn from Parker Palmer's *The Courage to Teach: Exploring the Inner Landscape of a Teacher's Life*. Copyright 1998, reprinted with permission of John Wiley & Sons, Inc.

3. Paulo Freire, *Pedagogy of the Oppressed* (New York: Continuum Publishing, 1985), 57 ff.
4. Parker Palmer, *To Know As We Are Known* (San Francisco: HarperSanFrancisco, 1993), 58.
5. Malcolm Warford, "Introduction," in *Practical Wisdom: On Theological Teaching and Learning*, ed. by Malcolm Warfoard (New York: Lang, 2004), xv.
6. See in particular Palmer's "grace of great things" in *The Courage to Teach*, 107–108.
7. See here, in particular, the Stephen Brookfield discussion in chapter 3 of this volume.
8. [Emphasis added.] Victor Klimoski, "Evolving dynamics of formation," *Practical Wisdom: On Theological Teaching and Learning*, ed. by Malcolm Warford (New York: Lang, 2004): 33.
9. Robert Kegan, *In Over Our Heads: The Mental Demands of Modern Life* (Cambridge, MA: Harvard University Press, 1995), 37–70. See also his *The Evolving Self: Problem and Process in Human Development* (Cambridge, MA: Harvard University Press, 1982).
10. Parker Palmer, *The Courage to Teach: Exploring the Inner Landscape of a Teacher's Life* (San Francisco: Jossey-Bass, 1998), 107–108.
11. See, for example, the work of P. Kitchener and K. King, *Developing Reflective Judgment: Understanding and Promoting Intellectual Growth and Critical Thinking in Adolescents and Adults* (San Francisco: Jossey-Bass, 1994) or Kenneth Bruffee, *Collaborative Learning: Higher Education, Interdependence and the Authority of Knowledge* (Baltimore MD: Johns Hopkins University Press, 1993).
12. For specific examples of Kegan's theorizing applied to communities of faith, see Anita Farber-Robertson, *Learning While Leading: Increasing Your Effectiveness in Ministry* (Herndon, VA: Alban Institute, 2000), and Walter Conn, *Christian Conversion: A Developmental Interpretation of Autonomy and Surrender* (New York: Paulist Press, 1986).
13. See in particular Robert Kegan and Lisa Lahey, *How The Way We Talk Can Change The Way We Work: Seven Languages for Transformation* (San Francisco: Jossey-Bass, 2001).
14. Ibid.
15. This, of course, is also part of the energy behind the research methodology known as "apppreciative inquiry." See David Cooper-

rider, Frank Barrett, Suresh Srivastva, "Social construction and appreciative inquiry: A journey in organizational theory," *Management and Organization: Relational Alternatives to Individualism*, ed. by Hosking, Dachler and Gergen (New York: Ashgate, 1995). Also, Mark Lau Branson, *Memories, Hopes and Conversations: Appreciative Inquiry and Congregational Change* (Herndon, VA: Alban Institute, 2004).

16. Stephen Brookfield and I have tried to make this point forcefully in chapter 1 of the volume you are currently reading, and Stephen explains a number of concrete ways to help students learn this respect through discussion in chapter 3.
17. Kegan and Lahey, *How the Way We Talk*, 102.
18. It is worth noting that Sharon Daloz Park's work on leadership education suggests that "it must be underscored that it is the reflection on one's own experiences of leadership failure that is the essential, vital feature of this leadership formation practice." Sharon Daloz Parks, *Leadership Can Be Taught: A Bold Approach for a Complex World* (Boston: Harvard Business School Publishing, 2005), 96. Further examples of how this works in teaching students how to participate in discussion can be found in chapter 3 of the volume you are currently reading.
19. The CIQ process is described at length in chapter 1 of this volume and then explored using particular examples in chapters 3, 5 and 8.
20. The interesting experiment at the heart of Luther Seminary's current curriculum is described by Donald Juel and Patrick Kiefert in "A rhetorical approach to theological education: Assessing an attempt to re-vision a curriculum." In David S. Cunningham (ed.), *To Teach, To Delight, and To Move: Theological Education in a Post-Christian World* (Eugene, OR: Cascade Books, 2004).
21. Kegan and Lahey, *How the Way We Talk*, 114.
22. Kegan and Lahey, *How the Way We Talk*, 128–129.
23. Kegan and Lahey, *How the Way We Talk*, 141. A similar set of principles can be found in the "Principles of dialogue" from the Catholic Common Ground Initiative (http://www.nplc.org/commonground/dialogue.htm), and in the ELCA's document "Talking together as Christians about tough social issues" (brief excerpt available online at: http://www.elca.org/youth/resource/riskydiscussions.html).
24. Mark Edwards names a series of Christian virtues in relation to

this kind of humility as being quintessential scholarly responses in his essay "Characteristically Lutheran leanings?" *Dialog: A Journal of Theology*, Vol. 41, #1 (2002).

25. Kegan and Lahey, *How the Way We Talk*, 143–145.
26. Palmer, *To Know As We Are Known*, 43.

CHAPTER 5

"How Do Students Experience the Teacher?" Knowing Who You Are as a Teacher (and Knowing that Your Students Do Not)

Rolf Jacobson

Classrooms are often areas of confusion where the teachers are gladiators of ambiguity.

—Stephen D. Brookfield[1]

I. A FEARFUL AND WONDERFUL AMBIGUITY

Teaching is a fearful and wonderful thing. When teaching works, it is mystical and marvelous. When it does not work, it is frustrating and frightening. But why does it work at some times and not others? Although an absolute answer to this question will remain elusive, perhaps a partial answer can be found in the reality that *teaching involves both teachers and learners*. And, to borrow from Psalm 139, both teachers and learners are fearfully and wonderfully made. As Parker Palmer has described it, "teaching is endless meeting"[2]—the endless meeting of teachers and learners, the endless meeting of infinitely unique individuals, the endless meeting of irreducibly complex creatures, the endless meeting of living people who can never fully know themselves or fully know each other.

And therein lie both the joy and the frustration of teaching. Teaching is people helping other people to learn. Because teaching is the endless meeting of people, the teacher can find her task to be an ambiguous one that takes place in an ambiguous environment. When it comes to human relationships, perfect clarity kills the relationship. Any relationship that unfolds with the clinical predictability of a physics experiment cannot give true life, in part because such a relationship will be too subject to control. But because people are fearfully and wonderfully made, teaching will also include randomness and unpredictability, which constitute true relationality. Therefore, the confusion of the teaching environment is not to be denied, but embraced; not to be conquered, but explored. So, rather than seeking to squelch the ambiguity of the teaching enterprise, teachers who embrace the confusion that is inherent in any genuinely relational circumstance must learn to be, in Stephen Brookfield's marvelous phrase, "gladiators of ambiguity."

None of which is to say that there is only confusion and ambiguity in teaching. To be sure, we are only able to see the teaching enterprise in part, as in a mirror dimly. But we do see! We do understand! Teaching is in large part about the interaction between teacher and student around an agreed upon subject matter. And as teachers, we know at least something about our subject matter, our students, and ourselves.

The focus of this chapter is on the *teacher*. To be more precise, this chapter is about the necessity and productivity of the teacher taking the time to understand himself or herself as a part of the learning environment. When we learn to know ourselves better as teachers and to teach comfortably as who we are, we can also learn to enter the teaching environment in a more productive way—which will make the students' yoke of learning a lighter load. That is to say, when we know ourselves a little better, we can enter into the confusion of the teacher-learner relationship at least a little more productively.

This chapter is in large part a conversation between my own confusing experiences as a teacher and three of my favorite books about teaching—two by Stephen Brookfield and one by Parker Palmer. Both authors share wise insights about the importance of self-awareness for teachers.[3] I commend these books heartily. I have structured this chapter around a few representative comments that I have received from students over the years.

Each comment in some way hurt, surprised, and/or upset me. The conversation and conversion that each comment generated has made me a more comfortable teacher.

II. WHEN I WAS A CHILD

Student Comment: "A lot of students say they like your courses. They say that you are an easy teacher."

A. Everything That I Needed To Know, I Learned at Tennis Camp

When I first began my career as a college teacher, I did so with a whole set of unexamined assumptions driving my teaching. In fact, it is not quite correct to say that I had not examined these assumptions as it is that I was unaware of these assumptions. One of the assumptions I held was that a good teacher is a demanding teacher. I still believe that. But I also held to a corollary assumption: A demanding teacher is one whom students experience as a difficult teacher. I no longer quite believe that.

When I was a child, I spoke like a child, I thought like a child, I reasoned like a child, I *learned* like a child, and I played tennis. As a child, tennis was a passion. The hours of my wasted youth were spent sprinting back and forth between white lines painted on green hard courts in chase of a yellow tennis ball. I had the passion to get better at tennis—to learn how to be a better player—so I took lessons, practiced, went to tennis camp, and did drills. When I was a child, I thought that a great tennis lesson was one that left me exhausted: doubled over with my head between my legs, searching between my feet for the breath that should have been in my lungs. A lesson in which the coach had run us mercilessly (tough love, don't you know) from side to side, pursuing excellence by chasing us all over the court.

When I was a young adult, I spoke like a young adult, I thought like a young adult, I reasoned like a young adult, I learned like a young adult, and I went to college and later to seminary and graduate school. Many hours of my young adulthood were invested in pursuit of intellectual and academic growth. I had the passion to learn and live. When I was a young adult—emphasis on the *young* more than on the adult—I thought that a great college course was one in which the amount of work was devastating, for which I would stay up late at night cramming for a tough exam, in which the demands were insane and the workload such that it left me exhausted: laid out flat on my bed at night, staring up at the bunk above me, searching for the wisdom that had evaporated out of the top of my head.

But when I became an adult, I put an end to childish ways. When I became an adult, I put an end to young-adult ways.

Along the way, in my journey from one who learned first as a child and then as a young adult, I realized something important about the best teachers that I had had: They were not always the teachers who demanded the most quantity, *but the best quality*. They were not always the teachers who assigned the most reading or piled on the most assignments, but the ones whose readings *made a difference* and transformed me in some way, whose assignments reshaped my mind. (Nor were the best teachers just the easiest teachers—I had plenty of easy teachers whose courses were not transformative.) The point is that the best courses I had were ones that provided learning experiences that transformed me.

As a 24-year-old I went back to a tennis camp, but this time I went as an instructor. The owner of the camp did not encourage the teachers to drive the students in frenzied, sprinting drills—although I noticed that the campers still thought that such drills were the best drills. The owner did not encourage such insane drills *because all they accomplished was to reinforce bad tennis habits*. In order to improve, most of the players needed to *transform some element about their games*. And in order to transform these elements, the players needed to *slow down*, not speed up, they needed time to understand why the adjustments needed to be made, time to make corrections, and then they needed deliberate (not frenzied) repetition so that the adjustments could sink in.[4]

B. A Tennis Player Teaching in King David's Court

In recent years, I have tried systematically to apply this insight to my teaching. I have tried to understand how my own experience as a learner—both in tennis and in academics—was in contrast to my practice as a teacher. To use a buzz word from a few years ago, I was teaching in "cognitive dissonance" with my own experience as a learner. But it is one thing to become aware of this cognitive dissonance as a teacher and quite another to own it and change my teaching behavior. The task of integrating what have been my most transformative learning experiences into my teaching approach is an unfinished work. I try to reflect regularly on the courses that I teach in the hope that someday I might integrate what I have learned about transformative learning experiences into how I behave as a teacher. In a way, this reflection is about knowing myself as a teacher and a learner. Because when I know myself and understand myself, then I can be a better teacher.

At the start of this section I mentioned that when I began my teaching career I held the unexamined assumption that good teachers are demanding teachers and that demanding teachers are difficult teachers. But as I have sought to illustrate using examples from my life as a tennis player, it is better to be demanding than to be "difficult"—at least, not "difficult" in the sense of piling unreasonable amounts of work on students or requiring so much reading that students cannot adequately engage with important ideas or have time to be transformed by those ideas. A more robust way to be demanding as teacher may be to slow the pace at which students are bombarded with information and instead structure learning experiences that require the students to own the material, to make mental adjustments, to be transformed.

A related type of demanding teacher is one who is very critical, who is very difficult to please, whose comments always wedge their way into the fissures in a student's work. But this type of demanding can also be counterproductive to transformative education if it is taken too far. Constructive criticism is necessary for transformation, of course, because unless a learner is made aware of something that needs improvement or change, he or she will be unlikely to work at changing it. But constant criticism in the absence of comments that support improvement and correction will only tear down and not build up. So here, too, a more robust way of being a demanding teacher can be found.

An example from my teaching might help to flesh out what I mean. One of the courses that I teach almost every semester is a survey course in the Old Testament prophets. The course is a challenging one to teach for several reasons: the students are by and large ignorant of the prophetic corpus; they are also ignorant of the Old Testament history that they need to know to understand that corpus; and the theological concepts that they meet in the prophets—such as divine judgment, righteousness, justice, sexist metaphors, and God's anger—are extremely challenging concepts.

I have found the concept of God's anger, in particular, to be an extremely difficult one for students to face. Most of them have no place in their theological imaginations for an angry God (or for a judging God, for that matter). Unfortunately they tend to equate the concept of God's anger either with acts of nature, with pre-Reformation medieval theology, or with lunatic fundamentalists from Topeka. The result of this "default mental setting" was that I often found students dismissing scriptural texts that portrayed a judging or angry God.

The default approach to teaching that I had learned would simply reinforce this dismissal. How so? It would reinforce this dismissal by requiring such a great deal of work that students would actually be forced to rush past the concept without engaging it, therefore making it very likely that they would dismiss it. The reason for such a dismissal is that *when students are under time pressure they are least likely to be able to reflect on their own assumptions and be transformed.*[5] Feeling crunched for time is one of the factors that interferes powerfully with transformative experiences. And transformation is exactly the outcome that this survey course needs to achieve. The course needs to help students first become aware that they have assumptions about a concept such as the anger of God, and second to help students shape their own thoughts about this concept.

Above, I mentioned that a similar type of "demanding

teacher" is one who is constantly critical, one who is very difficult to please, one who is always taking advantage of the teacher's hierarchical place in the classroom to point out to students the weaknesses in their work. Aside from what I hope are the obvious moral problems with this pedagogical approach, I think it is a counterproductive approach if the educational goal is transformation. Students are quite likely to shut down in the face of this judgment and simply give such teachers what they want to hear rather than engaging the ideas deeply enough so that transformation can take place.

My focus here is not primarily pedagogical nor specifically about the theology of the prophets.[6] Rather, I want to draw attention to the way in which awareness of *my own* assumptions about teaching and learning, and my own reflection on my biography as a teacher and as a learner, proved helpful in becoming a more comfortable teacher and in creating a better learning environment.

At the start of this section, I quoted a statement that one of my students offered to me of how some students viewed my classes. My immediate impulse was to be defensive and reactive. I thought, "Oh, they think that I am easy, I'll show them!" The comment was made about the prophetic survey course. My immediate reactive and defensive response showed me that I still have a long way to go in order to integrate what I have learned about transformative learning experiences into my teaching because it indicates to me that my "childish" and "young-adult" conceptions of a demanding teacher still have tremendous hold on me.

III. ON BEING ME AND NOT MOSES

Student Comment: "I didn't like it when you joked about Professor ________ in class today; you shouldn't belittle other professors."

A. "Our Strengths Are Our Weaknesses"

Whenever teachers enter a classroom, they enter as fully themselves. By saying this, I mean to assert neither some sort of touchy-feely absurdity nor a meaningless tautology. Rather, I mean to assert that *nobody can teach well as anyone other than who they genuinely are*. Some teachers may subconsciously change when they enter a classroom. They may feel forced—either by convention, by the expectations of the school at which they teach, or by their own ideas of how teachers should comport themselves—to try to become someone other than who they are. I would think it is obvious the damage and danger that such pedagogical *doppelgängers* must do, both to themselves and their students.

A wonderful Hasidic legend emphasizes the point:

> [There was] a young rabbi named Zusia. He was discouraged about his work. He would preach and his congregation would look out the window or doze off. The young people thought he was old-fashioned. He was not making an impact on the community. He knew he wasn't much of a scholar. He saw himself as a failure.
>
> So Zusia visited an older rabbit and said, "Rabbi, I'm so discouraged. What can I do?"
>
> The old rabbi said, "My son, when you get to heaven, God is not going to say to you, 'Why weren't you Moses?' But he is going to ask you, 'Why weren't you Zusia?' So why don't you stop trying to be Moses, and just be the Zusia that God made you to be?"[7]

On the other hand, entering a classroom as one's self poses its own set of challenges. An important teacher of mine taught me that rather than thinking about ourselves in terms of our strengths *and* our weaknesses, it is better to recognize that "our strengths *are* our weaknesses." To apply that lesson to the task of teaching, one might say that any given feature of a person's personality, or strength of a person's skill set, will be something that a person can rely on to help in the teaching task. But the opposite is also true: Any given feature of a person's personality, or strength of a person's skill set, will be something that a person can rely on to hinder the teaching task.

The specific example that I would like to discuss regards my use of humor as a teacher:

Humor is the number-two pencil that I use to fill in all of the bubbles on life's multiple-choice tests. If you offer me a compliment, I will deflect it with humor. If you lob an insult at me, I will deflect it with humor. If you ask me for advice, you'll get back something that passes for humor. If you ask me for my world-famous flourless chocolate cake recipe . . . well, you get the point.

Whenever I enter a classroom, because I am me and not trying to be anyone other than myself, it is a pretty good bet that humor will rear its ugly head somewhere along the line. (This is not, by the way, to assert that any of my jokes will actually *be funny*, only that at some point I will inevitably attempt a joke or fourteen.) *But humor is an ambiguous interpersonal phenomenon.* A quip that one person finds appealing may strike another as appalling. A remark that may tickle one person's funny bone may trigger another person's anger.

Among the necessary skills that all teachers must have are both the skill of communicating concepts and the skill of creating an environment conducive to learning. And that is precisely the rub with humor. On the one hand, because humor can grease the skids for communicating ideas and concepts, it is an invaluable strength for me as a teacher. Humor can contribute to a productive learning environment, because it can put students at ease by disarming apprehensions, by helping students to enjoy themselves, and by facilitating genuine relationality.

However, precisely because the same joke may lighten one person's mood and light another person's fuse, humor can also disrupt the communication of concept and undermine a learning environment. As Brookfield has written, "In human communication the potential for mutual miscomprehension is ubiquitous, especially in the complex relationship between teachers and students."[8] Humor, it seems to me, is especially volatile and ripe for miscomprehension. If humor offends, it can contribute to distrust. If humor doesn't connect, it can create a sense of disenfranchisement (especially if a person feels alone in not getting a joke or does not think it is funny). If humor is abusive or mean-spirited, it can create a hostile environment. If humor is used at the wrong moment, a student may feel that important concerns are being dismissed.

So what to do? How does a teacher for whom humor is as natural as breathing, for whom humor is a fundamental way of navigating life, enter the classroom, while being fully aware of both the promises and pitfalls of humor?

B. The Feedback Loop

A teacher must first develop ways to become "aware of how students experience learning," and second, learn to "teach responsively" to the realities of how students are experiencing the learning environment.[9] To borrow an image, it is important for a teacher to develop a feedback loop in his or her teaching—to find ways for students to give feedback about the learning process and then to teach and communicate in response to that feedback.

Toward this goal, I have found Brookfield's suggestion that teachers use a tool such as the Critical Incident Questionnaire (CIQ) helpful in my own teaching.[10] (This process is explained at more length in chapter 1 of this book.) I have found that by inviting students to name the incidents that they remember as being important from class, I am able to get some grasp on what the learning environment is like for students. This gives me some feedback as to how students are experiencing both me and each other, which in turn allows me to communicate with students in a more informed way. It also allows me to reframe student experiences, when that is appropriate.

At the start of this section, I included the following comment, which an anonymous student once wrote on a CIQ early in my teaching career: "I didn't like it when you joked about Professor _______ in class today; you shouldn't belittle other professors." I have to admit that this comment both hurt and alarmed me. It hurt me because the joke in question was meant kindly. It alarmed me for many reasons. I was alarmed that I might be creating a learning environment that some students found hostile, that I might be perceived by students and others as being mean-spirited or belittling of others, and most deeply, I was alarmed that I might have to stop using humor in the classroom—which would mean that I would have to stop being me in the classroom. At the most basic level, I realized that for at least one student, a joke that I had made misfired and had turned into a "vivid happening" that someone remembered as being significant. And my assumption is that if one student experienced the moment that way, others likely did too.

I believe it is important to recognize that this incident that centered around humor is illustrative of a bigger truth about classroom dynamics between teacher and students. This bigger truth is that every teacher has aspects of his or her approach to teaching that might be misunderstood or misinterpreted by students. We all make key assumptions about either the content of the material that we are teaching or assumptions about the purpose that the course is supposed to serve. But these assumptions cannot be shared by our students unless, first, we are aware of our own key assumptions and, second, we make an effort to communicate those key assumptions to students.

One of the best things about using a CIQ is that the form allows the teacher to become aware of when he or she has not adequately clarified some key assumption that informs either the course or that influences the learning environment. Brookfield recommends that teachers debrief the previous week's CIQs with students:

> At the start of the first class of the next week, I debrief students on the main themes that emerged in their responses. . . . If students have made comments that have caused me to change how I teach, I acknowledge this and explain why the change seems worth making. *I try also to clarify any actions, ideas, requirements, or exercises that seem to be causing confusion.* Criticisms of my actions are reported and discussed. . . . Quite often, students write down comments expressing their dislike of something I am insisting they do. When this happens, I know that I must take some time to reemphasize why I believe the activity is so important and to make the best case I can about how it contributes to students' long-term interests.[11]

Back to the example of my attempts at humor in the classroom. After processing this CIQ comment with colleagues in our teaching and learning group, I came to the conclusion that I cannot try to teach without humor. It is simply not an option for anyone to try to teach as someone other than who they really are. Instead, what I needed to do was to find a way to frame my attempts at humor so that they would stand a better chance of contributing to the learning process and less of a chance of undermining it. Obviously, this is a large issue. And just as obviously, there was no magic-bullet solution to the dilemma. Rather, I have had to address this issue in multiple ways.

One example of how I have tried to frame my attempts at humor can be found in my course syllabi. The comment about humor opened my eyes to the fact that I had not as a teacher clarified for my students many of my assumptions about learning. So I now include in all of my course syllabi a section on my values and assumptions. At the start of courses I do not make my students victims of a word-for-word tour through the course syllabus. I assume that they are smart enough to read and understand it on their own without me holding their hands. However, I do take them word-for-word through the "Core Values and Assumptions" section of the syllabus. Among the list of values and assumptions I include these:

- Learning ought to include some fun, excitement, and passion—as well as some threat, hard work, and friction.
- The professor values humor, at least as a way of negotiating the insanities of life and academy—warning: the professor will make fun of himself, his family, and his friends; if humor makes you uncomfortable, this might be a bad fit.
- A bad form of education is to play the horrible game of "figure out what the teacher wants to hear and then tell it to him/her."
- The professor will return assignments promptly, with comments; the professor will be on time and prepared; the professor is available for individual consultation.

I have listed four values here so that readers can get a sense of what I am trying to achieve by this section of the syllabus. I include the first bullet so that students can know that if they are alarmed or stressed by some of the difficult concepts that we will be addressing, such stress is proper. I include the third bullet so that students will understand why at certain points in the course I will intentionally *not tell* the students what I think about a certain topic. I include the fourth bullet so that students will understand that they have a claim on me and that I will be accountable to them in the learning process.

And I include the second bullet so that students will know—right from the start—that humor—or at least a reasonable facsimile thereof—will be present at every turn during the course. As I go over this point, I strongly emphasize that I only make fun of people I like, such as my wife, my friends, my family, and so on. I also insist that I am quite sincere about students having the option of leaving the course if humor bothers them. If students do not jibe with humor, they should consider leaving the course. There are other sections of the courses I teach that are taught by other teachers and students will learn as much or more in those sections.

I don't leave it there: A one-time warning at the beginning of the semester cannot perfectly frame the way humor operates in my classes. Throughout the courses I teach, I remind students quite often that I only make fun of people I like: my wife, my friends, myself. If I make a joke about anything or anyone close to the seminary community, I make a special point of reminding students that I only make fun of people that I like.

Since I incorporated the above changes into my syllabi and began feeding back to students my reasons for using humor and the caveats that govern my use of humor, I have witnessed a noticeable change in the classroom environment. For one, it has been years since a student has mentioned my humor critically on a CIQ—which I take to mean that the humor has at least been framed in such a way that the students can make sense of it. Second, the amount of positive feedback has grown concerning my use of humor as an affirming technique. Although I have concentrated mainly on humor in this section of the chapter, similar comments could be made about other values and assumptions that govern my teaching. For example, that learning is not repeating to the teacher what a student believes the teacher wants to hear or that learning that is truly transformative ought to include some degree of threat and friction as well as some degree of joy.

In closing, I will include a word about why humor is particularly useful in teaching Old Testament texts that students may find foreign and threatening. Again, I will use an example from the prophetic survey course that I teach. As was mentioned above, many of the basic texts and concepts that students encounter in the prophetic corpus are threatening and difficult. An example of this is the way that the prophet Hosea employed the marriage metaphor. (For those unfamiliar with Hosea, in order to communicate to Israel that the nation had been unfaithful to God, Hosea is said to have married "a wife of whoredom" and had "children of whoredom." Further, Hosea named two of his children NOT-PITIED and NOT-MY-PEOPLE in order to communicate God's judgment.)

This material is deeply challenging to students for a variety of reasons, but I will name just two. On the one hand, the idea of a prophet marrying a woman who may have been a prostitute in order to get across an idea can deeply disturb students. On the other hand, the equation of "God = the faithful husband" and "Israel = the promiscuous and unfaithful wife" can and has manifested itself in deeply sexist ideologies and behaviors. This is especially so because the text pictures Hosea as physically disciplining his wife Gomer and then accepting her back. Obviously, such a notion is highly problematic to the extent that it reinforces sexist notions that husbands have a right to abuse their wives and that such abuse is legitimated in the case of marital infidelity.[12]

I have found that humor is helpful both in communicating the basic content of Hosea's message and also in the process of helping students to reflect on the problematics of the sexist potential. In communicating the basic content of Hosea's message, humor can get the students laughing and thus reduce anxiety so that they can use words and images that they do not expect in seminary classrooms. Words such as, well, "whoredom." Who talks like that anyway?

In regard to the issue of the feminist critique of Hosea, the issue is trickier, but humor can be even more useful. This is especially the case because there are always some students present who want to dismiss the feminist critique of Hosea's use of the marriage metaphor (and those who want to dismiss it are not just men). Passions can ignite and students can become emotionally invested in having their side of the argument legitimated by the teacher. At this point, if humor were used to silence one side of the discussion or to dismiss a perspective, or if humor were used to trivialize a conflict between groups of students, the humor would be inappropriate. However, using humor to reduce anxiety so that the students can hear what others in class are saying is extremely helpful.

In fact, I do not know any other way that I could do it. And that is precisely my point.

IV. CONCLUSION

Raymond Brady Williams begins the lead essay in a volume on theological teaching by referring to "[t]hree components of theological education—teachers and teaching, students and learning, and theological disciplines and content. . . ."[13] It is not an accident that the first of these components is "teachers and teaching." The vocation of teaching—especially theological teaching—requires that the teacher learn to be at least partially aware of how his or her personality, gifts, and habits are impacting the learning process. This chapter has attempted to offer a case study from the perspective of one flawed and fallen human being on the pitfalls of not knowing and the promises of learning to know ourselves as teachers.

The chapter began by borrowing from both Parker Palmer and Psalm 139 in order to suggest that teaching is "the endless meeting of people" who have been "fearfully and wonderfully" created by God. As Clinton McCann has observed, the phrase "fearfully and wonderfully made" is an affirmation "that each human life belongs to God in every aspect."[14] The charge to one's self as a teacher, then, is neither some form of giving in to a narcissistic culture nor some form of self-serving pedagogical navel-gazing. Rather, learning to know ourselves as teachers serves the higher purpose of creating a better learning environment and is thus a necessary part of teaching. Recognizing the "otherness" of learners' perspectives, recognizing that students—yes, even students!—have been created by the Lord and "belong to God in every aspect," learning to know yourself as a teacher, all of these are, believe it or not, a form of loving your neighbor.

NOTES

1. Stephen D. Brookfield, *The Skillful Teacher* (San Francisco: Jossey-Bass, 1990), 2.
2. Parker Palmer, *The Courage to Teach: Exploring the Inner Landscape of a Teacher's Life* (San Francisco: Jossey-Bass, 1998), 16.
3. Palmer's entire monograph, *The Courage to Teach* (San Francisco: Jossey-Bass, 1998), revolves around this issue. Brookfield has written about the issue in more than one place, but I have profited in particular from Brookfield's work around this issue in chapters 1–5 of *The Skillful Teacher* (San Francisco: Jossey-Bass, 1990) and in chapters 3–5 of *Becoming a Critically Reflective Teacher* (San Francisco: Jossey-Bass, 1995).
4. Brookfield recommends that teachers develop teaching autobiographies (*Becoming a Critically Reflective Teacher*, chapters 3–4). In a sense, what I am doing in this section in which I draw upon my education history, is that I am drawing upon my educational biography. I also draw on this biography in the second half of this chapter, in which I discuss my wrestling with the effects that my humor has on my teaching. I could note there, but do not, that most of my favorite teachers incorporated humor greatly in their teaching.
5. Malcolm Gladwell, *The Tipping Point: How Little Things Can Make a Big Difference* (New York: Little, Brown, 2000) and *Blink: The Power of Thinking Without Thinking* (New York: Little, Brown, 2005) makes this point in multiple places.
6. For those who are interested, some of my thoughts on pedagogy related to these matters are available "Teaching Students to Interpret Religious Poetry (and to Expand their Avenues of Thinking),"

Teaching Theology & Religion (January 2004): 38–44 or in the volume *Teaching the Bible: Practical Strategies for Classroom Instruction*, ed. Mark Roncance and Patrick Gray (Atlanta: Society of Biblical Literature, 2005). On the theology of God's anger, see Terence Fretheim, "Theological Reflections on the Wrath of God in the Old Testament," *Horizons in Biblical Theology* (2002).

7. Told by James Limburg in *Psalms for Sojourners* (Minneapolis: Augsburg, 1986), 109.
8. Brookfield, *The Skillful Teacher*, 29.
9. Ibid., chapters 2–3.
10. Brookfield, *Becoming a Critically Reflective Teacher*, 114–39.
11. Ibid., 117. Emphasis added.
12. The finest treatment of this metaphor and its problems and prospects is that of Diane Jacobson, "Hosea 2: A Case Study in Biblical Authority," *Currents in Theology and Mission* 23 (1996): 165–72.
13. "The Vocation of Teaching: Beyond the Conspiracy of Mediocrity," *Practical Wisdom: On Theological Teaching and Learning*, ed. Malcolm L. Warford (New York: Lang, 2005): 16.
14. "The Book of Psalms: Introduction, Commentary, and Reflections," *The New Interpreter's Bible: A Commentary in Twelve Volumes* (Nashville, TN: Abingdon, 1996) V:1237.

CHAPTER 6

"How Can Students Learn to Trust Us as We Challenge Who They Are?" Building Trust and Trustworthiness in a Biblical Studies Classroom

Matthew L. Skinner

Many students in seminaries and divinity schools experience courses on the Bible and its interpretation as threatening. Students recognize that critical study of Christian scripture and honest engagement with other interpreters are about more than accumulating knowledge or acquiring skills. This work creates possibilities for religious discovery and reassessment, for students to arrive at new understandings of both God and the foundations of their faith. The prospect of a changed outlook in one's theological vision, especially when a student cannot foresee what that new vision will look like or what it will mean for notions of personal faith or vocation, easily generates fear. Fear's capacity to obstruct learning compels effective teachers to counteract it by making efforts to earn their students' trust.

I. THE TRAUMA OF DISLOCATION

As a professor at a seminary that is dedicated to preparing people for various kinds of Christian ministry, I find the pedagogy of my courses on the New Testament often causes students to experience *dislocation*. These courses, which aim to enable students to think deeply, critically, and imaginatively about Christian scripture, regularly require students to consider new ways of looking at the Bible and understanding how they are situated in relationship to it as people of faith. This dislocation comes when a course alters their intellectual and existential scenery: loosing their moorings, probing their foundations, and beckoning them to consider different perspectives on the Bible, its functions, and its relevance for life and ministry.

While new vistas of scrutiny and discovery can exhilarate learners, the movement to previously unseen locations can also unnerve them. Because I teach in an institution that construes theological education in explicit relationship to Christian vocation, most if not all of my students begin their studies already contentedly located in some kind of meaningful relationship with the Bible. They already know some of the Bible's content. Certain biblical passages have left a mark by inspiring and challenging their senses of identity and personal aspirations. They hold (whether or not they are conscious of it) particular hermeneutical assumptions that regulate how they read. They have theological leanings or deep-seated convictions that inform their understandings of what scripture is and what it is good for. My teaching inevitably dislocates—and disrupts—these preexisting locations, not because I consider those locations necessarily to be misguided, immature, or dangerous; not because I am opposed to people holding decided positions on questions of meaning, authority, and identity; but because I have been charged with the task of helping students become responsible and informed biblical interpreters.

Exegetical formation causes dislocation because my courses (like the courses of most biblical-studies professors I know) present students with a nearly constant flow of new information (about the Greek syntax of the New Testament, about relevant first-century historical contexts, about the Bible's literary structures, etc.), new perspectives from other interpreters (through options presented in lectures, through small-group discussions, through reading assignments, etc.), new methodological assumptions (as students discover and evaluate feminist readings, formalist readings, social-scientific readings, "third-world" readings, etc.), and new exegetical challenges (in assignments that require students to mount a defense of their interpretations, in the ways students integrate what they are learning in their other courses, in students' reflections on how a biblical document might still inform Christian faith and life in today's world, etc.).

Encounters with new information, perspectives, assumptions, and challenges routinely force students to reevaluate the locations they inhabit. A successful biblical-studies course gives students the information, tools, and space to engage in critical and creative reflection on the biblical material and on all it means for them to interpret that material in their own lives and in the work of Christian ministry. At the end of a day, students may return to their original locations in relationship to the Bible, situate themselves in new ones, or find themselves still scouting the terrain. But the dislocation they undergo remains key to learning what it means to encounter these ancient documents and to gaining facility in what it means to interpret them within, on behalf of, and even against Christian traditions.

This phenomenon of dislocation is undoubtedly familiar to anyone who has waded in the waters of biblical studies—and into the deeper sea of theological education, where God and religious knowledge are subject to critical investigation. Of course, theological education is hardly alone in its ability to dislocate students. Probably all pedagogies that aim to nourish deeper critical awareness, in disciplines ranging from anthropology to zoology, take learners into similar experiences where they must reevaluate and reconceptualize. Education is always more than the gathering of information; it involves an exploration of the world and how we as individuals and groups comprehend our place in it. Nevertheless, in a theological school I suspect that the dislocation stemming from a biblical-studies curriculum evokes a disproportionately large share of fear and resistance among students.

II. FEAR AND TRUST IN THE CLASSROOM

While the pedagogical rationale for encountering newness, discovery, methodological complexity, ambiguity, and broader horizons sounds like a lot of fun to those of us who are paid to teach, we do well to remember that exploring new evidence and ideas easily arouses anxiety in students—and not only in those students who come into a course brandishing unyielding commitments to particular positions. Discerning seminarians recognize immediately (and others might initially sense and eventually come to understand) that their views on scripture touch the nuclei of a host of other issues. These views, whatever they are, connect to students' theological worldviews, conceptions of Christian ministry, and self-understanding. The broader and more deep-rooted the potential implications of being changed by an encounter with a new idea are, the more such anxiety can derail or debilitate a student. The discomfort that can stem from dislocation *may* begin as a salutary defense mechanism, but when it becomes fear that impedes learning and genuine engagement with a course, then it exposes a teacher's responsibility to address it. Effective teachers recognize the part they can play. They respond proactively, making efforts to mitigate fear by cultivating a sense of their trustworthiness.

At the outset of this discussion, I want to make clear that my comments on the importance of a teacher caring about and gaining students' trust do not imply that I mean to dissolve or deny the gap in power that is a part of every formal teacher-student relationship. Instead, I want to advocate teaching in ways that do not allow that gap to be experienced as a weapon or a hindrance to learning. Also, I do not suggest that students' apprehensions about learning or about placing trust in their teachers are never well-founded; nor do the probing questions they put to their instructors always evince latent fear or distrust. It is usually an encouraging sign when students "check me out" as a theological interpreter of the Bible, when they ask questions that express a desire to know where an idea or a method might be taking them, or when they want to see how I would approach a theological or pastoral problem. These kinds of inquiries often signal that they are paying attention, that they glimpse where the class is headed. It should reassure teachers of the Bible to see that their students are aware that scripture does not interpret itself and that their professors bring to the classroom their own professed and tacit perspectives on how one should read the Bible and toward what ends.

My concerns, then, relate to a particular anxiety that can reside behind students' questions and behaviors, anxiety directed toward the professor's influence over the ways that they will encounter the course's material and will perhaps be changed. Manifestations of anxiety are evidence of neither the professor's failure nor the student's lack of virtue, but they remind us of fear's ability to impede learning. It is not difficult to identify the kinds of queries and reactions that expose a student's discomfort. In some students, these behaviors suggest trepidation concerning methodological assumptions that are unfamiliar or that trigger students' prejudices. In severe cases, they can betray a student's outright conviction that her professor is a dangerous person who advocates unhealthy ways of reading Christian scripture. The specific ways that fear might raise its head are legion; fear can emanate around various points and concerns:

- *Across a range of issues addressed:* Students may be alarmed by general assumptions of critical methods ("How can we dare to issue 'critical' judgments over God's word? Doesn't it judge us?"). Some are surprised when their deeper study brings them deeper uncertainty ("I thought learning Greek would answer all my questions about what a text means, but it has only opened up more possibilities and confusion!"). Others are unnerved by conclusions shared widely within biblical scholarship but not well known elsewhere ("If Paul didn't write the Pastoral Epistles, then why would they claim that he did?").
- *Across a range of theological commitments:* Students with certain views of biblical authority may fret that the professor's modes of inquiry are twisting "the word of God" into "a human word." Others express concerns about how the professor construes the New Testament's importance as a source for theological reflection, because they themselves have misgivings about ascribing *any* kind of normative value to documents riddled with patriarchal or anti-Jewish attitudes. As a

Presbyterian working in a Lutheran seminary, I sometimes field questions that suggest my students are seeking reassurance that my teaching will respect their particular Lutheran confessional traditions.

- *Across a range of students' expressions and responses:* Dismayed, nervous glances may greet a professor when she speaks about contradictions in scripture or about the ways in which even an embarrassing "text of terror" might yet contribute to theological reflection in a constructive way. Sometimes students' essays that avoid making strong claims suggest that their authors are afraid of putting their own ideas forward for scrutiny according to the course's ground rules for critical inquiry. Perhaps most disconcerting, although easiest to identify, are expressions of hostility in class discussions and written assignments, as well as a student's complete disengagement from the course.

The specific manifestations of these general kinds of behavior vary from course to course, from student to student.

Anxious behaviors and questions should be a concern for us who teach, not because they might express a student's refusal to emerge from the course just like us or to believe exactly what we believe. Rather, they often indicate a pedagogical problem, that a student is experiencing difficulty in engaging the basic commitments of the course. Such a student may be resisting dislocation simply because he cannot see where he and his ideas might eventually be relocated. His anxiety rightly falls upon the professor, for he justifiably wonders if his teacher intends to help him find viable bearings. He may be asking, "Does the professor only intend to cut me adrift? Will she locate my understanding of the Bible in some unfamiliar place that will hurt me? Does she know what the Bible means to me, and how it impinges on how I understand who I am before God? Is she aware of how much damage can be done when people pay too much attention to the Bible or misuse it for their own ends? What vision of God is the professor bringing to my encounter with the material of this course?"

These are good questions, and they reflect how important the Bible is within the scope of theological education, the practice of ministry, and Christian identity. They remind us that construals of biblical authority are usually at the center of theological and ethical disagreements, often making it hazardous for Christians to engage those who hold differing convictions. They suggest to professors that, if we are to be successful in leading all our students into new landscapes as part of their formation as competent interpreters, we need to make efforts to inspire their trust. The distinctively theological fabric of our subject matter and educational context intensifies our identities as role models to our students.[1] As a result, we implicitly ask students to put their trust in us on a theological level that acknowledges the spiritual dimensions of this kind of learning.

III. THREE DIMENSIONS OF GAINING STUDENTS' TRUST

Issues of trust influence teaching and learning in any academic discipline because they are integral to any teacher-student relationship and to the cultivation of a viable community of learners. I assert, however, that theological educators must tend to a layer of trust that is not immediately relevant to other fields of study. The dynamics of faith and theological education's overt attention to the reality of God make it crucial that students trust their professors as reliable theological guides who are attuned to distinct kinds of spiritual commitments. Moreover, study of the Bible in particular has the potential to make theological "trust issues" even more acute than they are in a seminary's or divinity school's other curricular areas. Before delving deeper into the particularities of trust and trustworthiness in a biblical-studies classroom, I will first review a general pedagogical rationale for building two categories of trust between students and their instructors. Then I will contend for the third layer of trust that effective theological education demands.

A. Professional Trustworthiness

Authors who reflect on the importance of trust between students and their teachers tend to focus on two general dimensions of trustworthiness.[2] The first of these has to do with the instructor's credibility as a scholar and a teacher. Students perceive their teacher as *professionally trustworthy* when he demonstrates that he is an able, judicious, and knowledgeable manager of the classroom and the learning enterprise. To foster this kind of trustworthiness, the professor must possess and show academic, pedagogical, and organizational competence. He must make it plain that he knows the subject matter well; that he possess the skills and insights that will enable even the most self-doubting students to grasp the content and skills that the course requires; and that he can guide the course from one stage to the next by crafting meaningful class sessions, communicating expectations clearly, and providing for contingencies. In short, students need to believe that they are getting their tuitions' worth and committing themselves to a specialist who can actually teach them something. Of course, professors who clamor for *only* this kind of credibility risk becoming exasperating know-it-alls or classroom autocrats; but neither are students well served by teachers who disingenuously soft-pedal the expertise they bring to the learning enterprise. Professionally trustworthy teachers inspire confidence that learning can indeed happen in a given course.

B. Personal Trustworthiness

The second area of student-teacher trust stems from the interpersonal learning environment that an instructor constructs and maintains. Students perceive their teacher as *personally trustworthy* when she exercises her pedagogy in a humane and inviting way. Classroom environment builds trust on several planes—not only a student's trust in the teacher as a benevolently attentive leader, but also trust among students as co-learners and trust within individual students as they learn to depend on their own abilities and value their contributions.[3] Students with a personally trustworthy teacher will perceive that their ideas are valued and that classroom discourse will be both fair and cognizant of the ways in which learning requires practice and experimentation to acquire, hone, and maintain skills.

This second type of trustworthiness is similar to the pedagogical expertise that makes one professionally trustworthy; ultimately, however, personal trustworthiness points toward something else insofar as it inspires a quite different kind of confidence. One can have a *professional* grasp of how to teach, be well versed in the theoretical foundations of a pedagogy, and even possess an impressive bag of tricks for the classroom. *Personal* trustworthiness, however, extends beyond this as it includes a teacher's ability to educate in a way that invites and encourages students. A former teacher of mine illustrates the distinction. He was an expert at both crafting discussions that isolated particular issues and at conjuring inspiring, revelatory moments in his lectures. But his penchant for ridiculing some students' contributions and intimidating those who held certain convictions left many deeply anxious about making mistakes or volunteering opposing perspectives. While the teacher demonstrated a deft ability to make learning happen, many hesitated to participate in the communal work of the course, presumably because they never knew when they might be victimized by his teaching. By contrast, teachers who are personally trustworthy take steps to lessen the potential for embarrassment and failure encountered by learners.

Personally trustworthy instructors, then, construct classroom environments—partly through their own modeling and admissions—that encourage risk-taking and acknowledge human fallibility. The ability to construct such environments stems from a professor's recognition that learning happens not through instantaneous events but through processes. To be sensitive to these relational factors is not to diminish the importance of making critical judgments or upholding serious academic expectations. Certainly a professor who tends to the interpersonal dynamics of learning to the neglect of all other pedagogical requirements risks transforming the classroom into a group-therapy session; but neither are students well served by teachers who promote, willfully or not, an environment of fear and intimidation. Many more learners are stifled than are motivated by education that is structured as a confrontational or perfectionistic gauntlet. Personally trustworthy teachers inspire confidence that the struggles of learning will be acknowledged in a given course.

The steps that teachers take to earn students' trust on both professional and personal levels certainly differ widely from teacher to teacher and class to class. Nevertheless, the importance of establishing a climate of trustworthiness in these two ways remains constant. Because students' perceptions of their professor's trustworthiness play a large role in students' evaluations, we might say that our future as teachers depends upon our ability to create such a climate.[4] More significantly, students' perceptions have consequences for our everyday effectiveness as educators, insofar as they reflect the degree to which students experience a teacher as committed to the subject matter, to the teaching vocation, and to students' intellectual and attitudinal development. Students who trust their professor's expertise and commitment to fostering a generative and humane learning environment will themselves be more willing to accept the risks that are inherent in the critical exploration of texts, ideas, assumptions, and their consequences.

C. Spiritual Trustworthiness

The nature of theological education requires its practitioners to cultivate a third kind of trustworthiness. My experience teaching the New Testament suggests that many seminarians react with anxiety to their experiences of dislocation in the study of the Bible but that this trepidation can be calmed when they perceive that there is a *spiritual trustworthiness* about a professor and the ways that professor shapes the course and its content. What this means is that students benefit from and are motivated by sensing that their teacher, as a person exercising significant authority over the ways in which the class considers biblical texts (including their contexts, their meanings, and their enduring significance), is a person who engages these documents with a commitment to their importance, to their vitality for Christian life and ministry, and to the God to whom they bear witness.

To have these commitments means more than—although it includes—being passionate and enthusiastic about the subject matter and being a teacher who can model thoughtful discourse with oneself, the Bible, and other interpreters. Spiritual trustworthiness comes as students become convinced that their teacher has passion and enthusiasm about understanding the Bible in a particular relationship to her own understanding of God and to her own vocation and obligations in service to that God. When students perceive such commitments they understand that their teacher recognizes and respects the ways that the study of scripture connects to a larger theological system or spiritual worldview and connects to intensely personal and foundational conceptions of who God is and how people come to recognize God.

In a way, to call for this dimension of trustworthiness is hardly peculiar. Scholars in religious studies have recently questioned the deep-rooted myth that university-based courses in religion must be taught without allowing room for discussion about personal belief or the ways in which the course's religious content matters for a person's meaning-making. In a summary of an essay by Kimberley Patton, Stephen Webb writes, "[E]very religion teacher is a theologian, in the sense that every professor is modeling ways in which faith does or does not hang together with various critical discourses."[5] Scholars in theological schools do this same thing as they help students navigate Christian commitments and inquire after what their studies suggest about God. The challenge for theological educators is to do so honestly, expectantly, and without resorting to manipulation or exhibitionism. This sounds simple, but the truth is that many biblical scholars have been trained under the myth of an objective, scientifically detached mode of critical analysis. Those who have been conditioned to bracket theological reflection out of the picture need to be especially intentional about modeling it for their students.

If professional trustworthiness relates to a teacher manifesting her commitment to the subject matter and the teaching vocation, and personal trustworthiness relates to her commitment to students and their positive intellectual and attitudinal development, then spiritual trustworthiness reflects her ability to communicate how a commitment to God imbues her work as a scholar and seminary professor. This commitment hardly requires displays of exemplary faith or sentimental expressions of piety. (The seminary professor aspires to be a trustworthy theological guide, not a guru or spiritual marvel.) Instead, a spiritually trustworthy teacher lets students know that *she understands* that the work of her course matters deeply for questions of personal faith and self-understanding. She allows students to explore and disagree about these mysteries. She willingly discloses the God upon whom her teaching is predicated—her theological assumptions and the ways in which her presentation of the course material implies complementary or other possible theological locations. She also makes it clear that students have in her course the potential to see their faith grow and change in positive ways as a result of deep engagement with the material. Notice that what I describe extends beyond recognizing the truth that there is a spiritual component to all kinds of teaching and learning, the spiritual dimension that Parker Palmer calls "the diverse ways we answer the heart's longing to be connected with the largeness of life."[6] In the context of explicitly Christian theological formation, spiritual trustworthiness comes from introducing into the course honest discourse about God and broader theological or practical ramifications. It also comes from including discussion about how various methods of interpretation and views of scripture might affect the ways in which future Christian leaders approach the "cure of souls." Spiritually trustworthy teachers inspire confidence that God can be glimpsed in new, meaningful ways in a given course.

D. False Forms of Spiritual Trustworthiness

Like any kind of trust, spiritual trustworthiness can be misconstrued or wrongly sought in ways that hinder learning or become otherwise manipulative. Describing some of the things that spiritual trustworthiness is *not* will better define what it is. First, in advocating a sense of their spiritual trustworthiness, I am not suggesting that professors should assume or present themselves as having reached ironclad conclusions about the totality of their field and the implications of their ideas. A teacher who himself is no longer capable of being dislocated by new information or perspectives hardly serves as a capable guide for others. I am fond of a statement from Paul Meyer: "No curse lies more heavily on our study of the Bible, especially in a theological seminary, than the confidence that we already know what is written on its pages. It is worse than ignorance or indifference, for like the unforgivable sin of blasphemy against the Holy Spirit, it is beyond being taken by surprise, even by God."[7] If these words are true for students, then they are also true for trustworthy teachers, who also must be on guard against domesticating the Bible and barricading themselves from discovery. To be trustworthy does not require one to be so settled as to adopt the façade of a saint or intellectual giant. It means that one is willing and eager to engage in the same kind of spiritual or theological reflection that one excites among his or her students.

The other side of this coin is that, even as they remain open to reading the Bible in new ways, professors obviously bring views on the Bible and its theological significance that are much more refined and comprehensive than those of their students. Students who become intimidated by the prospect of resituating themselves in relation to the Bible are themselves easily drawn to the stable footing they may crave in their professor's locations. A second false expression of spiritual trustworthiness resides in a professor's ability to attract theological groupies. When students latch onto a teacher's ideas because they find some kind of ideological or personal attraction to those ideas, the cause is not necessarily the professor's authentic trustworthiness. Students no doubt identify faculty members whom they regard as "safe" because their theology falls in an agreeable point along a liberal-conservative spectrum, because of their positions on hot-button topics, or because of other reasons. Professors do well to make their perspectives known in the classroom, of course. They also are right to acknowledge the ways in which they overtly and implicitly aim to persuade students to adopt particular views. But a professor who refuses to allow his students to reach a range of conclusions or who subtly rewards students who pledge unwavering devotion to his own positions is not equipping students to navigate on their own when they become graduates. This easily hampers true learning and is not what I mean by gaining the spiritual trustworthiness of students.

A third intimidation reveals itself when a professor tries to establish trustworthiness or theological credentials in such a way as to derogate others'. All communities—whether specific congregations, a seminary's faculty, or the guild of biblical scholarship—suffer from their tendencies to exclude interpretations and methods that come from outsiders. As students gain an appreciation for new data and new assumptions, as they grow into new identities as biblical interpreters, judicious professors will help them guard against exegetical parochialism. A responsibility of the spiritually trustworthy professor, then, is helping students develop the means by which they assess and listen to other interpreters.

Finally, a distinction should be upheld between a professor's efforts to foster spiritual trustworthiness and the problem of a subtle fideism that easily infects pedagogies in theological schools. My argument for the need to gain students' trust on a spiritual level neither calls for a retreat from academic rigor nor advocates shielding students from certain voices heard in and beyond the broader biblical or religious academic guilds. Likewise, the argument does not imply that only professing Christians (or Christians of a certain stripe) can effectively teach in a given seminary that pursues the kinds of pedagogical and theological goals that I describe in this chapter. In the end, spiritual trustworthiness is not totally reducible to the content of a person's own character or faith commitments. But it does require that a professor be committed to helping students make theological connections and be committed to exploring with honesty and vulnerability how his own teaching might lead students toward theologically viable outcomes.

E. Trust, Trustworthiness, and Biblical Studies

When done well, theological education is a tightly integrated enterprise. Its various disciplines intersect each other, such that one's theology matters for one's grasp of pastoral care, views of biblical authority matter for negotiating Christian ethics, and so forth. In a similar vein, as my discussion of spiritual trustworthiness highlights, theological education sits deeply integrated with students' own articulations of their faith and conceptions of Christian vocation. In the midst of these interwoven fabrics, however, every theological discipline can find its own reasons for why a professor's spiritual trustworthiness lubricates the learning process. From my perspective, biblical studies makes particularly insistent demands on its professors because of the regard that most Christian traditions give to scripture.

The Bible curricula at most seminaries and divinity schools I know have broad and multiple aspirations. They aim to shape every aspect of students' perspectives on their scriptures, from the meanings of particular words in ancient tongues to the disorderly documentary histories of biblical books to cherished hermeneutical assumptions to the nature of biblical authority and even to the God portrayed in the books themselves. At the core of these aspirations resides a common text. Biblical studies courses are unique within a seminary curriculum because their primary text is not a textbook but the Bible itself. Of all the books that a student will be assigned to read throughout her seminary career, this is perhaps the only one that she has already read (or, we hope, skimmed) before matriculating. It is also, more often than not, I fear, the only one she will read again after she graduates. Moreover, those people she will encounter when serving in Christian ministry will have read this same book, and they will be much more interested in her views on it than in her views on a textbook about pastoral care. Indeed, her views on scripture will be assessed and fretted over by others on a regular basis, beginning with her first interview. All of this is to underscore that the Bible is much more of a public, shared text than those populating the syllabi of other courses. Students recognize that their interpretations of this book will deeply shape who they are as Christians and as leaders of communities. And even the most naïve seminarian recognizes that the Bible is controversial and difficult, a source for all sorts of disagreements and anathemas. This makes it a particularly scary book to read, potentially even scarier to reread in a new way.

IV. CULTIVATING SPIRITUAL TRUSTWORTHINESS

Certainly not all students react to dislocation with fear or resistance. Also, some students are capable of deriving constructive academic and spiritual energy from their fierce *distrust* of a professor, although I suspect in the long run this antagonistic motivation is of dubious value. I believe that the potential for a given student's need to identify a professor as a spiritually trustworthy person does not easily align with particular categories. That is, I doubt one can predict a student's proclivity for fear by considering the student's age, academic abilities, theological leanings, or spiritual maturity (however one might define this). Those students who are unfamiliar with critical inquiry, or those who have never subjected their theological assumptions to serious analysis, may find the dislocation produced by a course to be alarming, but their subsequent responses may vary. This unpredictability should encourage us to think about how we might build trust proactively thereby lessening the chances that fear will create major obstacles for any one of our students.

Situated within relationships among persons, trustworthiness cannot be created instantaneously. Nor is it earned through executing a strategy or program. It can be gained or lost through all sorts of actions and comments. Indeed, everything a professor does in a classroom action, writes in an e-mail exchange, or implies in a remark scribbled on a returned essay has the potential to build or erode trust. At the same time, a teacher can take deliberate steps that give students opportunities to perceive her as trustworthy in a spiritual sense. Acknowledging that each individual builds trust in her own way, I offer these suggestions based on my reflections on my experiences.[8]

First, basic elements of course design contribute toward a more trusting environment. A course that allows students ample time for reflection and discussion, whether structured or unstructured, can be helpful. A former student recently commented to me that she struggled during her first year as a seminarian because she experienced many of her theological assumptions being dismantled, and she found no real opportunity to rebuild them into something new that she could embrace as her own. She lamented the fact that some of her courses did not maintain adequate time for class discussion. Some allowed for no discussion at all. The absence of discussion compounded her sense of struggle and made it difficult to forge her own path toward new conclusions. Professors who do not sufficiently allow for discussion risk communicating a lack of awareness or concern about those kinds of difficulties. Discussion, of course, also helps students test ideas and lets professors assess how students are responding. It can purposively check the pace of a course, making students less prone to feel as though too many ideas and points of information are coming at them at once. Increasing numbers of commuter students, whose schedules often prohibit them from engaging in impromptu discussions with others during meals or leisure time, make scheduled, in-class discussions all the more necessary. A professor's willingness to field students' questions and honestly participate in small group discussions also contributes positively to an environment of spiritual trust.

Second, a professor and her courses need to make room for people to consider the question, "So what?" Students want—and need—to explore how certain ideas matter for their understanding of who God is and how we come to know God. Those of us who delight in mysteries and want to maintain that there are irreducible complexities about life and God often cringe when students express desires for quick answers to elaborate problems. But we nevertheless must acknowledge that small ideas and points of data quickly unearth larger issues. Imagine a scenario: the class period ends in five minutes, but I still have three pages of notes I want to get through in my exploration of Romans 9–11 when a student asks, “So, does this mean there’s no such thing as free will?” I want to say, “No,” and keep going. Or, I could produce a convoluted answer about differing conceptions of divine agency and the philosophical problems that were not on the radar in the first-century world. Or, I could restrict my answer to what the Apostle Paul might have thought. Even though it is not immediately clear whether the questioner wants a brief or a detailed answer, he has asked a question that needs to be addressed in some forum because the biblical text has raised it for him. Furthermore, he probably glimpses how that same question will be asked of him in a pastoral context, perhaps in the midst of a person’s immediate crisis of faith. Behind the question surely are others: What does the Bible have to say to the hopes and trials of our existence? Why should we care what Paul thought? Who is this God we meet in scripture? Have you, professor, ever probed this issue? To dismiss the questions permanently is to sacrifice trust. To allow space for their exploration—whether through discussion, an assignment, a case study that reckons with biblical texts within the challenges of Christian ministry—communicates that the teacher understands the biblical text’s deep relevance for faith and life. It suggests to students that he knows his course opens doors to profound questions that we need to reckon with if we are to be responsible, authentic interpreters.

Third, a professor builds trust by performing as a theological interpreter in public contexts outside the classroom. There are venues that allow students to observe how a professor has reached conclusions and made constructive use of the same material and issues they are encountering in her course. For example, a professor who preaches in the campus chapel on texts or ideas that are currently under consideration in one of her classes helps her students see how their coursework connects to a different sort of analysis and presentation. When a professor preaches on difficult biblical passages (such as texts that report historical inaccuracies or reflect repellent presuppositions) or explores models of biblical authority in a sermon she takes steps toward helping students imagine how their emerging knowledge about the Bible might imaginatively play itself out in their future vocations. A professor who preaches also communicates her vision of God. Professors do similar things when they write essays and books directed toward pastors and others engaged in Christian ministry. These efforts tell students that a teacher is committed to providing viable theological leadership in light of her particular location in relation to scripture. They provide glimpses into the God she is teaching and how that theological vision emerges from her ongoing reflections on scripture.

Fourth, individual students are reassured to discover that they are not the only ones who experience, resist, and survive the dislocation that theological education effects. A professor can give students confidence and foster trust by counseling them to be patient and remain reflective. To return to the example of my former student who was unnerved by the dismantling of her theological assumptions, she found that she was finally able to reconstruct new and meaningful theological convictions in a course several semesters after her first year in seminary. Her experience reminds us that other courses and other experiences play a role in how a student undergoes transformation and finds new locations. Sometimes it takes time and the voices of other instructors and peers before the pieces can fall into place. A professor who remembers this and communicates it to his students can reduce the anxieties of students who despair over the elusiveness of quick, tidy solutions.

In addition to commending patient reflection, a professor also defuses fear and gains trust by regularly naming and acknowledging the spiritual anxieties that students may be encountering in his course. Exposing the potential for fear can deliver a learner from nervous suspicions that he is the only one with such struggles. When professors speak about the overarching theological issues that connect to the course material, and the difficulties that can visit believers who navigate these issues, they invite students into a community of other believers who are committed to ongoing theological reflection. In this way, the professor beckons students into the traditions that they are inheriting as Christian interpreters—longstanding and risky, yet *shared* exegetical traditions. My former teacher Brian Blount says it well as he describes introducing students to the hard work of interpretation:

> I've heard the words time and time again. "You're talking away my faith when you tell me all of this stuff about interpreting the words, understanding the words in light of our living, and not just taking all the words just as they are, no matter how tied they were to their first-century contexts. You're taking away my faith." And we listen, we struggle, and we wonder what to say as we tell them we'll try to help them rebuild their faith. When in truth, when they charge, "You're taking away my faith," we ought to respond, "No this *is* your faith. Your *living* faith. I'm trying to give it back to you. This is how the first Christians did faith, aggressively using it to interpret, not just recite their traditions."[9]

Teachers who make such a promise reassure students and build their trust, even as they refuse to dismiss the seriousness of the task to which they are introducing them. A commitment to cultivating spiritual trustworthiness does not mean that we reduce the complexities. Rather, to summon students into the complexities of interpretive practice reminds them that they undertake the work of interpretation with their ultimate trust not in their teachers but in God. Yet that foundational trust and their training as interpreters are made more inviting when they confidently understand that their teacher undertakes these tasks with them.

V. PERCEIVING ELIJAH'S TRUSTWORTHINESS IN 1 KINGS 17

I conclude with a loose analogy for my reflections on the importance of cultivating spiritual trustworthiness. The story of the Prophet Elijah's relationship with the anonymous widow of Zarephath in 1 Kings 17 illustrates that one builds trust not only through conveying accurate information and sympathy; a trustworthy theological interpreter also must display evidence that he himself has endeavored to explore the God implied by his words and actions.

The chapter begins in the wake of King Ahab's marriage to a Phoenician and his endorsement of Baal worship. Readers meet Elijah for the first time, and he announces a severe drought. God directs Elijah to retreat to the Wadi Cherith, where he can drink, and where God has commanded ravens to bring food to him. When the drought causes the wadi to dry up, God sends the prophet to Zarephath in Phoenicia, promising him that a widow there has been commanded to provide food. When Elijah arrives at the outskirts of Zarephath, either the widow he meets knows nothing of what the God of Israel has arranged, or she has elected to be disobedient to the command of this foreign God, for she tells Elijah that she is preparing to use her remaining provisions to prepare a final meal for her and her son. Elijah asks her first to make a cake to give to him before she and her son eat their meal. He explains by declaring that "the Lord the God of Israel" promises to sustain her supplies of meal and oil until the drought ends. The woman does as Elijah says, and in the aftermath his promise holds true: "she as well as he and her household ate for many days" (v. 15).

In the next scene, the widow's son falls ill and dies. She blames Elijah for this tragedy, for coming into her life and thereby attracting the attention and punishment of his potent deity. She cries, "What have you against me, O man of God? You have come to me to bring my sin to remembrance, and to cause the death of my son!" (v. 18). Elijah takes the dead child upstairs and laments, "O Lord my God, have you brought calamity even upon the widow with whom I am staying, by killing her son?" (v. 20). He presses God, charging God to make it clear whether God indeed is the source of this calamity and imploring God to restore the boy to life. God listens to Elijah, and the child revives (v. 22). When Elijah gives him back to his mother, alive, she declares, "Now I know that you are a man of God, and that the word of the Lord in your mouth is truth" (v. 24).

This story, as a part of the larger complex that extends through 1 Kings 19, establishes Elijah's authority as a prophet of the Lord. The activity in 1 Kings 17 highlights God's provision for Elijah and God's capacity to care for (perhaps also to threaten) even outsiders who do not initially recognize the Lord as God. Coming as they do in the midst of competing religious loyalties among Israel and her neighbors, Elijah's experiences stake a claim for the power of the Lord of Israel over Baal. What I wish to emphasize for the purposes of the current discussion, however, is the transformation that stems from the widow's growing trust in Elijah. Without overstating any illustrative connections between Elijah's role in this story and the role of a teacher in a classroom, we nevertheless can reflect on how Elijah's own theological struggles and commitments eventually result in the widow's perceiving him—and perhaps also the God he represents—in a new, trustworthy light.

The story contains a surprise when Elijah first meets the widow. The care that God commanded for Elijah at the wadi intimates that he can presume to enjoy similar support from the foreign woman whom God has commanded. But when these two people meet, their worldviews clash. Not only is she initially unwilling to bring him food, she calls on Elijah's God as a witness of her destitution (v. 12). She can interpret her circumstances for herself: all evidence indicates that starvation looms. Elijah tries to get the widow to see another possibility. He counsels her against fear and informs her of what God has promised (vv. 13–14). His contrasting vision, his different reading of the situation asks the woman to take a risk, to trust his words. She heeds his instruction, and God's word comes to pass. Her household survives the famine.

Given the result of the scene at the gate of Zarephath, which works out well at least for Elijah and the widow's household, the woman's words in the subsequent scene (vv. 18, 24) attract attention. First she accuses Elijah of bringing hardship to her life through the death of her son; later, after the boy's resuscitation, she declares that she now knows Elijah is a man of God and the word of the God of Israel is truth. Did the feeding miracle in the previous scene not convince her that Elijah was trustworthy and that his God was benevolent? Apparently not, but the miracle in Elijah's bedroom does. On one hand, this indicates that she regards raising the dead as more impressive than merely replenishing food supplies. But her transformed view of Elijah himself ("Now I know that you are . . .") also stems from the fact that Elijah previously did not disclose his own encounters with God, at least not until the widow's son dies. When Elijah and the widow first meet he merely comforts and instructs. He reveals no vulnerability, none of his own journey with the God whom he expects this woman to obey. Who exactly that God is is immaterial for everyone at that point of the story as long as the meal and oil containers stay full.

The tragedy of the second scene, however, requires Elijah to reveal more of himself. The boy's death raises the possibility that Elijah mediates a dangerous God, as the woman claims in v. 18. She had taken a risk by previously following Elijah's instructions, but now she thinks she has suffered a negative outcome by entrusting herself to this man and the promises of his religious vision. She raises the questions: what kind of man is this, who brings a vengeful God into my life? What kind of God is behind all this? Have I been used or misled?

Elijah's response shows that he is more than compassionate. He himself will struggle with the potential theological implications of the situation. Has God really done this? Is he truly the prophet of a God who punishes widows by taking their sons? In vv. 20–21 Elijah openly engages God, calling for justice and actively engaging God to make sense of God's motives in the world. In his questioning and imploring before God, Elijah demonstrates his own willingness to confront critical theological and existential questions, his willingness to wrestle with core issues of who this God is, and how this God is concerned about (or implicated in) the tragedy. As a prophet, then, he does not speak the word of God as merely a puppet, a passive beneficiary, or an unswervingly loyal employee. Rather, he does so as one with a deep stake in the words he speaks and in the God he intends to represent. His words reveal some of who he is as a person of faith. In the end, the widow comes to understand him and his God in a new, transformative way.

For the current chapter, the analogy is far from comprehensive, for the woman in v. 24 likely responds to the fact that

God listens to Elijah and is moved to act. The life of her child matters more than Elijah's honest struggle. I do not expect that, as a professor, I need to move God to raise the dead for me to earn my students' trust. Nevertheless, I emphasize that the widow now perceives *Elijah* in a new light, and part of that new light comes from Elijah taking her accusation seriously and himself engaging in serious theological reflection. I also admit that the widow is not present in the room when Elijah speaks to God in vv. 20–21. Let us assume that his anguish is palpable and that he speaks in his bedroom loud enough for her to overhear him. The point is that, within his associations with the woman, Elijah cannot capture her religious imagination and wonder merely by reporting information about how to stay alive during the drought and expecting her to follow his lead. To change her theological understanding he must also reveal that his life, hopes, and expectations are themselves connected to the God he teaches. Once he displays more of his understanding of this God, the widow of Zarephath does more than respond. She finds herself able to glimpse new realities. She and her world are transformed.

NOTES

1. See, in particular, Kimberley C. Patton, "'Stumbling along between the immensities': Reflections on teaching in the study of religion," *Journal of the American Academy of Religion* 65/4 (1997): 847–48.
2. See, for example, James M. Banner, Jr. and Harold C. Cannon, *The Elements of Teaching* (New Haven, CT: Yale University Press, 1997); Stephen D. Brookfield, *The Skillful Teacher: On Technique, Trust, and Responsiveness in the Classroom* (2d ed.; San Francisco: Jossey-Bass, 2006); Marshall Gregory, "Curriculum, pedagogy, and teacherly ethos," *Pedagogy* 1/1(2001): 69–89; and Marilla Svinicki, "If learning involves risk-taking, teaching involves trust-building," *Teaching Excellence* 2/3 (1989).
3. J. Dennis Huston, "Building confidence and community in the classroom," *Teaching Excellence* 3/1 (1991).
4. Gregory, "Curriculum," 69–89.

5. Stephen H. Webb, "Teaching as confessing: Redeeming a theological trope for pedagogy," *Teaching Theology and Religion* 2/3 (1999): 151. (The essay by Patton is cited in footnote 1 in this chapter.)
6. Parker J. Palmer, *The Courage to Teach: Exploring the Inner Landscape of a Teacher's Life* (San Francisco: Jossey-Bass, 1998), 5.
7. Paul W. Meyer, *The Word in This World: Essays in New Testament Exegesis and Theology* (ed. John T. Carroll; Louisville, KY: Westminster John Knox, 2004), 15.
8. Specific suggestions about the challenges of building trust in classrooms amongst diverse groups of students can also be found in chapters 3 and 9 of this volume.
9. Walter Brueggemann, William C. Placher, and Brian K. Blount, *Struggling with Scripture* (Louisville, KY: Westminster John Knox, 2002), 68.

CHAPTER 7

"How Does Team Teaching Model Trust In and Beyond the Classroom?" Teaming to Create the Conditions for Transformation

Janet Ramsey

Cast all your anxiety upon God because God cares for you.

I Peter 5: 7.

If we look at trust ecologically, we understand it as an atmosphere for living without which there can be no human life . . . Trust is the necessary habitat of freedom, its living space. Where other people trust me, I can develop freely and go out of myself. Fish need water to swim in, birds need air in which to fly, and we human beings need trust in order to develop our humanity.

Jurgen Moltmann[1]

Several years ago a respected colleague at Luther Seminary, Lois Malcolm, approached me about the possibility of co-authoring a book on forgiveness and healing. A systematic theologian, Lois wanted to work across disciplines on this complex topic and wondered if this project would interest me. "Why not teach a class first and write the book second?" I suggested. A collaboration began that continues to this day.

This new course received surprisingly positive evaluations from the thirty-three students who enrolled. We often heard them say, "This class is great, but it needs to be a semester long!" After the six-week session was over, we not only continued to receive verbal comments and emails of appreciation from students—we also realized that we ourselves missed the time spent together planning and teaching. I return to this experience here to reflect on why some team teaching courses are successful while others disappoint instructors and students alike. Why was this particular class so empowering and beneficial to us all?[2]

I. GOALS, PLANS AND REALITIES

Lois and I carefully planned the class over the course of several months. From the onset we determined that student transformation would be at least as important to us as cognitive learning. That goal would require building and maintaining trust and, although primarily the Spirit's work, creating a trust-filled *atmosphere for living.*[3] Of course, the responsibility was not all on our shoulders—the students would also need to work hard—not only by reading course materials, but also by remaining open to their own reactions and by taking significant personal risks when they shared their comments in class. The weekly journals we required would also mean they would need to reflect, critically and courageously, on the painful process of giving and receiving forgiveness. We believed that, as future pastoral caregivers, seminary students must do exterior and interior work to prepare them adequately for today's challenging ministry settings, locations where they frequently have to accompany persons dealing with situations of brokenness and hurt.[4]

One of the primary ways we saw to create a climate of safety and freedom would be to model a healthy, nonhierarchical relationship. We believed success in meeting our course goals would be enhanced by demonstrating our personal comfort with each other (including the use of humor and comments of genuine affirmation) and, naturally, by being consistent in our respect for the students. We wanted, in short, to embody the health and forgiveness we were teaching. We did not expect to agree with each other at all times nor interpret the case studies through the same lens. But these would be advantages, for we wanted the students to observe professors who could practice friendly debate and privilege trust and respect over competition and power.

Thus, as we planned details of how we would teach and structure this class, facilitating trust became a primary consideration. This meant that details of the course structure would not be chosen for our convenience or for didactic reasons alone but also for the impact they would have on class ecology. Considerations included, first of all, whether the students would email their papers to both or to only one of us.[5] We eventually decided to read all the final papers together, for these were less personal; we also needed to see the papers to agree on final grades. But we chose to read their more personal journals individually, giving students the choice of which professor they would like to choose to read that week's entry. We found that students often would send these journal entries to us both, but that was their choice.

We also wondered how to manage our different teaching styles. We both agreed that placing the chairs in a circle would facilitate discussion and would be particularly appropriate in a course where we spoke so often about *face* and its relevance for forgiveness.[6] But Lois typically walks around as she lectures while I use a seated, more conversational style. Would this confuse or distract the students? This aspect of the team-teaching experience is one I remember fondly, for Lois initially attempted to sit still to speak, gallantly trying to suppress her natural high energy level. Then, during the second class, she suddenly jumped to her feet and confessed, "I can't do this—I have to walk around!" Looking back at the way we all reacted to that moment, I know that it was a time when individual differences were enjoyed rather than made to feel awkward or problematic. The spontaneity of her "confession" contributed much to the relaxed and good-natured atmosphere that continued to be present in the room.[7]

We also needed to plan how we would arrange the subject matter for the course, and here we decided to begin with less threatening materials ("ordinary" forgiveness, as between brothers) and gradually move on to the horrors of systemic evil ("extraordinary" forgiveness, as in South African apartheid). This, too, we saw as a matter of building an environment of trust—bearing in mind the students' emotional need for time and space as they visualized the tragic results of human brokenness.

II. MAKING THE DECISION TO PRACTICE INTENTIONAL TRUST

Teaching can be a lonesome enterprise, and I believe that much of my enjoyment was the pure pleasure of getting to know a bright, personable scholar and teacher. As educator Mary-Jane Eisen wrote, "Many instructors are attracted to teaming precisely because it creates a social context among peers that promotes professional development opportunities and diminishes the isolation of the teaching profession."[8] It was not difficult to see why my personal needs were being met. But why was the course so well received by the students? I began to wonder if my own enjoyment and the students' appreciation were related and decided that, indeed, they were. I now believe that a team-taught course can only be as positive as the quality of the instructors' relationship. Without the trust and liveliness that result from a comfortable, collegial association, team teaching becomes more like parallel play—two teachers sharing time and responsibilities but not blending their presentations or engaging in meaningful exchanges.

Trust, above all, is crucial. As the comments of several disgruntled colleagues have taught me, team relationships in the classroom are not always positive or enjoyable. Sadly (and as anyone who has attended a faculty meeting knows!) we academics do not always deal with our differences in opinion constructively. Eisen wrote,

> At their best, teaching teams are model learning communities that generate synergy through collaboration. Because the fruits of their efforts are often very visible and since team members'

> excitement is often contagious, teamwork can also present challenges, such as time demands or potential conflict among teammates.[9]

As we initially planned this course, we certainly considered this last possibility, but we decided that, in a course focused on forgiveness, it need not frighten us. If hurt occurred, we would deal with it. We would work *intentionally* on our interpersonal relationship, particularly the process of building and maintaining trust. We saw this intentional privileging of our interpersonal relationship over individual agendas as a practice in keeping with both our Christian and feminist values. To use the language of feminist/therapist Laura Brown, we wished to "change the cannon"[10]—to shift our focus and strive to become relationship experts, rather than to aim, in traditional academic style, to being primarily distillers of information. "Feminist . . . theory also leads to a consideration of epistemologies and [to] the manner in which the sources of our knowledge claims have derived their information and authority."[11]

But, as teachers of the Church, we wanted trust to be present not only in our association as colleagues—it also needed to be at the heart of our relationship to God. Most fundamentally, we trusted (and spoke of this explicitly) that the Holy Spirit would be present in this course—as we and the students read, watched videos, and participated in conversations in and outside of class. We were, after all, dealing with the dark topics of individual brokenness and systemic evil; we needed to cast our fears on God. We recognized as well that the forgiveness and healing we were attempting to understand more fully could only be embodied through trust in God.[12] For this reason, we spoke often of the "impossibility" of human forgiveness and contrasted it to the forgiveness that occurs when persons who are broken cooperate with God and work to heal the world. Both trust and forgiveness needed to be integrated with our own and the students' spiritual lives, especially through prayer and worship. We attempted to articulate the importance of this integration when we wrote the class objectives for our syllabus: *To learn the importance of practicing forgiveness in our own lives, both personally and as caregivers, and to understand how our own refusal or inability to forgive may have an impact on our vocational tasks.*[13]

Our course topics inevitably dealt with some of the most difficult issues in pastoral care, including betrayals by friends, broken relationships between siblings and spouses, childhood sexual abuse, religious congregations in conflict, and ethnic genocide.[14] I knew, both as a marriage and family therapist and as a teacher, that one does not speak of these things without either opening old wounds in some students or making others very uncomfortable, particularly those who have not yet experienced high levels of personal suffering. Watching a clip from the film *Hotel Rwanda*, reading narratives from a concentration camp, and hearing the (video) testimonies of childhood sexual abuse survivors are all intense experiences, particularly when they occur in a group setting. Shattering the naïve perspectives of young seminarians who still view the world as a consistently safe and trustworthy place was not on our list of course objectives, but we knew it could easily happen.

While this disillusionment process is not necessarily all bad (we all have to grow up sometime!) rebuilding a more mature and balanced view of human existence and human nature certainly takes time. Not surprisingly, we experienced a heavy load of student counseling during this course and for some time afterwards. Talking with students who have been deeply hurt is not easy work in the midst of a busy week, and we knew that only trust in God's care and abiding presence would be adequate for this challenge. To use the language of pastoral care, we, as instructors, needed to be able to experience being held by God so that we could hold our students. When Lois and I met to review the previous week and to plan for the following class, we kept before us this crucial reason to trust in the Lord—the real needs and fears of our students.

Those were our goals, but we also recognized that it is not always easy to teach in the presence of one's peers, and it is certainly not easy to model trust consistently in either public or private life. Two teachers may not even agree about what constitutes trust or what actions and attitudes a trusting relationship should include. We found, for example, that the topic of forgiveness inevitably led us into murky waters in our own conversations. Since we sometimes chose to reveal to each other stories of past hurts, we needed to negotiate carefully what we would or would not speak of elsewhere. Some of our own exchanges were held in confidence while others could be shared in class, but only after checking carefully with each other.[15] Inappropriately revealing personal information is, after all, one of the most common ways trust can be broken between two people.

We also talked about how to advise those students who confided in us—when would it be appropriate for us to share with each other what they were telling us individually? We knew that God would be using us to support each other's burdens, but we also wanted to respect the students' confidentiality.[16] This was handled on a case-by-case basis, but it also required open and clear communication with each other and with the students. We wanted expectations and practices to be fair and congruent.

One of the joys of our relationship became clear early—as mentioned above, we spoke openly with each other about our faith and our own life experiences. We found that our trust in God was not only the ground we shared but, more importantly, crucial to our self identities. As the course began, we wondered together how it might make a recognizable difference to the students and to us that we, their instructors, were *Christian* women. That is, how might trust between colleagues in a seminary setting be similar to or different from the practice of trust in secular settings? Would it matter, in both our collegial relationship and in our relationships to the students, that, as Luther wrote, "In this church, God generously forgives each day every sin committed by me and by every believer"?[17] We opened each class with prayer and scripture[18]—would it change things to pray for trust in God and for the coming of the Spirit as we taught and advised?

III. THE IMPORTANCE OF TRUST

During my five years of teaching future church leaders I have occasionally thought that many students exhibit more trust and courage than members of our faculty, myself included. At other times I have marveled at students' reticence and sudden fearfulness in situations that do not appear threatening, at least from my perspective. Perhaps both of these impressions are accurate, for surely both students and professors find it challenging to experience trust in all contexts, with all people. We live, after all, in a demanding, complex, and anxious world where we are often, as Kegan put it, in over our heads.[19] Why should our seminaries be an exception?

Yet no other embodied practice is as crucial as trust. We sorely need this fragile dimension of faith for living out our Christian beliefs, for implementing transformative learning, and for experiencing joy in our life together. We want our seminary communities to be different in this way, if in no other—we want them to be locations where persons trust God and trust each other. Both our good sense and our theology demand nothing less, for it is at this point where, as Luther suggested, we define ourselves as both sinners and saints, where we know ourselves to be those imperfect ones who nevertheless cast all their fears on God. It is also at this point where we most want to help our pastoral care students prepare to be "called and sent" into a frightening world, ready to say to those they meet "I can accompany you. You can trust me—not because I am perfect, but because I trust the Lord!"

But what does it mean to learn to trust the Lord? Although our human nature readily allows us to trust things that are well-known—a recognized face, our own living rooms, a syllabus we have used before—this everyday comfort with the familiar does not equip us for new paths, untried practices, or uncertain futures. For these uncharted waters, we require a qualitatively different capacity—namely, the ability to trust in an unseen yet revealed God. This mature, far from common trust does not develop through life experiences alone but grows slowly through years spent intentionally relating to the Source of our existence and through extensive and intentional time spent in prayer, worship, and acts of loving kindness. Moltmann believes that this trust is not so much a reaction to the past as a pushing towards the future, developed not through our own power, will, or desire but by the power of the Holy Spirit, given to the whole community, as pure gift.[20]

Whether we reject or accept and nurture this gift is another matter, as the history of the People of God demonstrates repeatedly. This history is helpful, for it is often through well-known Bible stories that we get the best picture of what trust in the Lord can look like. Here we recognize that it was trust that allowed Abraham to obey God's call at the risk of being self-destructive, trust that gave Moses the patience to lead a grouchy group of people through wild places, and trust that made it possible for Paul to become a fool for Christ. I believe that it is also trust that we need as teachers of the church, both those of us who are new and those who are more seasoned. Only trust will allow us to risk our reputations to follow God's voice, give us the patience to lead our sometimes resistant students and colleagues through new experiences, and put aside our intellectual pride while we learn to teach together. The writer of St. Peter understood this when he wrote that trust is possible only when we turn over all our painful anxieties to God.

IV. TEAM TEACHING: OPPORTUNITY AND CHALLENGE

> The first step toward transformative teaching does not start with what the teachers prepare the students to do but rather with the teachers undergoing their own reflective process . . . Teaching to transform is a means of self-transformation as well as social transformation.[21]

Team teaching, formally defined "as two or more faculty in some level of collaboration in the planning and delivery of a course,"[22] appealed to us largely because of its transformative possibilities—transformative both for instructors and for students. As mentioned earlier, the personal and social changes we envisioned would be possible only by an intentional, reflective process—a process that, in turn, depended on our trust of God and of each other. But, although this transformation was our goal, it was difficult to articulate at the time just what we were hoping for or to explain how team teaching would allow us to reach that goal. In retrospect, there are a variety of advantages that we now feel ready to explain should the need arise to defend this (apparently) more costly teaching arrangement.[23]

As Allen, Floyd-Thomas, and Gillman wrote, a reflective process is the key to teacher transformation.[24] It is one thing to speak about this trust as a primary area for growth and reflection; it is quite another to embody it consistently. Neither Lois nor I had experienced institutional environments in which trust and collegiality are consistently valued over competition, be it subtle or blatant. Would we become distrustful and retreat into the corner that Moltmann spoke of, withdrawing into ourselves and feeling rejected? At this point we felt that our ability to speak freely about our faith in God, as teachers in a seminary, gave us a distinct advantage over persons working in secular settings, since we were able to explore our human damages and our need for God's help. Being part of a worshipping community was crucial, for here we received, with our community, the Body and Blood of Christ; here we were given the tangible assurance of forgiveness that we absolutely required before we could pass on that faith—to each other and to the students.

We found team teaching to be a dynamic experience, and we certainly hope that our course made space for God's patient, ongoing work to transform us—which is to say that it made room for Christ to live within us and our students more fully. This complex, irregular and fascinating form of human development, spiritual formation, was recently described by F. Leon Shultz as the process of *becoming wise* (being upheld by the Spirit to combine both scientific inquiry and spiritual knowledge), *becoming just* (achieving detachment from the desires of this world to await the Absolute Good), and *becoming free* (searching out truth and beauty in God's world to increase our joy). Shultz believes that spiritual transformation is one way to escape the dualism, extreme individualism, and mechanism that still permeate our society in these supposedly postmodern times.[25] Lois and I like to think that our course had a small part in this continuing process—for ourselves, for the students, and for the seminary community.

Team teaching is certainly not only a spiritual experience, but also has ideological and ethical justifications as well. As a form of collaboration, it is consistent with the shifts in education since World War II away from autocratic and elitist educational environments toward more democratic and learner-centered spaces. In team teaching, the goal changes from *How can I succeed in this class?* (i.e., by absorbing the knowledge of this instructor as I compete to get an "A"), to *How can we all learn more, together?* Team teaching is a good fit with what we've learned about cooperative learning, for it models this as the instructors engage each other. Students see their teachers as colearners and as persons practicing collegiality. As they witness their teachers' support for one another's growth and gifts, learners are more likely to respond by supporting each other. This, in turn, increases the flow of class conversation and decreases its staged and formal tendencies.

Students begin to believe that they can be at once vulnerable and safe because that is what they see happening with their instructors. For example, I spoke in class of my difficulties becoming ordained in a very conservative synod where women were not welcomed or affirmed. Lois spoke courageously of her challenges as a woman professor on a predominantly male campus and in a department where she was one of only two women. Women were a large majority in this class, and we wondered at times if having two women as team teachers might have been part of what attracted some students to enroll. This gender aspect of our experience is complex and might well be explored in a separate article, since both the personal as a way of knowing and shared power structures are so important to a feminist perspective. They are also important, we believe, for successful team teaching.[26]

We experienced a more mundane, pedagogical transformation as well. We were certainly not the first persons to discover the benefits of team teaching, which has become an increasingly popular learning arrangement, but this experience converted us—we want to team teach again, whenever appropriate. One quite obvious advantage is that each professor comes to the classroom with a different area of past knowledge and experience. In our case, Lois brought a rich depth and breath of familiarity with contemporary and classic theology, including her interest in atonement theory and in the fecundity of God, that rich, nurturing outpouring of God's love and Grace. Her past teaching, reading, and scholarship is scripturally based, and she brought to class deep reflections on biblical stories, such as the prodigal son. The intersections she found between these narratives and our topics were greatly appreciated by the students. My background as a marriage and family therapist and a parish pastor provided me with case studies that we used for class discussions.[27] I also brought years of experience with human brokenness along with a firm belief in the possibility of reconciliation in even the most damaged situations. I have seen remarkable things happen between estranged people, and my confidence in these wonders of God's healing work was perhaps my greatest contribution to the class. Thus the students were exposed to two varied backgrounds, to differing expertise and experiences and, hopefully, to wisdom based on those experiences.

Each professor on a cross-disciplinary team inevitably discovers overlapping areas of interests and knowledge that she had not previously realized—and this is true of students as well. Said one student, "I thought I wanted to study Old Testament, but now I realize I want to do my PhD in either pastoral or systematic theology!" The integrated work required in a team-taught classroom can challenge and inspire students to apply new, integrated learnings in other classrooms, contributing fresh perspectives all around. As a result of our work together, Lois has become more interested in object relations theory, narcissism and other personality disorders, as well as narrative approaches to pastoral care and theology. I became interested in reading more about the intersection of atonement theories, feminism, and psychoanalytical theories,[28] and I was powerfully impacted by how the cross reveals a tension between God's solidarity with victims of injustice and God's mercy toward the guilty. Our new interests and knowledge, we believed, enriched both our teaching in other classes and our advising of doctoral students.[29]

Some subject matters are more appropriate for team teaching than others. Because of its interdisciplinary nature (or multidisciplinary, in teams of 3 or more) this form of pedagogy is especially appropriate when the subject matter is highly complex and has been researched and practiced in a variety of disciplines. It is not sufficient to borrow, to cut and paste from other fields. One must accept the challenge to try new methodologies, to explore how the disciplines view a similar concept in dissimilar ways, and to wrestle with how the particular language of each field might contribute to understanding complex ideas.[30] This challenge is certainly true of our topic, forgiveness and healing. How can one discuss, for example, what happens between God and the victim of childhood sexual abuse without both theological rooting and psychological knowledge? Our differing perspectives also helped us notice things not otherwise obvious—for example, how both we and the students tended to portray ourselves as victims in our own narratives, never as perpetrators of harm. This was interesting in terms of theological anthropology (had Luther's teaching of sinner/saint really been internalized?) and psychologically (how powerful and inflexible are our defenses in situations of severe estrangement!).

It may be possible that an additional benefit of this teaching, and one specific to a seminary setting, is that it helps to prepare pastoral caregivers who will need skills for professional collaboration. Many of them will go on, after seminary, to work in interdisciplinary environments, e.g., as part of a hospital healthcare team. Team teaching, when successful, presents a positive model of what this collaboration might look like.

One of the most attractive aspects of team teaching for us is its implicit affirmation of diversity. In our classes at Luther we have significant numbers of international students; their captivating experiences and broad perspectives greatly enrich our classrooms. However, as we often lamented in our pre-tenure teaching-learning group, it can be challenging to find ways to draw into discussion those students for whom English is a second language. We also have a wide age span at Luther, typical of many seminaries today, along with differing denominations, sexual orientations, life experiences, and social-economic backgrounds. We found that some diversity in the professors (in our case, age, academic discipline, and teaching style) helped students feel more comfortable in their own differences. We believed that it also contributed to the lively class discussions that were so important for this course.

Team teaching also has its challenges. Ironically, the interdisciplinary or multidisciplinary aspects of this classroom structure appear to be more of an issue for educators than for students.[31] Team teaching can raise anxieties, particularly those of new teachers, in a variety of ways. As my former professor Katherine Allen recently wrote of her team-teaching experience, "We (those who team taught together) were restrained by our sense of vulnerability and desire to protect our self-interest. One of us was untenured. All of us felt outnumbered . . . And we were aware of the risks to our individual reputations as 'good teachers' at our university. Often, students' ratings of multiple instructors of team-taught courses fall below ratings for courses taught by those instructors as individuals. Thus, each of us was taking a risk in co-teaching this course by giving up our sole authority over the class."[32]

When I first taught, I would have resonated with those feelings. Now, at sixty, I am a bit more philosophical about my failures and successes, but I do not believe that my desire to be considered a good teacher will ever be completely obliterated. (Nor should it be!) Recently, I find myself overly concerned with others' perceptions of my teaching, chiefly when I have students in class who do not understand nor respect my academic discipline. I recently came across a paragraph I wrote a few years ago as part of a self-evaluation:

> Although these students (those who come to class with a negative attitude about pastoral care courses) constitute a very small minority, the first times I taught I allowed their anxieties to create anxiety for me. I believe I have developed some useful strategies for involving more immature and worried students and, in part, for helping most of them to move to a place where they

> can learn. Examples include genuine and appropriately timed feedback, opportunities to show what they already know, non-defensive reactions when they disagree with me, reframing their comments to search out positive motivations, etc. But I have also learned to expect this trust process to take time, and I am thus less impatient and self critical during the first few weeks, when defenses are high. This remains a growing edge, however, and I regret to say that, outside class, I still catch myself thinking frequently of these one or two students and obsessing a bit about how I can change their attitudes toward pastoral care.

Because of its very public nature, team teaching truly offers both challenge and opportunity, and the greatest challenges lie right here at our place of greatest vulnerability—the fear of being shamed. It would be easy for this form of teaching to be an occasion for unfair comparisons and harsh evaluations that would then overwhelm our creativity, fun, and sense of safety. I am very fortunate that, in my experiences both in this class and others at Luther Seminary, the fair, caring feedback of my peers has helped me grow more self-confident. They have sensitized me to the need to exercise that same care and balance when I am asked to write a teaching evaluation for a peer or PhD student! What trust it takes to place ourselves, as professionals, into our colleagues' hands!

V. THE TRUST TO EXAMINE OURSELVES

Christian self-examining can happen only on the basis of this premise—that Jesus Christ is in us.[33]

One of the many ways we asked students to practice trust in this course was to engage in self-examination. As I learned from mentor Stephen Brookfield, it is unfair and unrealistic to ask students to do what we will not do ourselves.[34] Thus Lois and I attempted to look at our personal and professional lives with courage and honesty, since this was precisely what we were asking of the students. This was mostly done privately, in prayer and in our journals, but, as described earlier, we also shared aspects of this process with each other. This is not something all team teachers would choose to do, but, in our case, it occurred naturally and led to greater interpersonal trust.

However, the intrapersonal work needed for honest self-evaluation is not easy; it is far more natural for us to fall into mechanistic, superficial, or narcissistic patterns. From a psychological point of view, one of two results seems most likely: either our own defenses are so inflexible that they immediately rush in to protect us, precluding the honesty and clarity we seek, or we will be stripped of all defenses and experience only shame, looking at ourselves too harshly and seeing only failure.[35] Of course, it is the mark of a differentiated and wise person to learn to think of herself with balance and even with self-deprecating humor, but we are all somewhere on the journey towards this maturity. The students often referred to the result of this process as self-forgiveness.[36]

Since this course was an attempt to integrate theology and psychology, we wanted to speak of self-examination and the trust it requires in language from both disciplines. Object relations theory was useful in understanding shame, splitting, and our human tendencies to introject good and bad "objects." Narrative theory was especially helpful in describing how we tell our own stories to ourselves and thus create roles that endure, such as victim, hero, rebel. This understanding—that we create our own realities—has been described as an *ah ha!* moment. Afterwards, we realize we have choices; we have the space and freedom to develop new stories, plots, and roles. This, in turn, increases our capacity for empathy with others who live in a locked-up, inflexible story. Often, hearing the narratives of hurting persons can break down our own private sense of hurt and isolation. As one student put it, "One discovers the meaning of one's life by remembering her story and how it intersects with God's story. . . . We receive a gift when we discover our story in that of another; we recognize our oneness."

But healthy self-examination is not simply a matter of psychological insight—it is a lived spiritual journey. Here Dietrich

Bonhoeffer can be particularly helpful, for he explained pharisaic vs. Christian self-examination. Wrote this theologian, whose absolute reliance on God is visible in his life and death, healthy Christian practice "rather than focusing on one's own knowledge of good and evil and its realization in practical life, daily renews the knowledge that 'Jesus Christ is in us.'"[37] Christocentric language, a focus on the New Being of the Christian, allows us to avoid dualistic, individualistic, and mechanistic tendencies in Western spirituality and leads us back to placing our reliance on God's forgiving and transforming love.[38] Since reading Bonhoeffer, I have found it more helpful in my devotional life to ask the question *To what extent has Christ's love lived in me today?* rather than *How upright and successful have I been today?*

Self-examination also raises the issue of self-labeling. We know intellectually and theologically that we are sinners, even if, as described earlier, we have trouble applying that to our interpersonal difficulties. But it can be even more difficult to call ourselves saints. This is an accurate description, Luther taught, only to the extent that we trust God. Based on trust, on faith alone, we are fit to be labeled saints, certainly not through our perfection or moral accomplishments. Labeling ourselves positively (on the basis of trust rather than through some sort of perceived superiority) not only breaks down many of the artificial barriers between victim and perpetrator, it is also a sign of the Kingdom of God among us.

VI. CREATING A LARGER CULTURE OF TRUST

I have a dream that these signs of the Kingdom will increase, that someday your seminary and mine will be places of joyful collegiality. I fantasize about a time when our common mission is so exciting and our appropriation of God's love so genuine that we can more frequently bypass our tendencies to exclude, blame, and gossip. Until that time, however, we are left trying to cooperate with the Spirit; we are left teaching future servants of the Church on imperfect campuses, preparing them to minister in an often disappointing, messy world. Until that time we are also called to keep the faith—to find, day by day, small ways to increase trust in God, in one another, and in ourselves. This hope, standing as it does against so much evidence to the contrary, is surely what it means to learn to trust in the Lord.

Surely it is not merely an individual matter, this business of building and embodying trust—there are, as Moltmann wrote, ecological ramifications. When one person trusts in the Lord, the entire community benefits. Trust allows people to join together to reject the addictions of this world—fame, wealth, power, all those illusions that constitute our *social security*. Through trust alone we find ourselves able to move as a community into a radically different space where we can thrive amidst enormous differences, find a haven from which to come and go without fear, and experience radical freedom from guilt and shame.[39] I believe that this place of tolerance, security, and safety is precisely the environment we want to create as we educate men and women to be full-time Christian public leaders.

We do not, however, always recognize the strong relationship of a healthy, trust-based ecology to what we do when we plan and teach a class. I believe that team teaching is one small but significant place where we can engage in the process of building cultural trust. It begins with the students, for when team teaching works well, they become energized, playful, and flexible, taking more risks to critique and self-reveal—precisely the ingredients we were seeking for not only our courses but also for the larger community. But professors are impacted as well—the collegiality of team teaching can be, along with many other practices, a tangible form of the noncompetitive, outpouring love that begins in the Triune God and overflows into our own lives.

It is challenging to describe how team teaching benefits a seminary using quantitative, concrete language. The elusive nature of trust and the invisibility of trust-building practices exemplified in team teaching are so difficult to articulate that administrators who are otherwise supportive may have problems justifying more than one instructor in a classroom at budget time. Therefore, in these days of cut backs and increased financial anxiety, those of us who have had positive experiences with team teaching may need to speak out. We may need to meet with our deans and presidents to explain what we have found this pedagogical method can do for students and how far it has deepened our faculty-wide conversations.

Emphasizing community trust is key, for administrators are well aware how important it is for our life together. I find myself talking about this course with my colleagues at lunch in the student center or on faculty retreats because I am eager to learn from them and to share my ideas and excitement about collaboration. I'd like to think that these conversations have translated, in some small way, into more tolerance and respect for pastoral care, an often disparaged discipline. And, hopefully, Lois and I, along with colleagues who team teach, may have contributed to less student entrenchment—we may have widened the narrow point of view in some of the more poorly differentiated students, playing a role in combating an unfortunate tendency they have to become the disciple of a particular professor. (How sad to see the difficulties we have with each other reflected in our students!)

Relationships are and always have been central to the slow process of expanding perspectives and building respect. Not surprisingly, Lois and I have had numerous conversations about the turn to relationality in contemporary philosophy. This trend suggests to us that teaching as a team might offer the possibility of experiencing more profoundly our reliance on the Triune God, who not only intends for us to relate to one another with love but who is relating, with perfect love and harmony, in precisely those ways within the dynamics of the Trinity. As George Cladis wrote,

> God exudes trust. It is the Lord's character to be trustworthy. The perfect community of the Trinity implies perfect trust. There is no sense that the Son betrays the Father or the Spirit lies and is deceitful. These things go against the character of God. . . . Ministry teams, filled with the Spirit of God, seek to mend broken community, and their members must therefore learn to trust one another and model trustworthiness . . . what a powerful force for good and God's sacred mission is the team

> that builds trust! In a world that thrives on betrayal and deceit, a culture of trust created by a trusting team is a wonderful source of healing and ministry in the church and the world.[40]

Clearly, the church needs this healing. But trust in a community of diverse individuals, such as a seminary, is a highly complex matter. Although it is indisputably true that "Fish need water to swim in, birds need air in which to fly, and we human beings need trust in order to develop our humanity,"[41] trust cannot be prescribed, legislated, nor artificially imposed. Rather, each small step toward breaking down systemic anxiety and toward embracing the stranger in each other is an act of potential transformation, a living participation in God's plan for humankind.

If nothing else, we hope that our course, along with those of our respected colleagues everywhere, will help break down the barriers of language and misunderstanding that have historically occurred on our campuses. One student wrote, "This course has provided a complex picture of forgiveness, and it is clear that forgiveness is not a subject that can be approached lightly or glibly. It cannot be demanded or commanded . . ." This complexity, and the need for a patient, organic process that it implies, is true of both forgiveness and of community trust building. We would all agree that true community, when it occurs, is a delightful gift, is recognizable as a sign of God's patient love, and is certainly one of the rich fruits of embodied forgiveness. Our seminary families, like our nuclear families, will not thrive without this process, this movement toward Christ.

At the end of a final case study, one student wrote, "May God's redeeming, restoring love make forgiveness and reconciliation possible for this broken family!" And all the people say, Amen!

NOTES

1. Jurgen Moltmann, From a Capps lecture, given April 27, 2005, *In God We Trust, In Us God Trusts: On Freedom and Security in a "Free World,"* http://www.theologicalhorizons.org/documents/CAPPStranscript1.pdf

2. Much of this chapter is simply a written form of the reflecting that was done with my colleague Lois Malcolm throughout the course and afterwards. I wish to acknowledge here my great debt to her.
3. Moltmann, *In God We Trust*, 2005.
4. These persons will be, of course, both the victims and the perpetrators of harm.
5. K. R. Allen, S. M. Floyd-Thomas and Gillman, "Teaching to transform: From volatility to solidarity in an interdisciplinary family studies classroom" *Family Relations, 50*, 4 (2001).
6. See further F. L. Shults and S. Sandage, *The Faces of Forgiveness* (Grand Rapids, MI: Baker Academic, 2003).
7. In fact, this particular difference became the subject of affectionate joking by the students. They gave us nicknames to capture our very different temperaments—Lois was "Robin Williams" and I became "Dr. Ruth."
8. Eisen, M. J., "The Many Faces of Team Teaching and Learning: An Overview," *New Directions for Adult and Continuing Education, 87*, (2000): 5–14.
9. Ibid., 12.
10. Laura Brown, *Subversive Dialogues: Theory in Feminist Therapy* (New York: Basic Books, 1994), 63.
11. Ibid., 63.
12. For more on embodied forgiveness, see Gregory L. Jones, *Embodying Forgiveness: A Theological Analysis* (Grand Rapids, MI: Eerdmans, 1995).
13. A complete listing of our course objectives is available online at: http://www.luthersem.edu/jramsey/PC4510/syl.htm.
14. We designed the course to move from the individual and normal cases of brokenness that require forgiveness to the systemic and extraordinary forgiveness that these evils require.
15. That "checking" includes this chapter which was read and approved by Lois before I submitted it for publication. Maintaining trust in writing as one interprets experiences is equally important.
16. This last issue, around advising students, became crucial on several occasions—one involving a history of childhood sexual abuse and one involving the murder of a family member.
17. Article Two of the *Small Catechism*, Martin Luther.
18. This mattered to our students. As one wrote in an email, "I want to thank you as instructors for opening our class sessions with prayer. I really appreciate that and feel the power of that practice

undergirding all that we do. Opening with prayer becomes a modeling, an invitation to create a holistic environment, and helps point to the importance of living out what we espouse."

19. R. Kegan, *In Over Our Heads: The Mental Demands of Modern Life* (Cambridge, MA: Harvard University Press, 1994).
20. Moltmann, *In God We Trust*, 2005.
21. K. R. Allen, S. M. Floyd-Thomas and Gillman, "Teaching to transform: From volatility to solidarity in an interdisciplinary family studies classroom" *Family Relations, 50*, 4 (2001): 320.
22. J. R. Davis, *Interdisciplinary Courses and Team Teaching: New Arrangements for Learning* (Phoenix: ACE/Oryx, 1995), 8.
23. I say "apparently" here because I believe that the costs are more than justified by the gains, but these are more likely to be long-term gains for the church, compared to short-term budget challenges for the seminary.
24. Allen, Floyd-Thomas and Gillman, "Teaching to Transform," 320.
25. F. L. Shults, "Transforming Spirituality in Theology," In F. L. Shults and S. Sandage, *Transforming Spirituality* (Grand Rapids, MI: Baker Academic, 2006).
26. See, for example, Webb, Walker, and Bollis, "Feminist pedagogy in the teaching of research methods," *International Journal of Research Methodology*, 7, 5, (2003): 415–428.
27. I altered them to protect confidentiality, of course.
28. See, for example, H. N. Malony and B. Spika (eds.), *Religion in Psychodynamic Perspective: The Contributions of Paul W. Pruyser* (New York: Oxford University Press, 1996).
29. My enlarged interests show in the required and recommended reading lists for my classes. What I learned from Lois has also enriched my research, advising and writing in aging and religion. For example, one of the doctoral students I advise has decided to do her dissertation on aging and forgiveness with a focus on Moltmann's theology.
30. W. H. Newell, *Interdisciplinary Essays from the Literature* (New York: College Entrance Examination Board, 1998).
31. Will Snyder, "Roundtables: A Way for Students to Develop their Internal Sources of Motivation to Learn and to Act," *International Research in Geographical and Environmental Education, 14*, 2, (2005): 150–154.
32. Allen, Floyd-Thomas, and Gillman, "Teaching to Transform," 320.

33. Dietrich Bonhoeffer, *Ethics* (Minneapolis, MN: Fortress Press, 2005), 326.
34. Stephen Brookfield, *Becoming a Critically Reflective Teacher* (San Francisco: Jossey Bass, 1995).
35. Many years ago, as a first grade teacher, I decided that people of all ages tend to hear criticism with the volume turned up, and praise as only distant, soon-forgotten sound.
36. I am more than a little uneasy with this terminology after reading Bonhoeffer—can we really forgive ourselves? Isn't this God's work alone? Yet it is language used so often that we are, to some extent, stuck with it.
37. Bonhoeffer, *Ethics*, 326.
38. Shults and Sandage, *Faces of Forgiveness*, 2006.
39. Moltmann, *In God We Trust*, 2005.
40. George Cladis, *Leading the Team-Based Church: How Pastors and Church Staffs Can Grow Together in to a Powerful Fellowship of Leaders* (San Francisco: Jossey-Bass, 1999), 14.
41. Moltmann, *In God We Trust*, 2005.

CHAPTER 8

"How Do We Teach Across Cultural Diversity?" Teaching in the Face of Cross-Cultural Conversation

Frieder Ludwig

I. PEDAGOGICAL CONTRASTS

It was one of those still warm afternoons in what is called "Indian summer" when I gave my first lecture at Luther Seminary in St. Paul, Minnesota. Since one of my colleagues had given an introduction into the Biblical foundations of mission, I could focus on mission history. I had lectured on this topic before in Bayreuth, in Munich in Germany, and in Jos in Nigeria, and had prepared my manuscript rather well, even with a few overhead illustrations. I felt confident. My main worry was that the evaluations would be too positive and that it would be difficult to keep to such a high level.

As it turned out, that worry at least proved to be unfounded. After half an hour or so, many of the students had stopped taking notes. Some of them were ostensibly passive, which in Minnesota, as I later learned, can indicate both lack of interest and silent yet aggressive disagreement. They were sitting there with their arms folded, looking at me with a critical view in their eyes which seemed to ask: "Do you understand what you are reading?"

There are various reasons for this first not-so-encouraging experience. Reading from a manuscript is the traditional lecture style in Germany and an overhead projector is usually the most modern technical equipment you can find in a classroom. (This form of teaching is accepted in Africa, too.) However, in the theological seminaries in the United States, where many professors speak freely, enrich their lectures with multimedia presentations and video clips, and encourage their students to interact, it is oddly out of place.

The different styles reflect different approaches, and these differences are probably nowhere as evident as in mission studies. David Kelsey's distinction between the "Berlin" and the "Athens" model in theological education may be helpful to clarify some of the issues at stake. According to Kelsey, the Berlin model is based on critical inquiry and research.[1] It was developed in the early nineteenth century when Wilhelm von Humboldt (who was then head of the Prussian government's section on cultural and educational affairs) appointed theologian Friedrich Schleiermacher to a committee which helped draft provisional statutes for a new university in Berlin. Kelsey described the model of theological education which was developed in that context as "a movement from data to theory to application of theory to practice."[2]

The Athens model, in contrast, stands for a type of schooling for which *paideia*—a process of "culturing the soul," schooling as "character formation"—is at the heart of education. Very early in the history of Christianity, the concept of *paideia* played an important role for leading theologians. Origen of Alexandria, for instance, affirmed that "Christianity is *paideia*, given by God in Jesus Christ, turning on to a radical conversion possible only by the Holy Spirit's help, and taught only indirectly by study of divinely inspired Scriptures in the social context of the church understood in some ways to be a school."[3] In the current discussion, it is especially Edward Farley's book *Theologia* which purports to promote a Christian *paideia*.[4]

There is some logic in the Berlin model, with its focus on critical inquiry, being more one-sidedly emphasized in the theological faculties of Berlin, Heidelberg, or Tübingen. This system is more likely to produce researchers who are experts in their fields, and one of the aims of theology in that context is critical reflection on church practices. Such an aim and set of practices has numerous implications for teaching. At least in theory, a lecture in Germany should be based on very new insights and the most recent relevant research. This requirement demands exact quotations and a balancing of nuances; one has to demonstrate the capacity for research, even in the lecture hall. (Lectures are free and open to the public, so everybody can attend.) Such nuancing and specificity is difficult without a script.

The system of the U.S. seminaries, on the other hand, while influenced by the European approaches, tends to emphasize, especially at the introductory level, foundational, ground-laying, praxis-oriented aspects of the topics under consideration. Theological education focuses directly on "forming excellent pastors" and "educating leaders for service." Any presentation of empirical and theoretical material is often followed up by an "application move"—questions such as "what can we learn from past mistakes?" "how can we develop better ministerial practices for the future?" and so on. Students have clear expectations and instructors repeat the same courses more often, sometimes three times a year.

In such a context, it is easier to speak freely. After four years of teaching in the United States I can give some lectures without a script, and although I am not the greatest rhetorician, I do occasionally have good moments. I know my audiences better, and I know which illustrations will work for them. (My dad worked as a veterinarian in a slaughter hall, and I have some colorful stories and jokes out of this context, but not all of them go well with my students here.) The tension, however, remains. There is something in the German system which I want to maintain, while at the same time it has become clear that without changes and adaptations to the local situation the impact of my teaching is rather limited.

In my first lecture, for instance, I had not only confronted my students with unfamiliar German names like Bartholomäus Ziegenbalg and Heinrich Plütschau, Johann Ludwig Krapf and Johannes Rebmann, Karl Graul and Bruno Gutmann, but I had also given a critical appraisal—pointing to weaknesses and failures in their work as well as to the reality that vivid and dynamic African and Asian congregations emerged from their mission. Yet I had nevertheless left my students without any indication of where they could or should go with this information in their own ministerial contexts.

Now I try to explain to my students at the beginning of a course why I am doing what I do and what my theological commitments are. This introduction includes, for instance, a reference to my teacher Hans-Werner Gensichen who described mission as an "altogether ambivalent enterprise executed in the context of tension between divine providence and human confusion."[5] This quote is helpful not only because it is sufficiently open to interpretation and integration (everyone agrees that there is human confusion; if we try to identify what exactly this confusion is, it becomes more complicated), but also because it opens the way for critical reflection while at the same time emphasizing the Christian conviction that God is at work in the world.

I have also learned to include other elements in my lectures, such as a walk across campus to consider local mission initiatives. Luther Seminary was established in the late nineteenth century by Norwegian immigrants: our first stop is a Celtic cross in front of Bockman Hall. It is a replica of the oldest cross in Norway, dating to around 1000 A.D. This brings out the ambiguity of mission, for while the "Celtic Way of Mission"[6] is associated with peaceful persuasion, the coming of Christianity to Norway was not peaceful.[7] We proceed to old Muskego Church, the first church building erected by Norwegian Lutherans in Wisconsin (and subsequently relocated to the Luther Seminary campus for historical preservation purposes). Here we reflect on the difficulties immigrants face in setting up a new congregation, and we discuss some of Martin Luther's ideas of how to organize worship in such a situation. Our next stop is the Luther Seminary archives, where our archivist, Paul Daniels, is always willing to share his vast knowledge of missionary initiatives especially to China and Madagascar. Afterward, we pass Bockmann Hall again, and I tell the story of old Bockman who was the Seminary's president during the 1920s and who always lectured in Norwegian. His lectures, it is said, never lapsed into English.[8] This short field trip usually leads into a general discussion of mission and migration. Luther Seminary is still dominated by Norwegian immigrant culture, but there are African, Asian, and Latin American congregations in the neighborhood, and these churches use Chinese, Yoruba, or Spanish in their services. They are also engaged in evangelistic activities in the United States; mission cannot be understood as a one-way road.

Another element which I have used to improve my teaching is the Critical Incident Questionnaire (CIQ) which was developed by Stephen Brookfield, Distinguished University Professor at the University of St. Thomas in St. Paul and consultant to our teaching and learning group formed by Luther Seminary's younger faculty. The questionnaire is comprised of five questions which ask students to note brief details of events that happened in the class that week.[9] These questions get the participants to focus on specific, concrete happenings that were significant to them.[10] When I started doing the seminary tour, for instance, most comments on the CIQ were positive. There were, however, two dissenting voices which pointed out that not all students were from the United States and that the particular emphasis given to the Norwegian experience was not very welcoming to others.

II. ENCOUNTERS WITH WORLD CHRISTIANITY

Yes, indeed. There is something more at stake in intercultural communication today than a German Lutheran teaching in a Norwegian Lutheran context at a U.S. seminary. One of the most important aspects of mission theology today is the "shifting gravity of Christianity." In his well-known book, *The Next Christendom,* Philip Jenkins points out that in the twenty-first century, the vast majority of believers will be neither white nor European nor Euro-American. According to an influential prognosis, there will be around 2.6 billion Christians in 2025, of whom 633 million will live in Africa, 640 million in Latin America, and 460 million in Asia. Europe, with 555 million, will have slipped to third place. Africa and Latin America will be in competition for the title of most Christian continent.[11]

The impact of Latin American, Asian, and African Christians in the West is significant. More than 100,000 Hispanic and more than 50,000 Asian immigrants live in the Twin Cities (St. Paul and Minneapolis). However, in the rest of this chapter I will focus particularly on African immigrants, African congregations, and African students of theology since that is the context with which I am most familiar.[12]

The number of African immigrants grew in Minnesota during the 1990s by 620.7%. This tendency continues. Data from the Department of Homeland Security shows 13,522 legal immigrants arrived in Minnesota in 2002—the highest number of legal immigrants since 1982, and 2,000 more than in 2001. It is generally acknowledged that religious institutions are a key forum among contemporary immigrants.[13] A good number of Liberian, Ethiopian, Nigerian, Kenyan, and Tanzanian newcomers are Christian and their congregations are of primary significance. Many of these congregations start as small prayer meetings in private houses. In preliminary research, we became aware of 75 African-led congregations in the Twin Cities. They include almost the whole spectrum of African Christianity—from Coptic and Ethiopian Orthodox churches to African Independent Churches, as well as Charismatic and Pentecostal and Pan-African congregations. There is little doubt that church life in Minnesota has been significantly affected in different ways by these new immigrants.

In theory, this shift should have far-reaching consequences for the way in which theology, and especially mission theology, is done. In actual practice we are only at the very beginning of a focused debate on theological education in these new contexts. One reason for the slow rate of change is that the divisions and rifts evident in such change are often stressed. Philip Jenkins, for instance, divides global Christianity into two streams—the "liberal west" and the "traditional rest." He writes that "there is increasing tension between what one might call a liberal Northern Reformation and the surging Southern religious revolution, which one might equate with the Counter Reformation."[14]

In such a view, there do not appear to be many points of easy contact. At a conference which I attended recently it was remarked that the theologies which emerge out of African congregations with their Biblicist and charismatic tendencies (singing, dancing, testimonies, prayers for healing) are not relevant for Western academic discourse. There is also the reverse form of the same argument—it can be said that our Western theological education is not relevant for these congregations. Such faith communities will continue to spread dynamically—with us or without us—and, so the argument runs, probably better without us, because they are neither affected by the critical self-doubts nor by the compromises with modern culture by which Western Christians are marked.

The assumption, however, that the theology coming out of these African congregations is more experiential, fundamentalist, or simplistic in character while "deeper thinking" is done in the West, is as misleading as the notion that these non-Western Christians represent a purer, more genuine form of Christianity than Christians in Europe or the United States do. Yet it is clear that theology emerges out of different contexts with specific questions. One of the challenges for African church leaders and theologians is to proclaim the gospel in a religiously plural context in such a way that it does not resemble African traditional religions too closely. (African traditionalists also believe in the direct intervention of God, healing by prayer, visions, and prophecies.) One of the challenges for European theologians and church leaders is not to be co-opted too closely into a state system (and thus to rely on church taxes and to become self-complacent). One of the challenges for U.S. theologians and church leaders is not to be too much compromised by concessions to the capitalist system. (Many immigrant Christians struggle with the fact that Sunday employment is generally and indisputedly accepted.)

It is a basic Christian conviction that we come together in Christ from different backgrounds and with different experiences (Eph 4). There is no question that there are many things that we can learn from this exchange. How do we apply this recognition in a U.S. theological classroom? It is fairly evident that good intentions alone are not sufficient. To put it in the words of Stephen D. Brookfield:

> "(O)ur attempts to increase the amount of love and justice in the world are never simple, never unambiguous. What we think are democratic, respectful ways of treating people can be experienced by them as oppressive and constraining. One of the hardest things teachers have to learn is that the sincerity of their intentions does not guarantee the purity of their practice."[15]

In regard to intercultural education, there are different patterns of teaching and learning.

While in the West, active student participation is seen as an indicator of a congenial teaching and learning atmosphere, students from Asian, African, or Latin American contexts may have different experiences and expectations. Regarding Chinese students, Alan Ka Lu Lai pointed out that:

> Chinese learners are not encouraged to exhibit verbal expressions in class since not just anyone is entitled to speak. This is based on their respect for the teacher: they may feel that asking questions suggests that the teacher did not teach the subject well enough. By speaking out, they may be perceived as assuming authority comparable to that of the teacher. As a result, "conversation" or dialogue is never a tool of teaching and learning in the Chinese context and students are not educated to participate verbally.[16]

And an Ethiopian pastor in the Twin Cities explained: "Back home, a girl or young women is admired if she doesn't look into the eye of a person. (. . .) This is expected from her. It is good. We say, 'she is wonderful. She can't even see in the eyes of a person.'" In the United States, people say "She must have a problem. She can't look into the eyes of the people and talk." But this is not a psychological problem, it is a cultural difference.

The use of the CIQ was helpful in my classes since it gave a voice to the less extroverted participants and also allowed expression of discontent without the danger of being publicly exposed (the questionnaires are anonymous). In this way, it was possible to analyze what was going on and to take some corrective measures in the next session. The insights gained by the responses to the CIQ led to another, more far-reaching question: How do we do theological education in a multicultural context? At first sight, the Athens model with its emphasis on Christian formation seems to be more attractive than the Berlin model with its focus on critical inquiry based on criteria developed in a particular European setting.

However, the protagonists of the Athens model have to ask very seriously: what is normative in the process of formation and who defines what is normative? Otherwise the process of Christian formation can easily be confused with a process of conforming to a particular culture. On the other hand, while the Berlin model is rather strict in regard to criteria established for research methods, it is sufficiently open in regard to content. We cannot simply neglect it, because it also provides the standards for publishing in most academic journals and books. To give an example: plagiarism was widespread in European literature of the sixteenth, seventeenth, and eighteenth centuries (and especially in accounts of travelers to Africa and Asia), while now there is a consensus that we should not copy from other sources without references. There is also an agreement that manuscripts submitted for publication should provide new insights or at least give precise and fresh summaries of the research done before. It is important to me that both our local students and our international students learn these methods so that they are able to interact with the wider academic world. There is also a missionary dimension in this; we do not want to do theology in isolated ways.

On the other hand, contemporary African theologians start by asking different questions than German theologians did at the beginning of the nineteenth century. Their insights about the Christian faith as a life lived in a community engaged in the world, about Christian witness in a religiously pluralistic context, about charismatic gifts and the theology of the cross, are relevant indeed for the general theological discussion of the twenty-first century.

A number of these same themes are also addressed in the book of Acts. In a recent publication it was pointed out that "perhaps no single issue . . . is more relevant to the church today than how Acts shows the church negotiating life and faith in a multicultural world."[17] Therefore I started to introduce some of my lectures with reflections on selected chapters or subchapters of the book of Acts and to draw the historical lines from there.

III. THE BOOK OF ACTS AS AN EXAMPLE IN TEACHING MISSION

I am not the very first missiologist who has discovered the significance of Acts. However, its potential for teaching in a multicultural classroom still needs to be explored. The way in which the book addresses vital questions in a concrete setting helps to engage students from different backgrounds and to address themes which have been underemphasized in Western Christian theological thought, but have received considerable attention from African, Asian, and Latin American theologians. Such diverse interpretations give us a unique opportunity today to read Acts with fresh eyes and ears.[18]

There are many rich, thought-provoking narratives in Acts. But the text which I use most often is the story of Philip and the eunuch in Acts 8:26–40. This passage is often interpreted as the beginning of the mission in a new land. The Church of Ethiopia, one of the most ancient in the world, which has millions of members, claims that its origins are precisely in this encounter between Philip and the Ethiopian eunuch. Furthermore, this passage may be read as the beginning of the mission to the Gentiles even before the Church at large authorized such a mission. It will only be after the episode of Peter and Cornelius that leaders of the church of Jerusalem will come to the conclusion that "God has given even to the Gentile the repentance that leads to life" (Acts 11:18).[19] Most importantly, it is a multi-layered account which can be interpreted in different ways and brings out many different dimensions of mission.

The text tells us about the deacon Philip who is directed by an angel of the Lord to the desert road between Jerusalem and Gaza:

> On his way Philip met an Ethiopian eunuch, an important official in charge of all the treasury of Candace, queen of the Ethiopians. He is on his way home from Jerusalem, sitting in his chariot reading the book of Isaiah the prophet. Instructed by the Spirit, Philip went to the chariot and stayed near it. He heard the man reading Isaiah 53:7–8, about God's servant who was led like a sheep to the slaughter 'Do you understand what you are reading?' Philip asked. 'How can I,' he said, 'unless someone explains it to me?' So he invited Philip to come up and sit with him. Philip then interpreted that very passage of Scripture to him and told him the good news about Jesus. As they travelled along the road, they came to some water and Philip baptized him. When they came up out of the water, the Spirit of the Lord suddenly took Philip away, and the eunuch did not see him again, but went on his way rejoicing.

Thus the text begins with Philip being directed to the desert road. Even the very first, simple question about Philip's background can lead to different directions and to different reflections. Philip is mentioned first in Acts 6:1–4 as one of the seven men who were commissioned to supervise the church's ministry to the needs of its widows and other poor so that the twelve could give their attention to prayer and the ministry of the word. (This is generally considered to be the beginning of the office of Deacon in the Church, although the Scriptures do not use this term in referring to the original seven men.) However, this division of labor did not work very well; the next chapters of Acts tell us that two of the seven, Stephen (who was martyred) and Philip, started to preach and evangelize. Philip proclaims Christ in Samaria and receives close attention because of many miraculous signs such as the healing of paralytics and cripples. As in other passages of Acts, there is no dichotomy between witness, social engagement, and charismatic gifts.[20] This integration of activity, of course, has implications for our own time and experience and can be followed up by a discussion on the relationship between the various elements of mission.

We also learn that Philip's job description obviously does not fit. That theme, too, is something we encounter in other chapters of Acts. Acts 2 tells us about the election of Matthias as the twelfth apostle, who is never again mentioned either in Acts or in the rest of the New Testament. Justo L. Gonzalez, a leading Latin American church historian draws our attention to the fact that this text resonates with the experiences of many Hispanic Christians:

> The "old guard," that is the eleven, seems to believe that the structure of the Church must forever be the same that they knew, and they even seek leaders whose experiences and perspectives are the same as theirs. The "Twelve," now reduced to eleven, think that the election of another like themselves is absolutely essential. They even set up requirements in the election—requirements that some of them themselves did not meet.[21]

However, the Spirit is ready to do new things, opening the church to a wider world which requires other leaders. The task of being witnesses, not only in Jerusalem and in Judea, but also in Samaria and to the ends of the earth, required people who could participate in that mission. The disciples chose Matthias, but the Spirit chose Paul, Stephen, or indeed Philip. This kind of discussion of the text of Acts can easily lead to a discussion about church leadership and the *missio Dei* in contemporary contexts.

Philip's success as an evangelist is related to healing miracles and charismatic gifts; later in the book, Acts 21:9, we learn that he had four unmarried daughters who prophesied. Phenomena such as visions, ecstasy, trances, healing the sick, and exorcism were of primary significance for the mission and spread of Christianity in the first four centuries[22], and they are also important for Christians in Africa, Asia, and Latin America today. It is usually worthwhile to include a brief overview on that particular theme. For, while a general outline of mission history leaves students with a bulk of abstract material, a presentation on health and healing often sparks stimulating discussions. One of my African students became much more interested in the theology of the three Cappadocians when she learned about the healing miracles associated with Macrina, the sister of Basil and Gregory of Nyssa.

In his work *Life of St. Macrina,* Gregory tells some vivid stories (for instance, how the sight of a blind girl was restored).[23] In *The Making of Man*, Gregory of Nyssa reflects theologically on the significance of healing, a theme which was central in the early church. In my classes we move from a discussion of Gregory of Nyssa to looking at the thoughts of other Christian theologians, for instance Martin Luther. While the German reformer indicates a belief in the possibility of healing by prayer, in general he is rather skeptical. The reason for this skepticism is that his theology is based on the cross. God is the hidden God, and for Luther it is not possible to recognize him by intellectual or sensual approaches. Belief is directed towards the future goods which we have *non in re; sed spe* Christians too, are *sub contraria specie*, and therefore suffering, humiliation, and carrying the cross are signs of the bonds/solidarity with Christ. Luther believed that the great miracles like healing were given in the beginning simply so that Church people could later do "greater works than these" by teaching, converting, and saving people spiritually.[24] Thus, in this session students working with classical texts can learn to appreciate the significance of charismatic gifts such as healing by prayer, while working closely with a variety of historical documents, and at the same time seeing the limitations of such experiences in historical context.

Back to Philip and the book of Acts. He who was so successful in preaching and evangelizing in Samaria (like a modern Billy Graham), suddenly finds himself on the road that goes from Jerusalem to Gaza. The narrator's aside that this is a "wilderness road" is puzzling because the road is not in fact a desert road. F. S. Spencer suggests that the story's geographical marker locates the prophet and the eunuch in a "liminal zone off the beaten path of regular traffic," where serious theological reflection and personal transformation is more likely.[25] Whatsoever it is, Philip is taken out of his successful ministry of mass conversion to a place where he meets but one person.

There are crucial implications in this story for our understanding of mission. In some contexts today, Christianity seems to be flourishing, with many converts coming from Traditional Religions. In other contexts, for instance in Muslim or also in secular environments, we cannot expect the same dynamic progress. Does this mean that we should not go to such places, engage in dialogue and exchange of views, and give witness to Christ? Philip is directed to the wilderness road. Then there is the missionary moment. Philip accompanies the carriage and is invited; he accepts the hospitality of the Ethiopian. Accompaniment and an awareness that missionaries are but invited guests are resurfacing themes in missiology today. The conversation which develops can be interpreted in different ways.

Thomas Menamparampil, the archbishop of Guwahati in eastern India, points out that:

> . . . the first important thing is that there be someone who explains. The second is that this evangelizer should begin from the point at which he finds the person who poses the question: from his passage of Scripture, his problem in life, his state of soul, his level of education, the aspirations of his heart, the nature of his culture, and the limitations of his scope and vision. In recent years one can note a sort of aversion on the part of many missionaries to assume the role of Philip. We should ask why. We can only guess at the reasons for such timidity or apathy.[26]

Others, Hans Schwarz for instance, emphasize that it becomes clear from this text that the Christian faith invites understanding (*Acts* 8:30). The Christian faith invites discerning reflection.[27] And in his book, *Teaching as Believing,* Chris Anderson points out that, inspired by the Spirit, Philip asks the question that all teachers ask their students: "Do you understand what you are reading?" The eunuch replies: "How can I, unless someone guides me?"

> All teachers,[28] [Anderson continues] are teachers of reading, whatever else they are, and what all teachers know is that reading requires community. It is not a solitary act because the texts we have to interpret are never self-evident. The eunuch cannot understand the Scriptures on his own, without context, without interpretive frame. There is always more than meets the eye, there's always complexity, and when Philip begins to interpret he immediately reads between the lines, looking past the literal meaning of the words of the Hebrew scriptures to how they symbolize the coming of this man Jesus Christ. (. . .)Philip . . . is thinking critically. He is looking beyond the surface to complexities and nuances that the eunuch cannot see because they first don't meet the eye. We need a method and a set of assumptions to see them. . . . The eunuch's response is the experience of freedom, and then, in that freedom, a public commitment to community, a plunging back into the tradition and stories and ways of reading that Philip has brought with him. First reading, then reading between the lines, then freedom, then commitment.[29]

The implications of process are huge, since it basically indicates that in this first text about mission into a new land the very critical thinking skills which are so central in the Berlin model do play an important role.

However, Philip's arguments are not the last words of the story. It is the Ethiopian who asks to be baptized, and after the baptism Philip is taken away by the Spirit, "and the eunuch did not see him again, but went on his way rejoicing." It is not Philip who is finally in control, it is the Spirit, and the focus also shifts more and more to the Ethiopian. This is reflected in the writings of Martin Luther, who drew far-reaching conclusions:

> If the eunuch converted by Philip remained a real Christian, which is exactly what one would assume, then he without a doubt taught many others God's Word since he was commanded "to proclaim the deeds of the one who calls us out of the darkness into his wonderful light" (1 *Peter* 2:9) The faith of many was surely a result of his preaching because the Word of God does not return empty (*Isaiah* 55:11). From faith, the church fol-

> lows. The church, therefore, through the Word had the offices to baptize, to teach, and all the remaining offices mentioned above. She fulfilled them all. All of this the eunuch effected by means of no other authority than the authority of his baptism and of his faith, especially since no others were there who could have done this.[30]

Luther was interested in the Ethiopian Orthodox Church partly for the reason that it was one of the churches which were not under the jurisdiction of the pope in Rome. In 1534, a visitor from Ethiopia, Deacon Michael, came to Wittenberg, and Luther recommended that the Evangelical congregations in Germany should receive him as a brother in Christ. With a letter, which was written to serve practical purposes, Luther illustrated that the unity of faith among Christians also implied their unity in love.

What do we know about the Ethiopian in Acts 8? He is a spiritual pilgrim who has come from a distant land earnestly seeking to understand Scriptures' prophecies of God's salvation. But he is also an outsider: Even though he is a "God fearer," he cannot become a convert to Judaism, for his sexuality excludes him. It was the law of Israel that "He who is emasculated . . . shall not enter the assembly of the Lord" (Deut 23:1, cf. Lev. 21:17–21). The eunuch must have been aware of this prohibition. On the other hand, he probably also learned about the promise in Isaiah (Isa 56:3–5—that is only three chapters beyond what he was reading), that the day will come when there will be in the house of Israel a place for the foreigner as well as for the eunuch.[31]

He is also an African, and that fact has been significant indeed for the history of Christianity in Africa. Although the Ethiopia of the Bible is more likely in Nubia (today's Sudan), the Ethiopian Orthodox Church traces its roots to Acts 8, and later this text became a key text for African self-assertion and emancipation from European domination. It was referred to, for instance, by Juan Latino (1516?–1597), one of the most influential black men in 16th-century Spain. (He is cited in Spain's most famous novel, Miguel de Cervantes' *Don Quijote de la*

Mancha). Juan Latino was enslaved and brought to Spain in chains. In Granada, he became a professor of Latin (hence his last name, Latino) and is reputed to have been sought after far and wide by students who were eager to learn from him.[32]

Addressing King Philip of Spain, Juan Latino bases his own claim to freedom on his self-proclamation as an Ethiopian. His use of Biblical Ethiopia as a rhetorical device brings him legitimacy but also a primacy over other Christians. In a Spain consumed by the socially exclusive practices of purity of blood, Juan Latino recalls the biblical story of the Ethiopian eunuch: "Philip, the disciple, taught Christ's word from his own mouth when he met the Ethiopian. Thus Christ sent a disciple to that Ethiopian. Philip therefore was sent by heaven to an Ethiopian as a part of a plan." For Juan Latino, the history of the Ethiopian eunuch is the birthright of all black Africans within the Christian fold. In Juan Latino's poem the place of the Ethiopian eunuch is now occupied by King Philip who is reading without understanding. The words from the Old Testament that foretold Christ's humiliation, his unspeakable destiny, and death, can be explained by Juan Latino the Ethiopian who takes the place of the apostle Philip. Juan Latino is an Ethiopian Apostle; Philip, while the king and white, is like the Ethiopian who seeks the word of God.[33]

Our text became even more important at the end of the nineteenth century when some African Christian communities in South and West Africa broke from the European mission churches primarily because of racial discrimination. The movement has been called "Ethiopianism" because of the many references to Ethiopia. Key documents were Psalm 68 "Ethiopia shall stretch out her hands unto the Lord" and Acts 8. An important interpretation was given by Edward Wilmot Blyden (1832–1912) in 1882. Blyden who was born in the West Indies became an outstanding scholar, Pan-Africanist, and politician in West Africa. In the late 1880s when African church leaders like the black Anglican bishop Samuel Ajayi Crowther were deprived of power by European missionaries, he was also one of the leading advocates of African Independent Churches. In his exegesis of Acts 8, Blyden wrote:

> It is evident that the Gospel of Jesus Christ is designed for all countries and all climes—for all nations and races; but it is also evident that we have this "treasure in earthen vessels," which subjects it to human conditions and limitations. . . . Now, after the Spirit had come, and had filled the disciples with power for their mission, and they began to organize for aggressive work, it was found necessary to add to the number of evangelistic agents. Accordingly, under the direct inspiration of the Holy Spirit, seven men were chosen as evangelists, among whom was Philip. This man, after the murder of Stephen, went away from Jerusalem, and preached with great success in the city of Samaria. The injunction not to enter into any city of the Samarians had been withdrawn, and the whole world was now opened to the preachers of the gospel. They went over into Europe, penetrated farther eastward into Asia, went south to Arabia. But there lay Ethiopia, with its inhospitable climate and difficulty of access. What was to be done? The Spirit which was to guide them into all truth met the emergency. An African had come up in search of truth to Jerusalem, and, having completed his mission, was returning to his home, and was so far on his journey as to have reached the southern confines of the Holy Land, when Philip the Evangelist received a message concerning him: "The angel of the Lord spoke unto Philip, saying, Arise and go toward the south, unto the way that goeth down from Jerusalem unto Gaza, which is desert. And he arose and went, and behold a man of Ethiopia, an eunuch of great authority under Candace, queen of the Ethiopians, who had the charge of all her treasure, and had come to Jerusalem for to worship, was returning; and, sitting in his chariot, read Isaias the prophet. Then the Spirit said unto Philip, Go near and join thyself to this chariot."[34]

This incident I take to be a symbolic one, indicating the instruments and the methods of Africa's evangelization. The method, the simple holding up of Jesus Christ; the instrument, the African himself. This was the Spirit's application and explication of the command. "Go ye into all the world," etc.—giving the gospel to a man of Ethiopia to take back to the people of Ethiopia.

We are told that after the singular and interesting ceremony, "The Spirit of the Lord caught away Philip, that the eunuch saw him no more; and he went on his way rejoicing." Philip was not to accompany the eunuch, to water the seed he had planted, to cherish and supervise the incipient work. If he desired to do so—and perhaps he did—the Spirit suffered him not, for he "caught him away."

In these ways Acts 8 opens the way for a whole set of reflections. Students from different contexts usually find at least one layer, one point of entry into the discussion, where they have more to say than others. Thus the story can help to integrate a diverse and multi-cultural classroom. In some classes, this works, in others it does not. My students will continue to ask me "Do you understand what you are reading?" and I will continue to ask my students "Do you understand what you are reading?" And we will be on our way, rejoicing.

NOTES

1. David Kelsey, *Between Athens and Berlin: The Theological Education Debate* (Grand Rapids, MI: Eerdmans, 1993), 12–13.
2. Ibid., 22.
3. Ibid., 11.
4. Edward Farley, *Theologia: The Fragmentation and Unity of Theological Education* (Philadelphia: Fortress Press, 1983), xi, quoted in Kelsey, 7.
5. Hans-Werner Gensichen, *Glaube fuer die Welt: Theologische Aspekt der Mission* (Guetersloh, Germany: Mohn, 1971), 16.
6. Cf. George Hunter, *The Celtic Way of Mission: How Christianity Can reach the West . . . Again* (Nashville, TN: Abingdon, 2000). I am not very convinced by this book, but this does not hinder my students from reading it.
7. Cf. Philip Schaff, *History of the Christian Church*, Volume IV: Mediaeval Christianity. A.D. 590–1073 (New York: Charles Scribner, 1903–1912). "The first time Christianity really gained a footing in Norway, was under Olaf Trygveson. . . . Invited to Norway by a party which had grown impatient of the tyranny of Hakon Jarl, he easily made himself master of the country, in 995, and im-

mediately set about making Christianity its religion, 'punishing severely', as Snorre says, 'all who opposed him, killing some, mutilating others, and driving the rest into banishment.'"

8. Alvin N. Rogness, "Centennial Article: Marcus Olaus Bockman," *Luther Theological Seminary Review*, Spring (1975): 19–21, 45.
9. 1.) At what time in the class this week did you feel most engaged with what was happening? 2.) At what moment in the class this week did you feel most distanced from what was happening? 3.) What action that anyone took in class this week did you find most affirming and helpful? 4.) What action that anyone took in class this week did you find most puzzling or confusing? 5.) What about the class this week surprised you the most?"
10. Stephen Brookfield, *Becoming a Critically Reflective Teacher* (San Francisco: Jossey Bass, 1996), especially chapter 6: Understanding Classroom Dynamics, 114–139. [There is also more description of the use of this process in chapter 1 of the volume you hold in your hands.]
11. Philip Jenkins, *The Next Christendom* (New York: Oxford University Press, 2002), 2, 3.
12. Together with six African pastors, I am involved in a project on "African Congregations in the Twin Cities" which brings together leaders (pastors and lay leaders) of African congregations in the Twin Cities area and members of Luther Seminary's faculty in order to develop a network and to connect potentials.
13. Jacqueline Copeland-Carson, "Black Philanthropy Today: Embracing the New Diversity," in the newsletter of the Minnesota Council of Foundations: http://www.mcf.org/MCF/forum/2005/newdiversity.htm.
14. Philip Jenkins. "The Next Christianity." The Atlantic Volume 290, No. 3 (October, 2002): 53–68.
15. Stephen D. Brookfield, *Becoming a Critically Reflective Teacher* (San Francisco: Jossey-Bass 1995), 1.
16. Alan Ka Lun Lai, "Educating Chinese Seminarians in North America: A Cross Cultural Understanding of Teaching and Learning," *Consensus* (1999): 69–91.
17. A.B. Robinson, R.W. Wall, *Called to be Church. The Book of Acts for a New Day*, (Grand Rapids, MI: Eerdmans, 2006), 8.
18. Robinson/Wall, *Called to be Church*, 9.
19. Justo L. Gonzalez, *Acts. The Gospel of the Spirit*, (Maryknoll, NY: Orbis Books, 2001), 116–118.
20. Robinson/Wall, *Called to be Church*, 5.

21. Gonzalez, *Acts*, 27–28.
22. Adolf von Harnack, *The Mission and Expansion of Christianity in the First Three Centuries* (New York: Putnam, 1908), 253.
23. Gregory of Nyssa, *The Life of St. Macrina*, translated in *Gregory of Nyssa: Ascetical Works* (Washington: Catholic University of America Press, 1967), 188–189.
24. For a general overview see S. Pattison, "Health and healing," A. Hastings (ed.), *The Oxford Companion to Christian Thought* (New York: Oxford University Press, 2000): 285–287.
25. F. S. Spencer, *Journeying through Acts* (Peabody, MA: Hendrickson Publishers, 2004), 90–91.
26. The full text of the archbishop's reflection was published in the number 1, 2003, edition of "Omnis Terra," the periodical of the Pontifical Missionary Union in Rome. It was reprinted by "Mondo e Missione," the monthly of the Pontifical Institute for Foreign Missions in Milan, in its April 2003 edition. Taken from the web on January 2, 2007: http://www.chiesa.espressonline.it/printDettaglio.jsp?id=6937&eng=y.
27. Hans Schwarz, *Christology* (Grand Rapids, MI: Eerdmans, 1998), 1.
28. Anderson refers to teachers at the university, but this also applies for teachers at a seminary.
29. Chris Anderson, *Teaching as Believing: Faith in the University* (Waco, TX: Baylor University Press, 2004), 71.
30. Martin Luther, *Briefwechsel* VII [1534–1536] (Weimar, 1937), 188–190.
31. Justo L. Gonzalez, *Acts. The Gospel of the Spirit*, (Maryknoll, 2001), 116–118.
32. Mario Andr, Chandler, "Mario's Journal: An Early Return" (June 14, 2000) taken from the web on January 2, 2007: http://wow.uab.edu/spain/show.asp?durki=30011.
33. Baltasar Fra-Molinero, "Juan Latino and His racial difference", J. F. Earle, K. J. P. Lowe, *Black Africans in Renaissance Europe* (Cambridge, Cambridge University Press, 2005): 339.
34. E. W. Blyden, "Philip and the Eunuch. Discourse delivered in the United States in 1882," In E. W. Blyden, *Christianity, Islam and the Negro Race* (Edinburgh: U.P., 1967): 160, 161.

CHAPTER 9

"How Can White Teachers Recognize and Challenge Racism?" Acknowledging Collusion and Learning an Aggressive Humility

Mary E. Hess and Stephen D. Brookfield

I. THE CHALLENGES WE FACE

Sitting down to try and write a chapter on dealing with race in theological classrooms is not an easy task. As people who live with the unearned privileges that bearing white skin in the American context brings us, there are many places and times in which we hardly feel like we have an appropriate voice to raise in this discussion. Yet, race should not be thought of as a question or issue only for people of color, something that white people need not concern themselves with. Whites need to deal with race as much as any other group and an inability to appreciate this is one more way white supremacy stays unchallenged, even unnoticed. Racism is not going away. The question of how diverse our faculties are, and how that diversity—or lack thereof—affects the teaching and learning process is a lively one. No matter how regularly other colleagues seek to dismiss the question by arguing the concern is solely a matter of political correctness and therefore no longer relevant, our students and faculties, indeed our communities of faith, still live in the grip of the dangerous and destructive currents of oppression.[1] How has it come to pass that concern for diversity is seen as a marginal issue and of interest only to people of color? Or that engaging issues of race has come to be understood primarily as a concern for appropriate language?

Perhaps in the general run of challenges facing theological educators, dealing with racism evokes a bone-deep and enduring fatigue that suggests there is little that can be done.[2] White theological educators often affirm that racism must be engaged but can't think of how to do so, or they live in deliberate ignorance of its pervasive impact on our classrooms. Theological educators who do not carry the conferred dominance or implicit privilege of "whiteness" often have all that they can do to marshall their own research and teaching within a predominately white context, and have little energy left for engaging these issues.

If one of the key reasons why white theological educators do *not* take up these challenges has to do with this form of fatigue, then that dilemma in turn has to do with having little sense of agency. Years' worth of study and writing and research and teaching have led us to a situation in which the "numbers" are still not promising. DeYoung, Emerson, Yancey, and Kim, of the Multiracial Congregations Project, noted that:

> The nation's religious congregations have long been highly racially segregated. If we define a racially mixed congregation as one in which no one racial group is 80 percent or more of the congregation, just 7.5 percent of the over 300,000 religious congregations in the US are racially mixed. For Christian congregations, which form over 90% of congregations in the United States, the percentage that are racially mixed drops to five and a half.[3]

Further, the statistics about faculty at institutions of higher education—and more specifically, of theological higher education—are just as disheartening:

> In 2001, 85% of male faculty at ATS schools were white, as were 85% of female faculty. That number has shifted somewhat, since in 2005 84% were white men, while only 81% were white women.[4]

Given that these numbers include all of the faculty at historically black schools, as well as schools within denominations that do not ordain women, they are not numbers of which any of us can be proud. Yet the very reality that the numbers are being kept, that we have this description available to us, suggests that there is at least some interest in engaging the issues. As Gary Gunderson writes, "what *might* be is embedded in what is, however painful it might seem to be."[5]

Proponents of anti-racism begin from an understanding that racism is a complicated process deeply embedded in human institutions. They draw out clear distinctions between "bigotry"—the practice of holding specific prejudices—and "racism"—the institutionalization and continued dominance of certain prejudices through the exercise of structural power.[6] In this analysis, racism is not entirely—or even primarily—a matter of individual persons and their individual responses to people with differing skin tones. Rather, racism is a complex process of developing structural power that has been inscribed in institutions over hundreds of years and that grows out of specific patterns of practice, legal definitions, and institutional norms that lead to clear benefits being conferred, in unmerited and usually unremarked upon ways, upon people solely on the basis of the social construction we label "race."[7]

Racism is structural, prejudice personal. Racism is embedded within permanent practices and socially learned ways of thinking, prejudice a matter of personal choice. Racism moves in white people whether they wish it to or not. Having several decades of socialization into racism, both of us are aware of how it moves within us, merely by the fact of our skin color. This is one reason for our ambivalence around the praise heaped on the Oscar-winning film *Crash*. Written and directed by a white man (Paul Haggis) the film presented racism in a very white way, as a matter of individual choice that the characters opted into and out of depending on the situation. Although traces of systemic, institutionalized racism could be glimpsed in some of the more painful dilemmas, the primary impact of the film remained for many white people one that was personal, on the level of prejudice. Prejudice and privilege both exist in individuals, but racism must be understood as something embedded within a whole political, economic, and cultural system. It follows, therefore, that it is a deeper, more enduring phenomenon than individual prejudice and can only be successfully understood and attacked structurally.

If you accept this argument—even if only for the purposes of this chapter—then notice what immediately becomes possible in a theological context. Perhaps the first and most important assertion we want to make is that grasping the systemic nature of institutionalized racism provides a vivid and compelling example of the vitality and resonance—even for white people!—of certain theological claims that Christians make. Such an assertion might seem confusing at best or oxymoronic at worse, but consider the ways in which Christianity defines sin and the persistent conviction on the part of Christians that we are bound from birth into sinfulness, and yet freed from that sin by the loving grace of God. Different denominations will specify how this process works in different ways, but at heart is a common conviction about a reality often labelled "original sin" and the concomitant belief that God's grace releases us, saves us from this brokenness, and liberates us into new, more just, relationality.

Language about original sin is often heard by contemporary ears as nonsensical or irrelevant, but when imagined anew in the midst of the systemic and complex nature of institutionalized racism, it takes on new cogency and urgency. Further, keeping in mind that Christianity has at its heart a number of convictions about deep relationality and about the necessity of kenotic posture—of pouring oneself out in love, of upending typical power structures, of seeing God in the darkness—all of a sudden theological language becomes a new set of powerful metaphors for engaging racism, and particularly for sustaining even weary—*and white*—theological educators in the midst of dismantling it.[8]

Consider, for instance, one of our favorite illustrations of how a "null curriculum" operates. A null curriculum, at least as described by Elliott Eisner, is that which is taught by virtue of not being taught.[9] This is a contradiction of sorts, and hard to illustrate. Yet for many white students, discovering how racism is socially constructed is an excellent example of this curriculum in operation. When we ask white students to consider how race functions in their own lives, most of them have to pause and wonder. For many of them race is a category they hardly think about and do not even notice except perhaps in filling out census forms, applying for financial aid, or reading news accounts of violent "others" found in "other" places.[10] In all of these instances "race" is a category that slips beneath their view, that eludes their consciousness, that can be defined as "not mattering" except insofar as they might want to make claims about the necessity of multiracial congregations (without, of course, having a clue how to create and sustain such congregations). Yet students of color usually have immediate, and voluminous, responses to this question; everything is viewed through the lens of race. Race is not a construct they can ignore, even if they want to, because it so thoroughly shapes so many of their experiences.

Using Peggy McIntosh's groundbreaking essay[11] as a jumping off point, eventually white students can come up with a list of the "benefits" of being white in a seminary context:

- Knowing that your theology will be the norm, rather than the "specialized" or "marginalized" discourse
- Knowing that the research upon which your primary textbooks are written was done in communities of people that look like you do
- Knowing that the hymns you grew up with are likely to be present in "typical" worship, and don't need to be part of "enculturation"
- Knowing that no one will wonder if you "belong" when you walk into the cafeteria, or into the library, or across the campus parking lot

Clearly these are benefits that anyone would—and potentially, could—enjoy. They are not aspects of a theological education to deplore—except insofar as they are denied to certain students, while promised implicitly to others. Yet they also point to the perpetual, exhausting burdens that students who do *not* benefit from these privileges carry. Our white students—we, ourselves!—experience both grief and guilt in this recognition.[12] Yet, rather than withdrawing into defensiveness, our recognition of this systemic process can give birth to a deeper sense of how God's grace liberates one into energy and action. Paul's exclamation that "I do not do the good I want, but I do the evil I do not want" (Rom. 7:19) becomes a more personal affirmation in such a context. Sr. Paul Teresa Hennessee, S. A., quoting Adrian van Kaam, noted that "the primal act of violence . . . is the defensive refusal of the potential fullness of our awareness."[13] For white students, *awakening* to the system in which they have been implicated begins to refuse such a refusal, it invites awareness which in turn connects to the deepest parts of Christian spirituality.[14] Sharon Welch suggested that "it is far better to see and empathize with suffering than it is to be oblivious or indifferent to human loss and misery. The ability to care for others is itself a precious gift, one we have received from those who first loved and cared for us."[15]

The issue, of course, is not simply how to illustrate the cogency and coherence of Christian theology. For us, in this discussion, our chief question is how might we, as teachers bearing white skin privilege, activate learning around this clear challenge while at the same time seeking to transform the very sinews of the bodies we operate within? How do we deconstruct these destructive systems, while working at the same time within systems of power that grant us the authority we rely upon for teaching and the agency we require for that teaching to function well?

What does it mean to be a "bearer of Christ" in this context? What does it mean to come into a classroom convinced that one bears witness to a power that is quite different from the primarily hierarchical forms of power that are common currency? Here again theological discourse comes alive, because the notion of *kenosis,* of a power that is experienced in the pouring out, takes on a quite specific vitality in this context.[16] Clearly it means, among other things, a deep and ongoing humility. It means and requires a giving of self that invites a renewed and reciprocal engagement.[17] There is indeed a kind of spiritual discipline at the heart of this set of questions that can enliven the entire enterprise, that embodies theological reflection in the heart of the academic task, that requires a re-membering—a pulling together again of the body of Christ.

This is the humility of the broken, the epistemological stance of bending one's head, the posture of prayer that comes when we are forced to our knees by the depth of our sorrow at the brokenness we inhabit. But that same brokenness, that same sorrow is also the birthplace of joy, the moment in which comes the liberation of knowing that we, alone, can do nothing to make this right—and yet God *loves deeply* and brings to birth freedom and grace in spite of us. In the words of the Lutheran book of worship, "we confess that we are in bondage to sin and cannot free ourselves"[18]—but only through the freely given gift of Christ poured out upon us all can we emerge from this brokenness into the glory of God's kingdom.[19] This is a humility that we dare to claim might even be "aggressive" in the sense of being willing to confront the distorting dynamics of racism.

Mark Edwards has written about this kind of discipline in scholarship in an essay about "characteristically Lutheran leanings" where he notes that:

> . . . a Christian scholar who views her work in terms of vocation will cultivate a range of Christian virtues that will, in turn, undergird her approach to life and learning. For example, humility in a scholar is expressed in openness of mind and a willingness to believe that she does not know everything and can in fact learn from others. . . . Charity finds expression in the willingness to construe the work of others fairly and sympathetically . . . serious attempts at understanding precede attack.[20]

What does it mean to hold off on saying something in order to invite someone else's words into one's heart? What does it mean to risk "believing in" something very different from what one has treasured, as an effort to imagine something different?

What does it mean to allow oneself, as a scholar and a teacher, to be surprised into a new understanding?

Consider some of the questions that students of color face when they walk into a predominately white classroom:

- Will I be welcomed here?
- Will my distinctive voice be allowed to participate, or must I couch my insights in language that will be acceptable in this place?
- Will I be invited to read texts that bring my experience into the classroom inquiry, or must I make those inquiries entirely on my own, and almost in spite of the classroom structures?
- Will my patterns of practice be honored, or will I find myself hiding them so as not to be ridiculed?
- Will my claims to authority share space with my colleagues, or will they fall on deaf ears?

Many students of color have learned the habit of "hiding" in plain sight so well that their passion and vision and commitments will not be activated in a given classroom unless specifically invited to be so. Yet those who have ears to hear and eyes to see can create spaces in which participation is possible, and in which the practice of kenosis, of making room for the other, of exploring power *with*, not power over, is so deliberately invited that lively new insights and engagement *with passion* occur.

There is no way for a person bearing white skin privilege to fully understand what it means *not* to carry that privilege in our cultural contexts. If we start from that position, then pedagogy becomes interesting. If we do not understand experientially the dilemmas of living within racist constructions, how can we teach ways to deconstruct them? What does it mean to learn in such a context? How do we invite inquiry? What are the specific classroom practices that are clues to creating this kind of space? Empathy is at the heart of this kind of stance, and humility of practice is key.

Kathleen Talvacchia suggested that "teaching demands a profound de-centering of self so that we can attend to the learning needs of our students,"[21] and she notes that "empathy for another's experience cannot be an excuse to appropriate that experience and make it our own."[22] In the spirit of her assertion, here are a few such practices that we have stumbled upon, sometimes by accident or sheer serendipity, most often through the graciousness of students who risked sharing their criticisms of classroom spaces.

II. MEETING THESE CHALLENGES HEAD ON IN PRACTICE

In this section we explore a number of specific practices that we have learned through bitter experience. Although we reject the idea of racism as purely personal prejudice, and although we believe racism can only ultimately be addressed structurally, we also think that throwing one's hands in the air and absolving oneself of any need to work individually in antiracist ways is also not an option. We describe a number of practices below because both of us, located in different institutions and working with different students and colleagues, have found that these behaviors have been commented on favorably by colleagues of color and students of color.

A. Personal Practices on the Teacher's Part

Acknowledge your own collusion in racism and how it moves in you—as a teacher never suggest you are free of racism. If racism is a structural reality—bolstered by ideology, then most, if not all, whites have learned at an instinctual level all kinds of racist stereotypes. There is no point in denying this. It should be mentioned, almost matter of factly (not as a dramatic confession) since a racist society in which white supremacy is a dominant ideology would mean that of course you have racism embedded in you. Making yourself study why and how this process lives in you should be a teachable moment—best done right in class.

There are different ways this can happen, some fairly superficial, some much deeper. On a fairly superficial level we have both become aware of how using "black" and "dark" as negative terms (it's a black day, that's a dark perspective etc.) is noticed by colleagues and students of color. To white colleagues who say this is political correctness run amok, and that using white and black, light and dark, as something that is totally independent of racial overtones in colloquial speech, we can only say that this view is a very white perspective. As an African-American colleague told one of us, "To me everything—everything—is seen through the lens of color." Several times both of us have had students of color come up and thank us for catching ourselves using "black" and "dark" as negative terms and talking publicly about this.

On deeper levels White Supremacy moves in us as it does in all whites. First, our skin color means that for our whole careers we have been used to seeing people who look like us as the gatekeepers in our fields. We have never had to question our right to publish something. Racism—the structural manifestation of the ideology of White Supremacy—moves in us in ways that constantly catch us by surprise. A black pilot enters the cockpit of the plane on which you're traveling and you catch yourself thinking, "Will this flight be safe?"—a reaction Nelson Mandela also had and which he writes about in his autobiography, thus illustrating the all-pervasive nature of ideological conditioning. In classes, both of us have caught ourselves holding back from challenging students of color and realized that our so called "concern" masked an embedded racist consciousness which says that "they" can't take a strong challenge from a white person. Clearly, racism moves in us to exercise a double standard in class, to practice what the *European American Collaborative Challenging Whiteness* calls "withholding."[23] Withholding is a behavior whites fall prey to in multiracial environments. It is the self-imposed silencing of self with the intention of creating space for the racial Other to speak. Withholding underscores the white center by implying that a white voice is so powerful it will overwhelm all else. It is seen quite clearly by students not as the empathic act of an ally, but as a racist practice.

Clearly, white teachers need to challenge students of color just as vigorously, but also as courteously, as they challenge white students. It is deeply sobering, shameful, and alarming to realize how strong and enduring is the successful ideological conditioning of White Supremacy.

Discuss how working with a multiracial teaching team is crucial for being able to model talking across difference and working through racial tensions. This is based on our own experiences in multiple contexts. The team should talk out how their racial memberships manifest themselves in decisions about process, e.g., how you ask students to address you, what behavior you regard as respectful, your level of comfort with *gumbo ya ya* (Alice Walker's description of overlapping speech patterns amongst African American students), etc.

Don't expect colleagues of color to "teach" you about racism and white supremacy. They already have enough to do trying to combat racism in their own lives. You're putting a double burden on them of having to educate you. This is your responsibility. You must conduct your own serious learning on this topic.

Don't ever suggest you understand how it feels to be the victim of racism. To students and colleagues of color, race can trump everything. Saying you're from the working class, have suffered under patriarchy, and can therefore understand what students of color experience will come across as naïve and condescending. You lose credibility in an instant.

Be prepared to be called a racist. It comes with the territory of this work. You may feel you're working with sensitivity and goodwill but as soon as you stir the waters with racial discussions you will inevitably inflame some students. As a white person and a representative of white supremacy you must expect to be mistrusted and not let that get you down. You must also expect white colleagues to accuse you of politically incorrect reverse racism. This is *not* a sign that you are somehow failing. It comes to every white person in this work.

Before you open your mouth make sure you have truly engaged with scholarship of color. You expect your colleagues of color to be well acquainted with Eurocentric theologies, Enlightenment philosophers, Greek biases in moral theory, etc. They have every right therefore to expect you to be similarly well versed in Africentrism, the many varieties of African philosophy, the debates between critical race theorists, and Africentric theorists, etc.

Never ask a student to speak for his or her race. Among other things it implies that all people of a particular race think and behave the same way. It would be infuriating for you to have to give the "white American" or "Anglo-Saxon" perspective on something given the multiple ethnicities, religious, ideological, and historical groups and variables in American culture. Don't demand it of anyone else. Never assume there is a unitary black/Latino/Asian or other perspective. After all, there is not a unitary white perspective on most issues. On the other hand, point out how race is evident in everything—how we name ourselves, what we consider respectful behavior, how we think a good discussion goes, etc.

Be aware that most principles of responsive teaching—the importance of modeling, using the CIQ, etc.—are just as relevant in teaching about race as in other teaching contexts.

B. Creating a Syllabus

As we've discussed in earlier chapters of this book, the very first gathering of a learning event—whether the opening session of a semester-long class or an informal bible study—sets the tone and expectations for much that follows. Based on what you know about your students, what kinds of "signals" will help on a syllabus? Consider asking yourself these questions.

How diverse are the authors on your reading list? Ensuring that some of the required reading comes from non-dominant authors signals that you are open to multiple voices and begins to lay some foundation for helping your students to begin the process of valuing other voices. If they are already able to do that, then diverse voices provide more room for getting into another space, for risking the transformation of learning.

What kind of teaching/learning process statements do you include? Incorporate paragraphs that invite students to recognize that diversity in terms of race, class, and gender is a gift in the classroom, one to be respected and cherished, honored through civil discourse.[24] Here again, a warm invitation to engagement suggests that these differences are respected and will provide substance for direct exploration—even as such statements signal that simply asserting difference is not an engagement with it.

How do you make yourself accessible to your students? Many teachers will list office hours, for instance, while others suggest making appointments in advance. How might you signal to students who have been hurt by previous encounters with faculty that your own commitment is to respect and openness? Providing room for email encounters, going to meetings and worship experiences where students of color gather informally, and sharing your own experiences of risking engagement (if helpful, and done with appropriate boundaries) are all appropriate.[25]

Does your syllabus include explicit time within the progress of the semester to engage issues of systemic oppression within whatever content you are exploring? Are terms such as race, class, gender, etc. visible on the syllabus itself? Providing clear acknowledgment that such dynamics will be explored alerts students to their importance.

C. The Opening Session

As your class begins, there are multiple ways to express your openness and interest in facilitating as lively a discussion as possible.

How is the room arranged? Is everything in straight lines? Is there space for you to walk around and talk with students from a variety of positions in the room? Straight lines of chairs or desks with a clear presentation of the professor in control in the front of the room reinscribe notions of authority and power, which in turn can subtly suggest that systemic forms of power are not to be directly confronted, but rather relied upon.

What quotations or images do you have on the chalkboard or presentation screen as the class begins? Many times it is not the images or words we use that are the problem, but rather the clear *lack* of such images. For example, you might use images of all white people simply because they were close at hand and easy to put together. Consider that the message you are sending to your students could be one that invites them to consider "white" as normal, as typical, and anything else as somehow "exotic," "alternative," or even "deviant."

Do you begin in prayer? If so, what does that prayer invite? Is there room within it for silence? Do you name your own hopes and vulnerabilities for the class? As you begin a class it is worth keeping in mind the work of organizational consultants such as Edgar Schein who point to the formative character of a shared emotional experience early in the life of a new collectivity—whether that is a classroom of students, a committee of employees, or so on.[26]

The first session of a class—where often students have not yet read any texts in common—can be an opportunity to introduce your students to a shared experience. Mary often uses a video reality exercise to provide a low threshold, high enjoyment way into collaborative learning.[27] Stephen asks students to reflect on their best and worst previous experiences working in groups and then builds on these to help the group develop norms for how members are going to treat each other. At the same time, these exercises can raise issues of race, class, and gender in ways that open up the questions and suggest that it is both appropriate and welcomed to investigate systemic forms of power.

One of our colleagues, Diane Jacobson, begins her class via a discussion of women in the wisdom literature. Another, Dick Nysse, invites his online course students to consider the ways in which their own interpretations will shape the conversation of the course. Yet another, Craig Van Gelder, asks students to imagine the neighborhood around their contextual placement churches, and to see all of the markers of power embedded in the landscape. Each of these opening moments provides an opportunity to invite students into the "meat" of the class right away, and to do so in a way that also names systemic power as an issue under consideration. If such content issues are engaged in a way that invites participation and collaboration in seeking answers, then the initial experience shapes a "norm" for the continuation of the course.

D. The Substance of Your Course

As we noted above, teachers need to be familiar with the conceptual frameworks that define systemic oppressions before designing learning environments that seek to deconstruct such dynamics, let alone help our students to learn about them.

In this vein, drawing conceptual frames from your specific disciplinary context that name and describe systemic power structures can be useful. This can help to draw students beyond the "personal discrimination" blame game to more complex and grounded descriptions of systemic power flows. In biblical studies there are many resources for doing this. In the arts of ministry systemic oppressions can be engaged directly as they impact specific questions of community and leadership. Here Elizabeth-Conde Frazier's work is particularly useful for the way in which it defines a shared hospitality of learning.[28] In history there are several very good examples of texts that explore how gender has been defined, for instance, or the ways in which race has structured how communities of faith have developed over time.

It is easy to fall into the trap of using the texts you're most familiar with and comfortable using, only to discover that they're all written by people who carry the same privileges (or lack thereof) that you do. The Wabash Center maintains a collection of Internet resources that are a great place to begin searches—in terms of syllabi, critical texts, web-based resources, and so on—to broaden your range and depth.[29]

Taking seriously the notion of "multiple intelligences" provides yet another way into reshaping the classroom to make it possible to engage systemic power dynamics more directly. Most students within higher education are capable readers and writers, and they have demonstrated at least some element of what Gardner would term "linguistic intelligence." Yet an overemphasis on linguistic intelligence narrows learning in any classroom and can contribute to students experiencing themselves as disadvantaged or unable to contribute from their most fluent and capable gifts. Providing room for kinesthetic learning, for exercises that engage logical analyses, for highly interpersonal engagement, can at the same time provide room to help students understand what it means to feel disadvantaged in one frame and empowered in another. That in itself can contribute to moving them towards more mature understanding—both in terms of perspective and of empathy.

Using a portfolio frame for assignments can help students to track learning over time and can provide numerous opportunities for tracing their own development. It can also be a framework that invites the kind of self-reflection that leads to seeing "power in action" and thus moving beyond simplistic notions to more systemic engagement with various ways of thinking about race, class, and gender.

We have discussed in chapter 3 some of the ways in which role-playing can help students to learn better dialogue practices. Role-playing has also proven useful in relation to exploration of the dynamics of class, race, and gender. Several good exercises have been developed, with specific instructions, to help classes do this.[30]

In chapter 1 and many subsequent chapters, we have talked about the use of the CIQ. In this context using the CIQ externalizes power dynamics that people are unwilling to confront directly in class. For example, in groups when there is a racial minority, these students will often sit together for self-protection. White students usually record their frustration with this on the CIQ which is a good opening to discuss different, racially grounded experiences of higher education.

E. Reflection throughout a Course

This entire book is a sustained attempt to support reflective practice in theological education. Engaging in such practice yourself is one of the best ways to support it with others. Here are specific suggestions that could be implemented throughout a course. Our goal here is to provide methods to "see through your students' eyes," and in turn help them to see through each other's eyes.

Teaching in a classroom where students have several different native languages provides an immediate entry point into discussions of how language can construct experiences of power. Even in a classroom in which only English is spoken, reference to varieties of slang—and the cultural etiquettes developed for using them—can be an interesting entry point for work in systemic power awareness. Try allowing students to write in their native languages and then verbally explain their essays to you, or allow them to summarize in English the learning units they have created in another language.

One relatively simple way to provide a range of assignment choices in a class—and thereby minimize some of the unequal power that can come with unearned privilege—is to invite students to choose one entry from a bibliography to read, and then have them present it to their colleagues in a way that both shares the material they've learned and demonstrates alternatives for presentation. Opening up the choice of what to read, as well as how to present it, opens up possibilities for yet again engaging the power dynamics.

For some students, participating in a free-wheeling large group discussion is simply not possible, given the power dynamics that swirl around them, making it difficult for them to speak. One alternative is to provide asynchronous opportunities for classroom discussion via online technologies. Students who flourish in the give and take of immediate discussion often find online discussions difficult, while students who have been silenced in the more typical classroom can prepare their responses carefully and feel more able to share them in the asynchronous environment. Here again, once having had such an experience, there is lots of room to "go meta" and discuss the experience of the experience with students, thus leading them to reflect upon the power dynamics.

Several examples of ongoing assessment have been sprinkled throughout the foregoing chapters, each of which provides yet another means by which teachers can share power with students, and in doing so model and articulate intentionally the deliberate exposure of systemic power, and the ways in which misuse of that power can warp and distort human relationality.

What is the range of discussion present in your classroom? How have you responded to challenges from divergent theological viewpoints? Often it helps to imagine what questions you could ask of a student, rather than what "corrective" responses you might offer.

When students experience resistance to specific points you're trying to make, how do you engage it? Simply asserting that they are wrong may make a point about your own authority, but it does not necessarily or even typically invite them into questioning their own beliefs.[31]

What are your practices of grading/evaluation? Have you made clear the rubrics by which you will evaluate written work? Do you practice consistency with respect to grading so that students can learn to trust that you will evaluate their work against a clear ruler, rather than in terms of other attributes? To what extent do you consider a wide range of elements of understanding in your rubric?[32]

One of the gifts of this practice of humility in teaching is that it is deeply freeing. It is *not* the kind of "political correctness" that invites one to question one's every utterance, but rather the freeing gift of grace which argues (to use the Lutheran formulation as an example) that since we are at one and the same time a saint and a sinner, we are indeed free to attempt to follow Christ—and will be absolved accordingly in all the ways that we fall short. Rather than worrying whether or not we are "passing on the faith" with sufficient regard to its purity and sanctity, we are freed to engage in the messiness of living into that faith. We are, as Robert Kegan notes, able to practice the hospitality of deconstructive criticism that urges us to suspend our claims long enough to enter into another's space.[33] Doing so does not imply that our claims are by definition not true, but it invites deep inquiry of a sort that makes it possible to test such claims with deeper resonance.

III. ENGAGING SYSTEMS

Thus far this chapter has focused on practices rooted in individual classrooms, practices that have been broached for a specific teacher in a specific classroom, ideas that might create a space that attempts to mitigate some of the more destructive elements of institutionalized racism. But this kind of work is only a first step, and an admittedly small one at that. As the definition of racism makes clear, it is a system built upon and enforced through structures of human institutions that are kept in place by collectivities, not simply individuals. It is in this point of the analysis that it becomes crucial to consider how it might be possible to open up teaching, to make a classroom bigger than simply one room with one teacher and multiple students.

Kenda Creasy Dean makes the point, within her study of youth ministry, that

> . . . young people are among God's most forthright, frustrating, and often unwitting prophets, reminding us that salvation is at stake, for they will not give up on true love until they find it. . . . The adolescent quest for passion reveals a theological aneurysm in mainline Protestantism. . . . For youth, ridding faith of radical-

> ness and transcendence amounted to castration, and rendered Christianity impotent for reordering the self. With nothing left "to die for" in Christian teaching, it became increasingly unclear whether or not Christianity offered something worth *living* for.[34]

It is entirely possible that this same kind of aneurysm has permeated graduate theological education. What if our work leads up to a particular point of transformation, but then we back away from it? What if at the heart of the academic disciplines in which each of us is formed as we move our way through the measured ladder of becoming a PhD-credentialed educator, what if in the midst of that process of formation we've lost our way?

What if the spirit of academic formation has become, instead of a path and process by which one retains the humility and self-critical posture necessary to pursue truth, it has become a structure by which more "worldly" forms of power are kept in place? Consider the myriad mission statements of some of our most elite institutions of theological education.[35] They ring with commitments to fighting racism and sexism, to inclusive communities of inquiry, but often students come away from these programs knowing what they should fight against and not always knowing what they are seeking to build. Indeed, academic socialization at this level—for a variety of good reasons, given the historical record—has tended to require that scholars hold their most intense convictions at arm's length.[36] The last two decades have seen an enormous amount of literature published detailing the distinctions between objective, arm's-length approaches to religion versus intimate, insider, faith-based scholarship. Yet this very dichotomy has in some cases contributed to a "passion-less" Christianity, a form of scholarship so disconnected from actual patterns of practice, and so detached from these convictions that it can continue blithely on in concentrated, "super white" forms, without once recognizing the emptiness of its content claims.[37]

To return to the questions we asked at the beginning of this chapter, how is it that communities of faith—in the United

States in particular—can continue to be so obviously separated by race? How is it that theological school faculties can continue to be so segregated, particularly when their most central faith claims would lead one to conclude that they ought to be deeply *integrated*?

The spiritual formation of an academic discipline *can* be rooted in a form of inquiry that shapes the task to be one in which one's deepest convictions must risk being challenged, or it can become instead a process by which one is formed *into* a set of convictions not to be challenged. One of the reasons scientific discourse is so powerful right now is that the integrity of its convictions shares a congruence and coherence with the patterns of its practice.[38]

Lee Shulman notes that religious education should include exposure to one of the empirical disciplines precisely so that it invites this kind of self-critical engagement.[39] For white educators, engaging racism is both a thoroughly appropriate and immediately urgent instance in which empirical information provides such a vital exposure, and indeed invites us to shape—and critique and challenge—our practices. This is the kind of learning we want to invite our students to share. And it is this kind of learning that can be rooted, founded, indeed *funded* by the spiritual commitments at the heart of Christian practice.

A. Institutional Practices

What are possible ways to move beyond the classroom in engaging issues of racism in theological education?

This book grows out of a teaching/learning reflection group shared by junior colleagues in a seminary. Such a group gave us space in which to test our own assumptions, share our "highs and lows" in teaching practice, and eventually, as trust grew, come to real discussion about points of resistance and opportunities for transformation. In the numerous and varied rubrics that have been published to place institutions on anti-racism spectra, most share in common an understanding that antiracist work must ultimately create and sustain communities of accountability.[40] A reflection group can be a space in which such accountability can be planted and nurtured. Even if the faculty at your institution is completely white, learning how to open up one's teaching to more shared engagement can be a first step towards learning the habits of heart and mind that make antiracist work possible.[41]

Distributed learning is another context in which accountability can grow. Many schools are experimenting with placing courses in distributed—mostly online—environments. An online course offers a context in which teachers can work with students from vastly differing backgrounds who are learning in myriad contexts. One of the first courses Mary taught in an online environment was a course that directly engaged race, class, and gender. It was possible to do so primarily because the institution at which she was working valued her ability to teach online to such an extent that they gave her permission to design a course around any content she desired. New technologies can offer such opportunities, but even beyond the opportunity of "newness," that early course gave Mary the chance to invite into a learning context students who otherwise had little interest in the issues. Their experiences in engaging the challenges, in turn, provoked her to look at the materials she was using through new lenses.[42]

Cross-disciplinary team teaching is yet another opportunity to subvert the institutional structures that have placed constraints around engaging institutionalized racism. Mastery of a limited amount of specialized material has, for a long time, been one route to advancement in the academy. Such a route tends to narrow one's perspectives to such an extent that exploring the impact of institutionalized racism may never even arise, or, alternatively, one might become an "expert" on *only* the ways in which such processes work. Choosing deliberately to work with a colleague from another disciplinary setting—perhaps a biblical scholar and a practical theologian, for instance, or a systematic theologian and a sociologist—provides multiple opportunities to explore new lenses, and/or the ways in which specific disciplinary definitions highlight or obscure how racism functions.[43]

Shifting the roles of teacher and student from hierarchical "power over" into collaborative coinquiry is not only "best practice" as defined by numerous recent studies within education, it is also more congruent with a biblical imagination, with certain practices of Christian formation throughout the tradition, and with contemporary notions of theological scholarship. While we've mentioned several ways to do this within the section of this chapter that considers classroom practice, it's important to remember that classroom practices are to a large extent shaped by institutional structures. Thus, searching for and hiring new faculty with a commitment to such practices provides a good entry point into confronting institutional practice on this issue.

Shifting the definition of what counts as appropriate and legitimate scholarship is also an important, long-term effort in this regard. Several womanist theologians provide excellent examples of ways to do this, as they have taken first-person narrative accounts, women's fiction, and other kinds of sources not ordinarily presumed to be appropriate sources of theological reflection and claimed them as crucial *theological loci.* Scholars who work with popular culture materials are another example, and it is not coincidental that many of the theologians who work with popular culture materials have also directly interrogated issues of race and other institutional oppressions.[44] Giving students access to this scholarship and helping them to experiment with new methodologies can open up spaces in the classroom of profound transformation—not solely for students, but for teachers as well.

Following in that vein, there are clearly many more ways in which to express theological engagement than through written text. More and more scholars are experimenting with inquiry into movement, art, music, and so on. It is not simply within the classroom that multiple intelligences can be engaged, but also by shifting and transforming what counts as a classroom in the first place. Online formats are perhaps the most obvious example of this kind of transformation, but many seminaries are exploring myriad other ways in which teaching can be *contextualized* by changing its location. Increasing accountability to communities previously marginalized within theological education by shifting teaching into locations that privilege such communities is a concrete and tangible way to do so.

All of the ideas presented in this chapter are the fruit of ongoing learning. Nothing discussed here is suggested as the *only* response, or even the *best* response, to engaging racism. Rather, we hope that as two white educators seeking to create liberatory learning experiences we have presented an opportunity to explore possible alternatives to current practice and to invite new energy into the process of reinvigorating contemporary theological education. At heart we, as white educators, are committed to healing the "aneurysm" suggested by Kenda Dean as existing at the heart of Christian practice. In doing so we need to take very seriously the wounds and brokenness evident in our sinful attachment to structures of oppression such as racism. We do so in the full and free grace offered by Jesus Christ—not with any self-righteous claim to being able to do so by ourselves, but rather in the graced presence and power of the Christ at whose feet we kneel, and with whom we live into transformation. It is our hope that this chapter might invite you into conversation with us, with these practices, and with the Hope that we witness to amidst them.

NOTES

1. On the topic of "political correctness," Kathleen Talvacchia has a wonderful section in her book *Critical Minds and Discerning Hearts: A Spirituality of Multicultural Teaching* (St. Louis, MO: Chalice Press, 2003) where she notes explicitly why a "multiculturally sensitive pedagogy is not political correctness," 4.
2. Tony Campolo and Michael Battle refer to this feeling as the "politics of resignation" in *The Church Enslaved: A Spirituality of Racial Reconciliation* (Minneapolis, MN: Fortress Press, 2005), 8.

3. DeYoung, Emerson, Yancey, Kim, *United by Faith: The Multiracial Congregation as an Answer to the Problem of Race* (New York: Oxford University Press, 2003), 2. This book reports, in part, on the results of a multiyear project on multiracial congregations funded by the Lilly Endowment. More information on the web at: http://hirr.hartsem.edu/org/faith_congregations_research_multiracl.html.
4. These figures are drawn from the Association of Theological Schools data tables, available online at: http://www.ats.edu/resources/fact_book.asp.
5. Gary Gunderson, *Boundary Leaders: Leadership Skills for People of Faith* (Minneapolis: Fortress Press, 2004), 97.
6. A particularly compelling example of how this institutionalization has occurred over time is found in Ian Haney López's analysis of the legal construction of race, found in *White by Law* (New York: New York University Press, 1996).
7. This definition is so common as to become the consensus, and you can find iterations of it throughout all of the books referenced in this chapter. In our own teaching, we rely on the definition put together by the Minnesota Anti-Racism Collaborative (http://www.mcari.org): "race prejudice plus the power of systems and institutions = racism." This definition is elaborated upon at some length in the MCARI workshops.
8. Mary Hess articulates more explicitly the connections between a posture of kenosis and teaching in chapter 4 of this volume.
9. Elliott Eisner, *The Educational Imagination: On the Design and Evaluation of School Programs* (Columbus, OH: Merrill/Prentice Hall, 2002), 97 ff.
10. Melanie Bush documents this reality more substantially with appropriate sociological research (and its accompanying statistics) in her book *Breaking the Code of Good Intentions* (Lanham, MD: Rowman & Littlefield, 2004), 65.
11. Peggy McIntosh, "Working Paper #189: White privilege and male privilege, an account of coming to see the correspondences through work in women's studies," Wellesley Center for Research on Women. Paul Kivel also has a list of white benefits in his book *Uprooting Racism: How White People Can Work for Racial Justice* (Philadelphia, PA: New Society Publishers, 1996), 32–34.
12. James Perkinson writes eloquently of the pain of this process in his book *White Theology: Outing Supremacy in Modernity* (New York: Palgrave Macmillan, 2004), 234.

13. Sr. Paul Teresa Hennessee, S. A., "Violence in the household," *Ending Racism in the Church* (Cleveland, OH: United Church Press, 1998): 82.
14. Norman Peart makes this point in *Separate No More: Understanding and Developing Racial Reconciliation in Your Church* (Grand Rapids, MI: Baker Books, 2000), 105.
15. Sharon Welch, "Ceremonies of gratitude, awakening and accountability: The theory and practice of multicultural education," in Harvey, Case, and Gorsline (eds.), *Disrupting White Supremacy from Within* (Cleveland, OH: Pilgrim Press, 2004): 250–251.
16. Lois Malcolm is particularly compelling in her work on this topic. A good place to start is "Teaching as cultivating wisdom for a complex world," in L. Gregory Jones and Stephanie Paulsell (eds.), *The Scope of Our Art: The Vocation of the Theological Teacher* (Grand Rapids, MI: Eerdmans, 2002): 135–154. The language of kenosis can also be found written in a specifically feminist tone in Deanna Thompson, *Crossing the Divide: Luther, Feminism and the Cross* (Minneapolis, MN: Fortress Press, 2004).
17. There are clear connections here to the argument David Lose makes in chapter 2 of this volume, on teaching with conviction.
18. *Lutheran Book of Worship* (Minneapolis, MN: Augsburg, 1978), 56.
19. Fumitaka Matsuoka makes this point eloquently in *The Color of Faith: Building Community in a Multiracial Society* (Cleveland, OH: United Church Press, 1998), 126–127.
20. "Characteristically Lutheran leanings?" in *Dialog: A Journal of Theology*, Vol. 41, #1, Spring 2002 (8).
21. Kathleen Talvacchia, *Critical Minds and Discerning Hearts: A Spirituality of Multicultural Teaching* (St. Louis, MO: Chalice Press, 2003), 9. Aana Marie Vigen uses similar language of "decentering of self" in "To hear and to be accountable: An ethic of white listening," in Harvey, Case and Gorsline (eds.), *Disrupting White Supremacy from Within* (Cleveland, OH: Pilgrim Press, 2004): 224.
22. Ibid., 41.
23. "A Multiple-Group Inquiry into Whiteness" European-American Collaborative Challenging Whiteness. In L. Yorks & E. Kasl (eds). *Collaborative Inquiry as a Strategy for Adult Learning*. San Francisco: Jossey-Bass, 2002.
24. Parker Palmer's articulation of such a stance through the "grace of great things" has become a mantra of sorts in Mary's own teaching. She explores its use in chapter 4 of this volume.

25. Stephen writes about appropriate personal sharing in chapter 3 of this volume.
26. Edgar Schein, *Organizational Culture and Leadership* (San Francisco: Jossey-Bass, 2004). Also, Mary further explores issues of prayer in chapter 10 of this volume.
27. This exercise, as well as two others, are detailed in "Seeing, hearing, creating: Exercises that are 'low tech' but that engage media cultures," *Engaging Technology in Theological Education* (Lanham, MD: Rowman & Littlefield, 2005): 133–143.
28. Elizabeth Conde-Frazier, Steve Kang and Gary Parrett. *A Many-Colored Kingdom: Multicultural Dynamics for Spiritual Formation* (Grand Rapids, MI: Baker Academic, 2004).
29. The Wabash Center Guide to Internet Resources is available at: http://www.wabashcenter.wabash.edu/resources/guide_headings.aspx.
30. Several examples would include Jane Elliott's "brown eyes/blue eyes exercise" (http://www.janeelliott.com/), several cross-cultural learning games (http://wilderdom.com/games/MulticulturalExperientialActivities.html), Jean Kilbourne's documentary "Killing us Softly" (http://www.mediaed.org/videos/MediaGenderAndDiversity/KillingUsSoftly3), etc.
31. Two books that have been out for years continue to be treasure troves of useful exercises: Judith Katz, *White Awareness: Handbook for Anti-racism Training* (Norman, OK: University of Oklahoma Press, 1978) and Adams, Bell, and Griffin, eds. *Teaching for Diversity and Social Justice* (New York: Routledge, 1997).
32. Grant Wiggins and Jay McTighe have developed a particularly useful rubric for assessing understanding that identifies six facets of understanding: explanation, interpretation, application, perspective, empathy, and self-knowledge. For entry points into their work, see *Understanding by Design* (Upper Saddle River, NJ: Merrill/Prentice Hall, 2001).
33. Robert Kegan and Lisa Lahey make this point in *How the Way We Talk Can Change the Way We Work* (San Francisco: Jossey-Bass, 2001). More description of how this practice works can be found in chapter 4 of this volume.
34. Kenda Creasy Dean, *Practicing Passion: Youth and the Quest for a Passionate Church* (Grand Rapids, MI: Eerdmans, 2004), 7, 9.
35. Vanderbilt Divinity School (http://www.vanderbilt.edu/divinity/viewbook/introduction.htm) and Harvard Divinity School

(http://www.hds.harvard.edu/history.html) might be good places to start.

36. There is a growing literature questioning the central commitments and processes of graduate theological education. Keeping in mind his particular theological stance and location, Robert Banks's *Reenvisioning Theological Education: Exploring a Missional Alternative to Current Models* (Grand Rapids, MI: Eerdmans, 1999) is a good place to begin. See also Lewis Tait *Three Fifths Theology: Challenging Racism in American Christianity* (Trenton, NJ: Africa World Press, 2002), 126.
37. James Perkinson makes this point in more depth in *White Theology: Outing Supremacy in Modernity* (New York: Palgrave Macmillan, 2004), 224 ff.
38. Although of course this is not necessarily true of the technological outcomes to which scientific inquiry is put.
39. Hanan Alexander quotes Shulman in *Reclaiming Goodness: Education and the Spiritual Quest* (Notre Dame, IN: University of Notre Dame Press, 2001), 186.
40. The Minnesota Collaborative Anti-Racism Initiative has an organizational rubric that is very useful (http://www.mcari.org/). Also, see the table in *United by Faith: The Multiracial Congregation as an Answer to the Problem of Race* (New York: Oxford University Press, 2003), 165, and the reconciliation continuum described by Norman Anthony Peart in *Separate No More: Understanding and Developing Racial Reconciliation in Your Church* (Grand Rapids, MI: Baker Books, 2000), 129–142.
41. Kathleen Talvacchia's book, referenced above (*Critical Minds and Discerning Hearts*), is an excellent resource for this kind of discussion, particularly pages 33 and following.
42. Mary Hess, *Engaging Technology in Theological Education: All That We Can't Leave Behind* (Lanham, MD: Rowman & Littlefield, 2005), 79–93.
43. See chapter 7 in this volume for a sustained discussion of collaborative team teaching.
44. See for example, the work of Anthony Pinn, Elizabeth Conde-Frazier, Cornel West, Thomas Beaudoin, Mary Hess, etc.

CHAPTER 10

"How Do We Enter Students' Worlds We Cannot Know?" Praying and Teaching When Not "At Home"

Mary E. Hess

Many of us who teach in seminaries must think about the process of living amidst several competing realities, crossing several community borders. I am a Roman Catholic teaching in an ELCA Lutheran seminary. I am a layperson in an institution whose primary mission is preparing people for ordained ministry. I am someone deeply immersed in visual/musical culture, teaching in a context which glorifies print. And I am a woman academic in a field—theological education—still largely populated by men. These are just a few of the borders I regularly find myself crossing. In some ways I am tempted to carve out my own small space, delimit its boundaries and refuse to let anyone cross them, but far more often I have found that I really am "better off for all that I let in."[1]

The things that we let in continue to cross my mind as I reflect on the questions of what it means to pray, to worship, to teach in a theological context that is not my own. It is far more common now than it was even twenty years ago for faculty from one denomination (increasingly, even one faith) to be invited to teach at a school rooted in another. What are the dilemmas that arise in such a context? What are the practices of teaching and learning that emerge? What does it mean to "let something in"—particularly if that "something" is different from what one has been formed to recognize as "home"? What can it mean to be better off for doing so? And if indeed that is a goal, how does one prepare oneself to do so? What are the disciplines and the practices that might provide an open form of attention for shaping authentic religious identity in an age of pluralism?

Religious identity formation in the twenty-first century, at least in the contexts I inhabit (which are admittedly quite narrow—United States, middle class, seminary, etc.), is now a fluid process, shaped by dynamics often far beyond the control of individual congregations, let alone larger institutional religious structures. It is at heart a highly experiential and relational process, and its markers are less those of doctrine than they are of style and process. The recent reception of Mel Gibson's film *The Passion of the Christ* is an interesting case in point. The film is essentially a vivid representation of the Catholic stations of the cross. It draws on the eighteenth-century meditation of Anne of Emmerich and expands the text with visual images drawn from the genre of horror. It is not the kind of interpretation of the gospel that one might expect to appeal to evangelical Christians. Yet that has been the community that has been most actively supportive of the film.

That the film has found the audience it has may have more to do with its ability to draw on the grammar and language of pop culture than any explicitly Christian assertions. The doctrinal choices embedded in a depiction of Satan as an androgynous person carrying a grotesque child, for instance, owe far more to a peculiar form of Catholic piety than they do to scripture. It is not so much the content of a film that has power on its own, but the meanings we make *with* it as we respond to music and image, bringing our lives to our interpretation. Thomas Boomershine has suggested that in our current context we reason more by means of sympathetic identification than philosophical argument, and the evangelical Christian community's embrace of Mel Gibson's film is a good illustration of that assertion.[2]

Even as I trace this example, I need to be clear that I am not—particularly as a professor of education at a seminary—

especially thrilled at this shift in identity production. The systematic approach of theologians to explicating doctrine within religious communities has had important implications over centuries, and that tradition is not one I'm interested in ignoring. Nor do I believe that emotional engagement alone makes for strong religious communities. I am simply trying to point to the ways in which our current context shapes and contains, and perhaps resists and defers, religious identity construction.

So what can we do? What might I, as a Roman Catholic teaching in a Lutheran seminary, propose? Indeed, I call that particular aspect of my identity back to mind because there are facets of my experience in that intersection that can prove helpful here, too. Like any religious practice, the process of constructing religious identity is best understood as a discipline, as a sustained practice over time that is not about "getting better" but about "paying attention." So what are the disciplines of religious identity in a pluralistic world? What might be the appropriate ways in which to "spend" or "pay" attention? How might we attune ourselves to letting in that which might enhance our ability to hear God in a postmodern context? Three schema in particular have helped me. The first is a practice of relational learning, which I've described at some length in chapter 4 of this volume. Palmer's image map for learning as a "community of truth" is a passionate one that bears critical reflection, particularly in his description of the "grace of great things." Diversity, ambiguity, conflict, honesty, humility, freedom—these are not characteristics often cherished in contemporary communities of faith, and they are not easy commitments to inhabit.[3]

When I reflect upon my own experience as a Roman Catholic teaching in a Lutheran seminary, I remember far too often feeling a deep internal uneasiness. Opening myself up to considering a different way of looking at the world, particularly if that different way challenges what has been "home" to me, requires real and conscious intention and attention. Sometimes it even requires an effort of will to draw a deep breath and simply wait on my feeling. Am I uneasy because something is unfamiliar? That doesn't make it wrong. How do I know if I am uneasy because something is wrong? How do I define "wrong"? And what ought I to do about it if it is? Ambiguity is a painful place in which to rest.

The second schema that I have found helpful relates to how I handle such unease or "dis-ease." It grows out of the work of cultural anthropologist Richard Shweder and is a framework for understanding a variety of ways for "thinking through others." The framework is complex, and I have written about it in a variety of other contexts, but at this moment I want to speak primarily in personal terms. Shweder speaks of "thinking through others" in four ways: "thinking by means of the other," "getting the other straight," "thinking beyond the other," and "witnessing in the context of engagement with the other."[4]

"Thinking by means of the other" is his first mode and tends to be the kind of place in which I suddenly notice that something is different, that the Lutherans around me, for instance, have a different form of prayer. Many of my colleagues, for instance, find it very easy to pray spontaneously in a public setting. All of our meetings, no matter how small, begin in prayer, and people appear to have no difficulty at all in voicing quite eloquent prayers. My first response to them is generally one of admiration. As Shweder notes:

> Thinking through others' in the first sense is to recognize the other as a specialist or expert on some aspect of human experience, whose reflective consciousness and systems of representations and discourse can be used to reveal hidden dimensions of our selves.

I have admired my colleagues, and I assumed that here was a form of prayer that they are particularly adept in and that I might one day learn, but in the meantime can simply enjoy. This form of engagement with difference is certainly positive and has the advantage of positioning me as the learner. On the other hand, I all too quickly also begin to feel stupid, or at least somehow "lesser" for not being able to pray in the same way. Every time a meeting begins and I am invited to pray, the words catch in my throat and I become immediately aware of how inarticulate I am and how clearly lacking in appropriate pastoral skill. Such engagement with the "other" does not allow the other to have its own separateness and being, but instead makes it simply a reflection—whether for good or for ill—of myself. I see the other, but only by way of comparison to myself. I am still the central focus.

Shweder's second mode, by way of contrast, is something he terms "getting the other straight," by which he means "providing a systematic account of the internal logic of the intentional world constructed by the other. The aim is a rational reconstruction of indigenous belief, desire, and practice."[5] This mode requires me to seek to inhabit the practices of prayer in my current context, to stay with this example deeply enough to understand their internal dynamics, the logics by which they function. I have learned, for instance, that one element of the prayer I took to be so spontaneous is actually a reliance on a particular rhythm, a cadence for drawing scriptural verses and particular experiences together in a pattern that proves familiar to listeners. This kind of prayer, far from being as spontaneous as I had at first experienced it, is actually quite scripted. At the same time as I have come to cherish and value this form of prayer, I have also come to value in a different way the practices of prayer with which I am most familiar.

Like many Catholics, I suppose, I can rattle off "Hail Marys" and "Our Fathers" at great speed and with little consciousness of what I'm doing. What I am beginning to recognize, however, is that these tightly scripted prayers have given me room to train my body into a meditative place that allows a different kind of inner prayer to rise. In some ways such prayer has its own kind of spontaneity. So, again, I have found myself comparing my prayer practice with their prayer practices. In this mode, however, Shweder's second mode, the comparison does not so much reflect badly on one or the other, but instead it enhances both because it requires me to immerse myself in the other and to seek to understand it on its own terms. This is an improvement over the first mode, but it is still a position that draws clear lines between me and you, between us and them.

Shweder's third mode, "thinking beyond the other," is:

> a third sense, for it properly comes later, after we have already appreciated what the intentional world of the other powerfully reveals and illuminates, from its special point of view. Thinking through others is, in its totality, an act of criticism and liberation, as well as discovery.[6]

This mode moves beyond, is a form of criticism and a way of appreciating the other by taking the other seriously enough to challenge it. To return to my example, as I have learned about prayer in my current teaching context, I have pondered the ways in which the unremarked, the "so often done as to be unnoticed," forms of prayer that we employ demand their own kind of conformity. The prayer with which we begin meetings, for instance, carries so often the same rhythm and cadence that changing it, stepping outside of that pattern, is felt as breaking it. Since I very often choose to bring prayers from my own tradition to such contexts—one of my favorite hobbies is collecting books of prayer—I am often the person who "breaks" the pattern. Breaking patterns is often uncomfortable. If I am uncomfortable doing so, as a professor at an institution carrying all of the power and privilege that such a structure accords me, how much harder must it be for our students?

We have students who come to us from all over the world and from multiple traditions (including those beyond Christianity). How am I inviting their diversity into our midst? How am I stepping outside what is familiar to me to meet them where they are at home? Here is where Shweder's schema helps me live more fully into Palmer's "grace of great things." I look for the ambiguity; I cherish the conflict because it is a sign, a "welling up" of the learning that points to real engagement with difference. Stepping beyond my own comfort levels, seeking not only to understand deeply but to stretch that understanding in new ways, is its own form of "making room," of the deep hospitality that the Christian tradition demands of me. As Jane Hotstream notes:

> When you cross your own border, that means you're going into a strange territory . . . One challenge is to look at yourself and to

> say "what is it that I have to learn in this new area, at this new table so that others can come to the table fully and equally, and there's nothing in me that would block them?"[7]

Shweder's final mode, "witnessing in the context of engagement with the other," is a mode in which:

> . . . the process of representing the other goes hand in hand with a process of portraying one's own self as part of the process of representing the other, thereby encouraging an open-ended, self-reflexive dialogic turn of mind. . . . .[8]

I suppose this mode is closest to what many might term a post-modern practice. Whether or not you apply that term to it, it is the mode that always reminds me that we do, indeed, "make each other up," and thus must be extraordinarily attentive and respectful in doing so. Every time I begin a class by reading a prayer written by someone else, I am teaching something. What am I teaching? I wish that I was sure! Most of the time I hope that I am teaching our students that it is permissible, perhaps even enriching, to use someone else's words to open prayer space. Sometimes I think I am teaching them that Catholics cannot or do not choose to engage in spontaneous prayer. Obviously such a conclusion would be wrong, but it might arise if for no other reason than that the only Catholic many of my students come in contact with is me, and they generalize from one to many. The only stance that makes sense to me, and the one I try to model and support for our students, is precisely the one that Shweder points to—an "open-ended, self-reflexive, dialogic turn of mind"—which is, incidentally, also the outcome of attending carefully to Palmer's "grace of great things."

Such attention is never done in isolation or individually, however. As I struggle to maintain this kind of engagement with otherness, I am supported by a community which shares the search with me; indeed, several communities—Luther Seminary, my local Catholic parish, the cluster of religious educators who struggle with issues of difference, and so on. It is tempting in a cultural context, in which experience governs so much of knowing, to rely on one's own individual experience. But I cannot. Using the language of my community of faith, I would argue that I must pursue this engagement in community because we confess a relational God, we understand God as Trinity. There are other ways to make the argument, as well, but the point is that Palmer's notion of learning in relation requires relationality to be at the heart of the process. Shweder's description of thinking through others assumes as an essential element of its schema that such engagement is done "in relation."

The final piece I turn to, as I seek to practice the living of life amidst many border crossings, is something that a group of scholars came up with as they studied people who had maintained commitments to the common good over long periods of time. These scholars noticed that most of the people in their study maintained what the scholars termed a "responsible imagination."

> They pay attention to dissonance and contradiction, particularly those that reveal injustice and unrealized potential. They learn to pause, reflect, wonder, ask why, consider, wait. . . . [this] requires discretion and responsible hospitality . . . to what may be unfamiliar and initially unsettling. . . . . [9]

". . . Hospitality to what may be unfamiliar and initially unsettling" is a habit I hope that I am developing. One of the advantages of working in a community that is committed to a different set of practices than my home community is that I am immediately invited into the "unfamiliar" and the "unsettling." I don't have to wander far, or work too hard, to seek out such practices, such images. Where the difficult work comes in is in the patience of wonder, in the process of "pausing" as Daloz et al. note. I have had no other experience as difficult but also as profoundly prayerful as trying to enter this space of wonder, this space of "pause." Here again, the many communities of which I am a part support this kind of search and value both the "wonder" and the "pause."

Yet many people in our contemporary context do not have such a community from which to draw. Far too many of our communities of faith practice "thinking through the other" in the first sense of Shweder—seeing the other only as a mirror in which to know oneself, or against which to compare oneself, or by which to distinguish oneself. This pattern is particularly clear in the ways in which communities of faith relate to mass mediated popular culture.

Here again the Mel Gibson film is an interesting example. The film is both enormously popular—achieving sales near the record-breaking level of the *The Lord of the Rings* phenomenon—and enormously problematic, given its representation of religious leadership. Many Christian communities of faith have practiced the first two of Shweder's modes of engagement in relation to the film, but not the latter two. Some of us have seen the film as a brilliant evocation of the gospel stories and used it as a vehicle for evangelization. We have recognized it as "expert" in conveying meaning and latched onto it in Shweder's first mode, not recognizing the ways in which other meanings might be made with it, seeing it only through our own eyes.

Others of us have sought to make people aware of the dangerously anti-Jewish representations embedded in the film—the ways in which the Satan character winds its way around religious leadership, the sympathetic portrayal of Pontius Pilate, and so on—and have spent significant time trying to help people "see" the internal logics of the film, the particular and specific ways in which light and music and framing combine to communicate a very specific Christology. Still, although we have entered the space of the film, explored it, tried to appreciate its "internal logics," we have ultimately seen it primarily as something from which to distinguish ourselves. In both of these instances we are not really "engaging the other" in a deep experiential and relational and interwoven sense, but merely seeing the other through our own lenses. Perhaps that is all that is possible, most of the time. Still, if communities of faith did not begin from the stance that pop culture in and of itself is other, if we instead found that our faith-filled and faithful meaning making emerges there just as much as in our churches and synagogues, our mosques and our temples, we might be open to immersing ourselves deeply enough to practice Shweder's third and fourth modes, and indeed begin to see beyond ourselves and to see in each other the ways in which we "make each other up."

A tantalizing glimpse of the possibilities of such a stance is visible in a recent episode of the television cartoon *South Park*. *South Park* is an adult animated series that airs on the Comedy Channel in the United States. It portrays a band of young children and their daily, often vulgar, bathroom humor as they negotiate life. Recently the children on the show encountered Mel Gibson's film *The Passion of the Christ*. One of the children is Jewish, one is fat and given to power plays, and two appear younger in some sense (one of them speaking only unintelligibly). This small band of children presented a diverse set of responses to the film, and the episode neatly explored a variety of issues—whether the film can indeed "lift" up Christian spirituality, whether it was only a money-making adventure, what role Mel Gibson's own life played in the making of the movie, whether it was anti-Semitic, and so on—all in the space of less than 30 minutes. The episode ended with an explicit call to reject violence:

> Child: "If you want to be Christian, cool, but you should follow what Jesus taught instead of how he got killed. Focussing on how he got killed is what people did in the dark ages and it ends up with really bad results."
>
> Adult: "You know, he's right. . . . We shouldn't focus our faith on the torture and execution of Christ."
>
> Other adult: "Yeah, lots of people got crucified in those times. We shouldn't rely on violence to inspire faith."

Many of the Christian communities I'm familiar with reject this cartoon series out of hand, refusing to watch it because of its crude and often ugly humor. It is certainly not a series I would invite children to watch, but then again, it's not a series aimed at them. It is, instead, a satirical and interesting perspective on contemporary U.S. life written for adults. This particular episode managed to engage most of the issues raised by the Mel Gibson film in an amusing and yet thought-provoking way. I can't help wondering if the biting satire of such a cartoon might provide yet another way into "thinking beyond" and "witnessing in the context of engagement with." By exaggerating the issues and putting them in animated form, the cartoon provides a way for us to look at them and to engage them with some degree of differentiation. It certainly provided a much more thought-provoking entry into the cultural debates swirling around the film than I encountered in the many "church" contexts in which the film was discussed. In that way it supported me, at least, in seeking a more "open-ended, self-reflexive, dialogic turn of mind."

I asked at the beginning of this essay what might be the disciplines of religious identity in a pluralistic world? What might be the appropriate ways in which to "spend" or "pay" attention? How might we attune ourselves to "letting in" that which might enhance our ability to hear God in a postmodern context? I hope that I have now suggested a few that will provoke your own imagination. Remembering that learning is about practicing the "grace of great things," opening ourselves to engagement with others and practicing a responsible imagination are the disciplines that I am attempting to practice. We could, as people of faith, enter into the wider streams of popular culture and practice such disciplines there as well. In so doing we might indeed enter a space in which we're better off for the things that we let in.

NOTES

1. "All That We Let In," from the compact disc All That We Let In, by the Indigo Girls (Sony, 2004).
2. Thomas Boomershine, "How to be a faith witness in the communications media? Conditions requisite for the public communications value of faith witnesses," paper presented at the *Witnessing to the Faith, An Activity of the Media* conference, St. Paul University, Ottawa, Ontario, May 30, 1999.
3. These image maps are found in chapter 4 in this volume, and the "grace of great things" is explored in Section II of chapter 4.
4. Richard Shweder, *Thinking Through Cultures: Expeditions in*

Cultural Psychology (Cambridge, MA: Harvard University Press, 1991), 108. My own work on the topic can be found in chapter 5 of *Engaging Technology in Theological Education* (Lanham, MD: Rowman & Littlefield Publishers, 2005).
5. Shweder, *Thinking*, 109.
6. Shweder, *Thinking*, 110–111.
7. Personal transcription of an interview with Jane Hotstream contained in the CD-ROM *Beyond Borders: Ministry in a Multi-Cultural World*. Produced by JMCommunications, and available through the Mexican American Cultural Center in San Antonio, TX (http://www.maccsa.org/).
8. Shweder, *Thinking*, 110.
9. Daloz, et al., *Common Fire: Lives of Commitment in a Complex World* (Boston: Beacon Press, 1996), 151–152.

CHAPTER 11

"How Do We Know What Our Students Are Learning?" Assessing Learning in the Context of Pastoral Engagement and in Candidacy Processes

Alvin Luedke

Several of the previous chapters have focused on "seeing through our students' eyes" in the context of particular classrooms. In this chapter I am trying to provide a window into what we might be able to see if we look "with institutional eyes"—with the hope that in doing so we might further reflect on the information that can be gathered across a curriculum, or what some literatures name "assessment."[1]

The people of Israel were looking in two directions during their wilderness wanderings after their Exodus from Egypt. They looked to a future: former slaves living in freedom, a future in which the promises of land and descendants originally made to their patriarch Abraham and his wife Sarah would be theirs. While in the wilderness, however, this future was yet to be realized. In the absence of this full realization the people of Israel looked to their past:

> And the whole congregation of the people of Israel murmured against Moses and Aaron in the wilderness, and said to them, "Would that we had died by the hand of the Lord in the land of Egypt, when we sat by the fleshpots and ate bread to the full; for you have brought us out into this wilderness to kill this whole assembly with hunger." Exodus 16: 2–3 (RSV)

> Now the rabble that was among them had a strong craving; and the people of Israel also wept again, and said, "O that we had meat to eat! We remember the fish we ate in Egypt for nothing, the cucumbers, the melons, the leeks, the onions, and the garlic; but now our strength is dried up, and there is nothing at all but this manna to look at." Numbers 11: 4–6 (RSV)

Given their years of residence in Egypt, slavery was their primary frame of reference for living, and the knowledge and skills they had gained, developed, and used in Egypt were the skills they brought to their current situation, as helpful or unhelpful as they were.

Perhaps this story of looking in two directions, with all of the advantages and limitations of knowledge and skills from one context being applied to a different context, lives beyond the people of Israel in the times of the Exodus. Perhaps it remains powerful and applicable to many students within theological education. Generally such students have received an undergraduate degree before entering a course of graduate theological study. Some may have entered seminary directly from an undergraduate program, with no previous professional experience. Others may be second or third career students, intent on new horizons. Both of these groups may also include students who have responsibilities that constrain them to part-time study. In all of these cases students are managing multiple transitions, drawing on previous experiences and skills developed in other contexts. Are the knowledge, skills, and experiences gained in graduate theological education adequate and sufficient in preparing ministerial candidates for their calls to ministry?

This chapter focuses on this question through the lens of assessment and suggests places within a candidacy process where assessment of seminary theological education processes may occur. At this point a note on the relationship between evaluation and assessment is warranted. I understand evaluation to refer to the process of determining whether or not a candidate has met the minimum standards necessary to obtain approval in the candidacy process of their denomination (if such a process exists). As such, evaluation focuses on the individual candidate and asks if he or she has met the minimum standards for new pastoral leaders. Assessment, on the other hand, focuses on the adequacy of the curriculum, of the whole experience of a seminary theological education, for helping candidates achieve the knowledge, skills, and attitudes needed for pastoral leadership in the church. Consider this example, the mission statement of Luther Seminary: "Luther Seminary educates leaders for Christian communities called and sent by the Holy Spirit to witness to salvation through Jesus Christ and to serve in God's world."[2] Flowing from that statement, the Seminary argues that:

> To accomplish this mission, the faculty and community of the seminary will work to assure that our students
> - Know the Christian story;
> - Understand the interpretation and confession of the message in varied contexts;
> - Are able to lead others in the calling and commission God has given to them; and
> - Are disciples of Jesus Christ.[3]

A process of assessment asks whether the curriculum, indeed the whole experience, of Luther Seminary actually helps candidates accomplish these goals. While individual student achievement is a part of assessment, the primary focus is on determining whether the seminary is accomplishing what it claims to accomplish.

I. MULTIPLE STEPS

Most denominations have a process of reviewing ministerial candidates during their preparation and of evaluating the readiness of candidates, both theologically and practically, for their call to ministry. The main premise of this chapter is that while these processes have been used mainly for certification and credentialing of candidates, there is huge potential for using them to ascertain if candidates have actually learned what the curriculum claims to teach. There are several points at which denominational structures involved in the candidacy process can cooperate with seminaries or schools of theology to engage in conversation about how well candidates are being prepared for ministry. Such conversations would allow a seminary curriculum, as well as actual teachers, to participate in healthy assessment. The goal of such assessment would be to determine if candidates are indeed gaining the knowledge, skills, and attitudes that adequately prepare them for ministry.

Such conversation by way of assessment would have at least three important advantages. To use economic terminology, such a process would allow "consumers" of theological education (congregations, synods/districts/presbyteries/etc., and the church-at-large) to have a clear voice in articulating what ministerial candidates need to be able to serve faithfully and effectively in given contexts, and to assess how well the current educational processes are meeting these needs. Seminaries could then be engaged in a closer conversation with, and have clearer accountability to, the communities receiving their graduates, and they could receive regular and direct feedback concerning the knowledge, skills, and attitudes needed for ministry. Such regular assessment conversations could allow changes in ministry needs to be identified quickly, thus providing more timely development of curriculum. Ideally, ministerial candidates would also be better prepared for the transition from seminary setting to the ministry context in their first calls.

This chapter will review one denominational process of candidacy as a case study of places at which a seminary could engage in conversation that assesses its educational processes. This case is rooted in the processes with which I am most familiar, those of the Evangelical Lutheran Church in America (ELCA). Keep in mind that there is variation even amongst the different ELCA seminaries and synods in how they carry out their responsibilities in the candidacy process. Thus, this chapter will explore how the candidacy process is engaged at Luther Seminary, as one example.[4]

This chapter will proceed by presenting the steps in the candidacy process and then suggesting how conversations about assessment could be incorporated into each step. Several examples will be used to suggest points at which a process of assessment either helped, or could have helped, the educational process. My goal is to suggest ways in which seminary education and the candidacy process might work together in relation to assessment of learning in order to better prepare leaders for ministry in the church.

II. THE CANDIDACY PROCESS

Within the ELCA, the candidacy process is primarily engaged through the work of candidacy committees in each synod. A synod candidacy committee is generally composed of pastors and lay persons elected by the synod assembly, members of the synod bishop's staff, a seminary faculty member, and a regional staff person representing the ELCA. To date most such committees have focused primarily on evaluating individual students as they progress through the process of preparation for ordination.[5] While there has been little effort to assess the *learning process* in relation to candidates, I would like to argue that the candidacy process actually provides several good opportunities for ongoing assessment discussions. Keep in mind that this chapter is not an exhaustive presentation of such opportunities, but rather an exploration of some possible points of contact where such dialogue might occur.

The appropriateness of dialogue in the candidacy process is suggested in the *Candidacy Manual*:

> Interdependence within the Evangelical Lutheran Church in America means that there is a sharing of responsibility and accountability in the Candidacy Process. Each partner in the Candidacy Process has a discrete role, but always participates in cooperation with the other partners. Candidates, congregations, synod candidacy committees (which include bishops), seminaries, and the Vocation and Education Unit all work together and communicate openly to assure that the ELCA prepares gifted men and women who are called by God to serve in the rostered ministries of this church.[6]

This statement suggests that there are numerous persons within the candidacy process with whom the seminary partners, and with whom the seminary could be in dialogue with, about the adequacy of preparation of candidates.

The *Candidacy Manual* also lists three steps in the candidacy process at which interviews with candidates are conducted and formal decisions about each candidate's progress in the process are made. These steps are entrance, endorsement, and approval. In addition to these three steps, I will also address two additional portions of the seminary educational process that would allow assessment conversations to occur, Clinical Pastoral Education (CPE) and internship. For each of these a brief description of the step is presented, a vignette is offered, and then discussion about the opportunities for assessment conversations in relation to the seminary educational process is presented.

A. Entrance

The entrance step is the first formal step in the candidacy process. A candidate must have been an active member of an ELCA congregation for at least one year before the entrance decision. They are to complete a "candidacy application and entrance information form," a "congregational registration," and an initial interview with the synod candidacy committee. This process also includes a thorough background check and psychological evaluation. Normally a synod candidacy committee must make a positive entrance decision before a candidate can be admitted to the Master of Divinity degree program at an ELCA seminary.[7]

The entrance step is the beginning of "a process of discernment that explores an individual's potential for rostered ministry and readiness to begin the process of seminary preparation and candidacy in the ELCA."[8] It should be noted that the seminary is not involved in the candidacy process at this time. Entrance is strictly a decision at the synod level by the synod candidacy committee. The entrance step could, however, provide important opportunities to assess where a candidate begins their seminary study. Conversations with or reports from the synod candidacy committee could be helpful for teachers of first-year students in noting any special services that might help a candidate get a good start in the seminary endeavor. Physical challenges which might require modifications in housing or mobility assistance could be anticipated and addressed by the seminary prior to the arrival of a candidate. Likewise, learning challenges or other special needs, such as help with reading or writing skills to help the candidate perform at the level of graduate study, could be noted. Counseling or other support services that might assist with transition to a seminary community, as well as provide continuing support for the candidate, might be identified. Perhaps most importantly and broadly among candidates, the seminary could better advise candidates in their course selection and could make informed judgments about which type of advisor and group might help the particular candidate to grow and mature in seminary training.

As an admissions committee member, I noted Alan's strong sense of call to ministry and the strong recommendations on his behalf. However, his recommenders did mention Alan's "struggles" with academics, though the exact nature of the challenge was unclear. After significant discussion, and in spite of his rather low college GPA, I and the members of the committee decided to admit Alan.

Alan's struggles became clear early in his matriculation. He had severe dyslexia, which impaired his reading comprehension, his reading speed, his ability to read publicly, and his writing ability. Compounding these challenges was the course offering schedule that assumed full-time attendance. Particularly difficult for him were language and theology courses. As Alan tried to manage his academics, personal growth, and learning challenges, he soon was frustrated and failing in his educational endeavors.

What if, after admission, the seminary and candidacy committee had conversed about Alan's challenges at the en-

trance step, before he began his seminary career? The challenges to his educational experience might have been more clearly identified and communicated to all concerned.

Resources to support his reading and writing requirements might have been anticipated and secured. Perhaps the necessity of a less than full-time load of course work, as well as difficulties with particular courses, could have been anticipated. Such anticipation could have led to an adjustment in the pace and sequencing of his study. Certainly the frustration he experienced could have been anticipated and addressed. So, while the entrance step could have been used to help Alan get a better start at seminary, in his case such opportunities were missed.[9]

The entrance step could provide a good foundation for the assessment of where each candidate begins their seminary study, what resources might be needed by the candidate, and what support might best help the candidate grow during their seminary experience. Dialogue between the synod candidacy committees and the seminary could allow the broader church to be involved in the seminary educational process from the beginning. Further, such a partnership between the synod and the seminary might create many other synergies.

B. Endorsement

The endorsement step, the second formal step in the candidacy process, normally occurs in the fall of a candidate's second year of seminary study. An endorsement panel made up of two candidacy committee members and the candidate's seminary faculty advisor meets with the candidate and makes a recommendation to the synod candidacy committee about whether or not the student is ready for the full-year internship practicum required of all ELCA candidates for ordination, the so-called "endorsement" decision.[10] The endorsement step "encourages and affirms those who clearly demonstrate gifts and qualities for a specific form of ministry in the ELCA as well as identifies areas for growth and development."[11]

The endorsement step, by its organization and guidelines, could present an important opportunity for the seminary and synod candidacy committee to engage in a dialogue of assessment by addressing, in particular, how well the candidate is learning the necessary elements of ministry. This step embodies well the theme of this chapter: *looking backward to the past and forward to the future*. Endorsement visits the strengths and weaknesses of the particular candidate that were identified at the entrance step and asks how these have been both nurtured and challenged during the seminary experience. Some assessment of how the seminary curriculum has been beneficial, or not been beneficial, for the candidate would be appropriate at this step. Since at Luther Seminary candidates are required to participate in contextual education by being assigned to attend and be active in a congregation, the learning and experiences gained from this particular curricular requirement could also be incorporated into the endorsement step. While these questions reflect upon the past in the present moment, the endorsement step also looks to the future. Recommendations for what type of internship would provide the most growth in ministry skills, as well as recommendations for classes and other training deemed desirable, are duly noted at the endorsement step.

The candidacy committee was quite concerned about one of my advisees, Rita. With the exception of sporadic attendance during college, Rita had experienced membership in one congregation, with the same pastor, in her lifetime. The candidacy committee's concern was that she should be exposed to a variety of theological views and worship styles and would be able to develop flexibility of thought and leadership styles that would prepare her to serve in a variety of ministry contexts. Most of their concern was whether she was receiving exposure to a range of styles. Rita was able to present to her candidacy committee a compelling summary of what she had learned in her classes and experienced in her contextual assignment. The candidacy committee was convinced that Rita was indeed experiencing a wide range of theological views and worship and leadership styles. They were able to describe an internship context that would continue to broaden her experience and prepare her for a wide range of potential contexts in which she could faithfully and effectively serve.

Attention to the assessment process at the endorsement step could enable Luther Seminary to discern how well candidates are integrating their classroom and contextual experiences as they prepare for their ministry calling. Listening to students voice how they are growing in self-awareness and in ministry skills could help to assess whether the goals of our curriculum are being realized for candidates. Such determinations could then provide the basis for modifications in the curriculum where necessary and reinforcement of strengths where they are found.

C. Clinical Pastoral Education (CPE)

While not a formal step in the candidacy process, all candidates for ordained ministry in the ELCA are required to successfully complete a unit (at least 400 hours) of Clinical Pastoral Education (CPE) or other Supervised Clinical Ministry.[12] While the timing of the CPE training is not specified by the ELCA, many synod candidacy committees are requiring that the CPE requirement be completed prior to undertaking an internship. Often this requirement is fulfilled through a hospital chaplaincy setting. Learning contracts by students are to address the following goals:

- Expression of a personal theology of pastoral ministry
- Enhanced self-understanding and self-integration: spiritual, physical, intellectual, emotional, and relational

- Ability to initiate helping relationships
- Identification of personal strengths and weaknesses in ministerial functioning
- Ability to use pastoral supervision for personal and professional growth and to develop the capacity to evaluate oneself in ministry
- Capacity to engage a peer group for consultation and receive support and challenge in ministry
- Development of one's pastoral identity and authority while working collaboratively with interdisciplinary teams
- Formulation of clear and specific goals for continuing pastoral formation[13]

Bruce shared with me the difficulty he had with CPE. Due to struggles in his family of origin and some physical challenges, the group work with peers under supervision of the CPE director was particularly hard. At the conclusion of CPE Bruce received credit for completion of the CPE unit, but also was encouraged to work with a spiritual director to continue addressing some aspects of his life and experience further growth in some areas of his life. The CPE supervisor listed some concern about Bruce's ability to be a pastor in a congregation.

Bruce's candidacy committee, however, read some promising possibilities for ministry from his CPE evaluations. While acknowledging the CPE supervisor's concerns about pastoral ministry in a congregation, they noted with great interest the way that Bruce's experiences in his family and struggles with his physical challenges had given him insight into how others with these challenges experience life. They felt that Bruce might be able to relate and minister very well to such persons, knowing from his own life experience how they felt and what they had to deal with in life. They noted how Bruce had grown in this awareness during the CPE experience and how his ministry skills had grown through CPE. They also asked how the seminary, the academic program as well as community, supported persons with physical and emotional challenges. Did the program provide appropriate training for persons who might seek ordination but whose call was to specialized ministry settings? How did faculty, staff, and peers support those whose callings may be to places other than pastors of congregations? They felt Bruce's struggles indicated that the seminary might need to investigate how they trained and supported such candidates.

At the completion of a unit of CPE, the supervisor and candidate (if he or she chooses to do so) submit statements about the learning experience and how well the goals of CPE were accomplished. These statements are filed with the candidate's record at seminary, and the candidate forwards these reports to the synod candidacy committee. As can be seen from the guidelines for a CPE learning contract, many issues addressed in a CPE experience could also provide a foundation for assessment. How well did the seminary prepare the candidate in the knowledge and skills of pastoral care, confidentiality, and ethics? What continued learning is suggested by the evaluations of both candidates and supervisors? What resources are available to help the candidates gain needed knowledge and skills in their remaining seminary education? CPE would provide a foundation for dialogue between the seminary, the candidate, and the candidacy committee in evaluating the readiness of the candidate and assessing the ability of the seminary curriculum and experience to assist candidates in developing necessary ministry skills.

D. Internship

Like CPE, internship is not a formal step in the candidacy process, but it is required of all candidates. A positive endorsement decision for a candidate is required for internship. Normally a candidate is placed in a congregation for a year as an intern. Generally, the internship year is the third year of the four-year Master of Divinity program, though some fourth-year internships (where the candidate completes all class work before internship) are approved. "Internship facilitates the integration of academic study and theological education with the practice of ministry . . . where a candidate has an opportunity to give attention to contextualization, reflection, integration, and evaluation."[14] During internship the candidate is expected to participate in a wide variety of leadership roles in the congregation. These include preaching, teaching, leading worship, visiting, and other duties offered by the congregation.

Similar to CPE, quarterly reports are submitted by the candidate, supervisor, and congregation internship committee. These reports are filed with the candidate's record at seminary and with the synod candidacy committee. Since there is reflection on ministry and learning, internship provides another place in which assessment could be addressed. Internship would be particularly important for understanding how well the curriculum prepares candidates for the context of ministry. Can the candidate translate what is learned in the classroom to the context of ministry in a congregation? An assessment from internship would also provide direction for considering what may need to be emphasized with those candidates who are returning for their final year of class work at the seminary.

Mary was a second career student who had struggled with her call to ministry for many years. As she shared with me, internship frightened her a great deal because she felt inadequate to take on the authority of pastor in a congregation, even as she realized she was an intern serving under a resident pastor supervisor. Additionally, knowing how competent she felt in her previous career, the thought that she still had much to learn in order to master the tasks of ministry and preaching made her feel inadequately prepared for internship.

I had the opportunity to meet with Mary's internship supervisor a few times during the year. She informed me that Mary integrated her seminary training into her ministry work very well. Furthermore, she was impressed with Mary's willingness and ability to reflect on her training in light of her ministry context, and to continue to deepen her skills and understanding through this reflection.

Likewise, Mary was able to articulate a growing level of comfort with her call. In talking with her when she returned to seminary after the internship, she was able to reflect on which portions of her seminary training were most helpful in preparing her for internship, which had been most helpful in situations she faced on internship, and what types of training and issues she still needed to address in her final year of seminary. Mary was able to admit that, though she was sure she would continue to grow in ministry skills, seminary had prepared her to serve as a leader in her internship context. This, in turn, affirmed her call to ordained ministry. She finally began to believe she could be a pastor. She also realized that ministry would be an endeavor in which she would continue to learn and grow as a person and a leader.

E. Approval

The final formal step in the candidacy process is the approval step: "Approval comes near completion of all academic and practical requirements."[15] Candidates submit an approval essay, following guidelines developed by the ELCA, to the seminary and the synod candidacy committee. At Luther Seminary each candidate is interviewed by their faculty advisor and another faculty member partnered with the advisor, using the approval essay as a foundation for that interview. After this interview, and if the two faculty members agree that the candidate should be recommended for approval, the advisor constructs statements about the candidate in three areas: the candidate's academic and theological competence, the candidate's call to ministry and ministry gifts, and the candidate's practical readiness and leadership skills. The advisor's faculty partner reviews and approves the statements, which are then forwarded to a larger group of faculty for review, modification, and approval. When approved by this group of faculty the candidate's name and statements are forwarded to the entire faculty for consideration. If approved by vote of the entire faculty, the candidate's name and statements are then forwarded to the synod candidacy committee with the recommendation of the faculty for approval.

Candidates are then interviewed by synod candidacy committees. All documentation and past decisions are considered: "Approval occurs when the candidate articulates the call to ministry and demonstrates readiness to assume a leadership role as a rostered minister in the ELCA."[16] A positive approval decision means that the candidate is "available for assignment, ordination, and first call for service to this whole church."[17]

Dennis was not one of my advisees, but I had gotten to know him quite well. By chance, I was one of the faculty members who interviewed Dennis at the approval stage of the candidacy process. Dennis's candidacy committee had been concerned about an area of his theological development, and this had been noted in his endorsement report. As a response to the concern, Dennis spent a portion of his approval essay on the issue. From his writing in the essay it was clear that Dennis had studied hard in his theology classes. However, he was not clear in his conclusions and the implications of these conclusions for ministry. My faculty partner and I questioned Dennis quite closely in his interview. It was amazing to see how he gained new insight in that interview and how he was able to integrate and reflect on his class work in a way he had not done before. I was amazed at how one interview could help a student grow in understanding and confidence. Dennis had gained the basic tools through his class work. He needed help in integrating that work into his call and to see the implications for his leadership.

Dennis came to see me after his meeting with the candidacy committee. It seems that one person on the candidacy committee was concerned if he had addressed the theological issue that had been of concern to the committee. Dennis expressed some surprise that the question was very similar to the one my faculty colleague and I had raised with him. He stated to the committee that his faculty interview committee had addressed this with him, and he then stated where he stood. His answer satisfied the committee, and there were no further questions about the issue. Dennis's experience at the approval stage illustrated for me how, even late in a student's seminary training, the candidacy process can continue to challenge candidates to grow in their understanding of ministry. It also can help us identify where more clarity and integration may be needed by a student in order to better prepare them for service.

Given that approval is the final step in the candidacy process, it provides an opportunity to address assessment of overall preparation of candidates in the seminary educational process. All portions of the process are open to assessment at this step, and this assessment can be accomplished in light of a candidate's outcome and readiness as a result of experiencing the theological education process. It is likely that such an assessment could provide an important overall picture of the effectiveness of the educational process in a seminary for preparing candidates for ministry.

III. SOME SUMMARY THOUGHTS ABOUT CANDIDACY

The candidacy process, then, provides several places at which assessment activities could be initiated. Such assessment activities not only address the readiness of candidates, but also provide helpful assessments of both strengths and weaknesses in a seminary's theological educational process. Utilizing several of these places in the candidacy process would include the wider church, represented by candidacy committees, pastor supervisors, and lay people on internship committees as important participants in the learning and pastoral preparation process. Such wide-ranging participation is likely to provide helpful assessment to the seminary concerning the effectiveness of its curriculum, contextual education, and community life in preparing candidates for ministry in the church. Such assessment should help the seminary to know if it is delivering what it promises. Responding to such assessment should also help the seminary to better prepare its students to use their pasts and training to enter into their future of leadership in the church.

I am not suggesting that the seminary engage in these discussions over each candidate. Such an endeavor would not only require too much commitment of time and energy to be practical, but concerns about privacy and confidentiality, and the protection of private records and communication of individual candidates, need to be respected.[18] It is also unlikely that conversations at all the steps of the candidacy process can be conducted. What I am suggesting is that seminaries might find it helpful to consider at which points in the candidacy process information that could assist them in assessment should be gathered, and then give that information to those persons who could shape a summary assessment of the theological educational process in light of preparation of candidates. Such a report would likely provide important information about the educational process and might even be useful information to use in documenting various requirements for accrediting agencies and others interested in the effectiveness of a seminary's program.

Post-candidacy

While this chapter has concentrated on the candidacy process, a brief comment about the possibilities for assessment after the candidacy process seems in order. After candidates have received approval, information about candidates is distributed to bishops. Approved candidates enter into an assignment process where they are assigned to a region of the ELCA and then to a specific synod of the ELCA. Bishops, and their staff persons, then engage in placing the candidates into congregational call processes. One potential assessment source would be to dialogue with bishops and their staff persons about the type of contexts in which first-call candidates are likely to be placed, how candidates "fit" within these contexts, and the readiness of candidates for service in their synods. This could be a source of information about the practical personal and pastoral attitudes and skills that need to be emphasized in a seminary's curriculum and training in order to prepare candidates for the contexts they are likely to enter.

One bishop approached me at a church meeting. Her question came out of an interview experience with a recent seminary graduate. It seems that there were several things the senior pastor of a congregation viewed as inappropriate behavior on the part of one candidate interviewing for a call. While the pre-interview material clearly noted that much of the membership of the congregation, and the call committee in particular, was made up of senior executives of major companies, the candidate arrived for the interview dressed casually. At an informal gathering in the senior pastor's home, at which the associate pastor and the spouses of each pastor and the candidate were present, the candidate ignored coasters, set wet beverage containers on wood tables, and then placed his feet inappropriately on tables and other furniture. In the senior pastor's view the candidate presented an unprofessional, unpolished image and demeanor. The bishop asked me "Doesn't the seminary teach these folks how to act?"

I am not sure if this behavior exhibited itself at seminary for this candidate. Perhaps this candidate simply did not understand the transition from a more informal place in the seminary community to a more formal position in the congregation. However, this example does suggest that dialogue between the seminary and those receiving candidates around the topics of personal and pastoral attitudes of graduates might need to take place.

Another source of assessment could be congregations who receive first-call candidates. While there is likely to be a range of expectations, dialogue with congregations about what they expect in their pastor could reveal some important information that would inform the educational process. Patterns in expectations of preaching, worship leadership, pastoral care, and teaching might shed light on changes occurring in congregations, or at least some of the variety of values and conditions that candidates are likely to face in their first calls. Some assessment about how well candidates can translate and integrate their theological perspective into practice in their ministry in the congregation could be explored. Such dialogue would also allow congregations that receive a seminary's graduates to engage in the assessment process of that seminary's program. Such a gathering of information would allow the seminary to demonstrate its interest in the opinions of its "customers" and provide information from the field in its assessment processes for accreditation and other purposes.

Because my area of concentration is rural ministry, I am often in conversation with congregations about how well graduates are prepared to serve in small town and rural contexts. Two examples are ones I remember well. The first was Peter. He requested to be placed in a rural congregation. However, the congregation to which he was called was suspicious of Peter's request. They had experienced a succession of short-term pastorates where the pastor seemed to be pleased with the placement early in the call, but then within about three years looked for another call. They suspected that Peter would follow the same pattern. However, Peter was able to use his training and experience in rural ministry to build trust, and to let the congregation know that he understood their context and was committed to stay with them. When I last heard, the congregation deeply appreciated his commitment and pastoral leadership.

Linda was called to a small town congregation because of her interest in this context for ministry and because her family required her to stay in a specific geographic area. One important question for the congregation was how a female pastor would be accepted by the congregation, given that the congregation had never had a female pastor. As I have visited with members of the congregation, they are very pleased with Linda's leadership, noting that she is a strong leader. While not all always agree with her, they appreciate her willingness to state her views and particularly her ability to explain her views from biblical and theological foundations.

In both of these examples the congregations expressed gratitude for how Peter and Linda built and tended relationships in the congregations and communities. While such relationship building was emphasized in the rural ministry classes that they took, it is unclear how their personalities and training worked together to help them lead. This topic would be worthy of more conversation with Peter and Linda, as well as their congregations.

Another source of assessment information could be the First Call Theological Education (FCTE) program. Pastors are expected to participate in FCTE for their first three years after seminary. Dialogue with synod persons engaged in FCTE would provide information about patterns or challenges they are seeing in newly ordained pastors that might be addressed by the seminary curriculum or experience. This dialogue might also suggest some ideas for continuing education that the seminary could offer to pastors early in their ministerial careers.

FCTE has been a program mainly conducted by synods. Therefore, I do not have experience teaching in FCTE. However, I have had conversations with bishops and synod staff members about how seminaries may be used to support FCTE efforts. Out of my conversations several areas of training are suggested for new pastors: ability to understand the context for ministry and identify ministry opportunities, leadership challenges in multipoint parishes, skills in leading change in congregations, skills for leading in the areas of stewardship and outreach, and skills in administration. These, and other important topics, might be areas in which seminaries could support synods in their FCTE efforts.

A further avenue for assessment would be dialogue with pastors who are graduates of the seminary (as suggested with

Peter and Linda in the example above). Questions about what further training would have been helpful for them as they began their first calls, what situations were confusing or surprising, and what challenges to personal or professional development and care they face could suggest things that need to be modified in the seminary curriculum or experience. Such dialogue would also allow former students to reflect on their preparation at seminary and to provide input, from their perspective, about how the educational process could have been more helpful. These pastors might also suggest needed continuing education opportunities and could be participants in such programs.

Looking Forward by Looking Back

When it entered the Promised Land, the nation of Israel had to use its past experiences and knowledge to look to the future in a new context and calling. Candidates entering ordained ministry experience many of the same struggles. They enter the future in new contexts and callings, relying on past experiences and training. One important source in the new context and future is the training they experienced in seminary.

Assessment activities can help the seminary ascertain and understand which aspects of the seminary theological education process are adequately preparing candidates for ministry and which may need to be modified and improved. This chapter has suggested that there are numerous opportunities for the seminary to engage in assessment dialogue within the candidacy process. While this chapter concentrated on the candidacy process of the ELCA, and particularly as it is enacted at Luther Seminary, I suggest that all seminaries could engage in dialogue about assessment with partners in what is their equivalent of the candidacy process. Such dialogue provides a potential for receiving important feedback and information about the seminary's educational process from many portions of the Church. Perhaps even more importantly, such dialogue provides a potential for building stronger partnerships in the training and preparation of ministerial candidates. Such assessment activities can help seminaries answer the question, "Are we delivering what we have promised?" After all, this *is* the goal of seminary training and the candidacy process, to provide faithful and effective leadership for the Church.

NOTES

1. Several basic resources include: T.A. Angelo, ed. "Classroom Assessment and Research: An Update on Uses, Approaches, and Research Findings," *New Directions for Teaching and Learning, no. 75.* (San Francisco: Jossey-Bass, 1998). S. M. Brookhart, "The Art and Science of Classroom Assessment: The Missing Part of Pedagogy," *ASHE-ERIC Higher Education Report Series, Vol. 27, No. 1.* (San Francisco: Jossey-Bass, 2000). L. W. Anderson, *Classroom Assessment: Enhancing the Quality of Teacher Decision Making* (Mahwah, NJ: Earlbaum, 2002). S. M. Butler and N. D. McMunn, *A Teacher's Guide to Classroom Assessment* (San Francisco: Jossey-Bass, 2006).
2. Luther Seminary Catalog, 1.
3. Ibid.
4. I will use the general guidelines from the *Candidacy Manual* published by the Vocation and Education Unit of the ELCA, rather than any specific synodical procedures. It is available online at http://www.elca.org/candidacy/manual/.
5. The ELCA candidacy process relates to four rosters: Ordained Ministry, Associates in Ministry, Consecrated Deaconesses, and Consecrated Diaconal Ministry. While there are many similar steps in the candidacy process for all rosters, as well as some unique aspects depending on the particular roster, this chapter will use the framework of the process for Ordained Ministry as its guide.
6. *Candidacy Manual*, A-2.
7. *Candidacy Manual*, B-1.
8. Ibid.
9. Please note that names and other distinguishing characteristics have been obscured in these vignettes.
10. *Candidacy Manual*, B-1.
11. Ibid.
12. *Clinical Pastoral Education (CPE) in the ELCA*. Published by

the Department for SPCCE, Division for Ministry, ELCA. It is available online at http://www.elca.org/chaplains/mcpcce/clinicalpastoraleducation.html, taken from web July 2006.

13. Ibid.
14. *Candidacy Manual*, B-4.
15. *Candidacy Manual*, B-2.
16. Ibid.
17. Ibid.
18. *Candidacy Manual*, A-9–A-11.

CHAPTER 12

"How Can Technology Stretch Us Without Snapping?" Teaching with Technology

Mary E. Hess

I. QUESTIONING LEARNING, QUESTIONING TECHNOLOGY

Writing about technology is always a difficult challenge, given the rate of change we are currently experiencing in the development and circulation of various technologies (particularly digital technologies). In some ways it makes more sense to point readers to specific weblogs, websites, and other resources that live in the digital realm, and hence are more frequently updated, than it does to write about digital tech in print publications (particularly books that are months, if not years, in the production process).[1] At the same time, *teaching* with technology is increasingly a challenge most educators in the graduate theological context must engage, and this book would contain a glaring omission if we did not at least try to suggest some paths by which to meet the challenges.

More than anything, it's important to recognize that the basic patterns of reflective practice that we've been exploring throughout this book work well when teaching with technology. Whether teachers are using presentation software (such as *Keynote* or *PowerPoint*) to illustrate specific points, sharing audio examples using compression technologies such as MP3 files and podcasting, creating wikis to sort through shared knowledge, or writing weblogs with their students, the same tasks of "seeing through your students' eyes" exist and can be met.[2] Questions of matching a particular teaching strategy to a specific learning task are well documented in a variety of online forums, and increasingly schools are providing access to workshops on using specific technologies.[3]

Teaching a fully distributed, or online, class is perhaps an order of magnitude more challenging. While the different models for processes of teaching and learning we described in chapter 4 are also evident in the context of teaching with technology, the disadvantages of the first image or model, that which Parker Palmer termed "the objectivist myth,"[4] become particularly problematic. Many of the challenges of using such a model (unilateral control by the teacher, the encouragement of passivity on the part of the student, a tendency to view learning as an instrumental process) are not so easily mitigated in an online environment. In a typical classroom (that is, one in which students meet physically in the same space at the same time with a teacher who is also present) lecturing can be an effective pedagogical technique whose disadvantages can be modified by using buzz groups, two-minute essays, and so on.[5] In an online environment none of the "local clues" that exist in a typical classroom are present, and students cannot effectively "lurk" in the back of a classroom being "present" without participating.

In an online environment, teaching becomes—of necessity—a more collaborative, participatory process. Palmer's second image map, which he terms the "community of truth," is much more reflective of what faculty are encountering in their efforts to create effective learning environments online. Several authors have gone so far as to argue that digital technologies are in fact fundamentally altering the ways in which we think about teaching and learning.[6] Indeed, the MacArthur Foundation has just invested more than 50 million dollars in a project that will explore and learn from what young people are doing with new technologies in their "digital media and learning" project.[7] The white paper that forms one of the key foundations for that project points out that we are moving into a time and a series of cultural contexts in which participation is key, and several skills become far more important for learning than they have been in the recent past. Such huge shifts make learning to teach, indeed "learning to learn," in this environment much more of an adaptive challenge, rather than a technical one.[8]

One crucial difference that digital technology can make, therefore, in a graduate theological context is that it can provoke teachers to rethink their pedagogical models. Meeting adaptive challenges requires more than honing technical skills; it requires thoroughly rethinking basic assumptions. As might be expected in such a circumstance, theological contexts are full of anecdotes in which seminary professors who began to teach online found themselves rethinking the ways they were teaching in typical campus-based classrooms. Given the serious mismatch between the information transfer model of teaching and the convictions of Christian communities, this is quite a significant difference to produce. But are there other ways in which digital technology, particularly in an online environment, might contribute to relational pedagogies in the seminary classroom?

I would point to six in particular:

1. Providing a richer, more multiply intelligent environment within which to learn
2. Providing more opportunities for real collaboration
3. Giving teachers a better angle of vision on the challenges their students are facing and the specific assumptions with which they enter courses
4. Providing better access to primary source materials
5. Overcoming constraints of geography and time
6. Attending to the meaning-making contexts of our students and our communities of faith

As these are differences that are best seen in relation to specific examples, let me walk through each by pointing to a number of concrete examples.

II. EXAMPLES

A. Presentation Software

One of the first digital technologies that professors have begun to experiment with in seminary classrooms is presentation software (e.g., *Keynote, PowerPoint*). These software programs make it relatively easy to bring images and sound into a classroom, whether that classroom is located in a campus building (in which case digital projectors and speakers support the process) or online (in which case the easy conversion that these programs offer into formats that work on the web support the process). Teachers do not need to be experts in the manipulation of digital images or audio sound files but simply need to use standard interface commands ("insert file" "copy and paste" and so on) to import such files into a presentation. In doing so they can provide support for learning that engages more senses at once and that expands and layers the interpretations they are constructing. Of course, there is no inherent reason that faculty would not continue to use an instrumental or information transfer model in this instance, because presentation programs can become merely snazzier forms of a traditional overhead presentation, with long lists of bullet points reiterating a lecture's main points.[9] Still, to the extent that such software programs enhance a teacher's ability to connect students with the main topic around which they are gathered, such digital tools can have a significant impact that supports learning because they create an environment in which more than one form of learning is supported.[10] One of the more interesting ways in which teachers are experimenting with presentation software is in creating multi-user "webquests" and other kinds of scavenger hunts.[11]

B. Supporting Collaboration

Digital technologies can make the web of connection depicted in Palmer's second figure much more visible and tangible.

Students can use email to exchange papers in advance of gathering (either in a campus classroom or an online classroom) and in doing so refine and hone their thinking. The collaboration need not end at the boundaries of the classroom, however situated, because the web makes it possible to share materials and collaboration across much larger contexts. Students can post reviews of books they are required to read at *Amazon.com,* they can keep weblogs on course topics (in the process inviting comments from outside readers), they can evaluate religious education materials found on the web for use in specific congregations, they can create such materials themselves and post them for sharing with others, and they can work with other people scattered across the globe on topics of shared concern. One of our colleagues, Mary Hinkle Shore, a New Testament professor at Luther Seminary, has developed a wonderful site for teaching exegetical skills that utilizes problem-based learning and invites such collaboration from students in solving "messy" puzzles that draw on the specific skills she's trying to teach.[12]

These examples have been centered on ways in which students in typical seminary programs can utilize these technologies, but such examples point to much broader and more potentially transformative uses as well. What if communities of faith were more directly involved in the teaching and learning process? So that "learners" was a category that included not only those enrolled in degree programs, but also those worshipping in a local community who had decided to participate in the learning as well? Christian commitments to relationality compel us to understand Christian learning community in much broader terms than merely "graduate theological education," and if seminaries exist to prepare leaders for communities of faith, then the possibilities for collaboration with these communities throughout seminary education (not simply at the endpoint, when they must "consume" our graduates) are breathtaking! Indeed, the dawn of the World Wide Web was really the dawn of global networking.

Digital technologies can open up our classrooms on this same scale. Imagine students in a seminary context writing Bible study plans that a specific congregation has asked be developed for them in their unique context. Imagine members of congregations across the globe working with students within a seminary to plan prayer vigils for a specific social issue that will then be held simultaneously across the globe. Imagine digital images from one community's context bringing mission concerns alive in the prayers of another community. The possibilities for such collaboration are endless and point to the enormous opportunities available for helping students see the precise reasons why theological study is important.

C. Giving Teachers a Better Angle of Vision on Their Students' Thinking

One of the difficult challenges of supporting learning is that teachers must meet students where they are in their constructions of meaning if we ever hope to walk with them beyond those constructions into new understandings. As the famous video "A Private Universe" documents, if students' fundamental assumptions are not directly engaged—particularly their misconceptions—they can conclude a program of study with the same misconceptions they had when they began.[13] Many teachers have begun to recognize the extent to which they can "see their students' minds in action" when they include online discussion groups as part of their teaching (whether they are teaching in typical classrooms, or in distributed formats). As Nysse points out:

> . . . a threaded discussion allows time for everyone to contribute; everyone can "hear" by reading what everyone else has stated. There is no speaking over each other, and nothing is lost if there is a lapse in attention. If small groups are formed, the teacher can "hear" the contribution of every student.[14]

Digital technologies make it possible to create spaces in which most if not all students can find a way to participate—indeed, in which they can be required to participate—and that also shows their thinking *in process*. There are ways to do this without using digital technologies of course, but digital technologies can make the process much easier, and can contribute to helping such work to feel in some ways safer for students. Dividing students into small discussion groups is a venerable practice in theological classrooms, but no teacher can possibly "overhear" all of the groups. Doing the same division, but hosting the groups online in an asynchronous manner provides a way for a teacher to overhear what is going on, while at the same time easing the pressure to perform that often attends such groups when run in real time.

D. Providing Access to Rich Primary Sources

One of my colleagues, a professor of Hebrew Bible who also teaches our Hebrew classes from time to time, has been heard to wonder aloud if it still makes sense to require study of Hebrew. He is not in any way suggesting that it is no longer useful to know Hebrew when doing biblical exegesis, but rather pointing to new software programs that bring original Hebrew words with definitions, grammatical explanations, and other resources readily to hand. He questions whether it might make more sense to teach a class that helps students to use such programs wisely and well in the process of preparing for preaching and teaching. This is one concrete example of the rich primary resources to which digital tools have given us access.

Professors of history regularly utilize the many collections of primary documents now available on the web in digital formats, and professors of hymnody can access music recorded in mp3 files. Professors teaching cross-cultural mission courses can direct students to diverse collections of materials placed on the web by communities of faith in specific locations, and professors teaching comparative confessions (or other courses that engage ecumenical and interfaith concerns) can point students to websites full of materials written from within a specific communion, rather than simply giving them secondary textbooks to read.[15]

Recently the American Theological Libraries Association

and the Association of Theological Schools have collaborated on a digital image repository that makes the digital resources held by member libraries accessible—and more importantly, easily searchable!—in one location.[16] As theological educators grow more comfortable with the use of such resources, we will also grow more capable of creating additional collections. The American Studies Association has for years collaborated with a number of academic departments and philanthropic foundations to sponsor an innovative project that supports professors within that guild in creating and teaching with such resources—the Visible Knowledge Project.[17] The project has made a demonstrable difference in energizing and supporting creative teaching and scholarship. It should serve as both a vibrant example to us within theological education and perhaps a competitive prod as well.

E. Overcoming Constraints of Geography and Time

Perhaps one of the most palpable differences digital technology can make within theological education is that of overcoming the constraints of geography and time that many of our students face. This is the context in which distributive learning has become so important: learning that is "distributed" via online technologies allows people to access seminary education in ways never before possible. Many schools in the ATS now offer elements of their degree programs in online formats, most of them using asynchronous web technologies. Some schools have gone so far as to place large portions of degree programs into distributive formats, making it possible for hundreds if not thousands of students in the United States to attend seminary who might not otherwise have been able to do so. If we take seriously the community of truth model, then this easing of the constraints of time and geography is enriching our learning enormously, bringing many more people into the fabric of our teaching and learning contexts. A community of truth model, however, also requires us to recognize that teaching in this way demands full support for *all* of the curricular elements that contribute to this model. More informal elements of learning—communal worship, library research materials, spontaneous gathering places, and so on—must all be made accessible to students studying in online formats.

F. Attending to the Meaning-making of Our Students and Communities of Faith

This category of significant impact is perhaps the one that is least visible within more traditional, historically grounded institutions of theological education. Although there are frequent calls to reform theological education, even going so far as to suggest that we move beyond the "theological encyclopedia," or the "current fourfold academic division" (biblical studies, church history, theology and ethics, and practical theology), few if any of these proposals actually take much notice of the digitally mediated environments we inhabit.[18] Consider just the ways in which younger people living in the United States access news sources: "less than a fifth of 18–34 year olds rank newspapers as their primary source of news, while 44% check out internet portals such as Google and Yahoo for updated information."[19] When combined with another interesting statistic—

> . . . more than one-third of Americans under 30 now get their news primarily from late-night comedians, and that 79 percent of this age group (and half of the adult population generally) say they sometimes or regularly get political information from comedy programs such as *Saturday Night Live* or nontraditional outlets such as MTV . . .[20]

—theological educators should begin to ponder how to give students access to meaningful ways in which to critique their constructions of reality through news consumption. But we must also ask ourselves if we are sufficiently aware of such contexts to pursue our work in faithful ways. Quite frankly, the satirical edge to news events that is regularly promoted on shows such as *The Daily Show with Jon Stewart* requires more awareness of current events than most regular TV news broadcasts impart.

Yet how are we to add "becoming aware of mass-mediated news" to the already overwhelming tasks we face? Simple digital tools—good RSS feeds from a limited assortment of the common sites our students visit, for example—exist that can help us to stay current with the meaning-making contexts we are embedded within.[21] Using such tools would be one good response to our predicament. But this example also illustrates a key advantage of the relational mapping of learning over the information transfer model. In a world of exponentially increasing numbers of information sources, there is no realistic way to attain expertise or mastery. Instead we must be increasingly attentive to the multiple webs of knowing that we are embedded in and increasingly alert to ways to make our learning and teaching more collaborative and participatory.

Indeed, a recent review of "elements of effective e-learning design" in the prestigious *International Review of Research in Open and Distance Learning* points to the utility of the relational model: five of the six elements they identify cannot be described apart from such a model. The six elements are: "paying attention to the provision of a rich learning activity, situating this activity within an interesting story line, providing meaningful opportunities for student reflection and third-party criticism, considering appropriate technologies for delivery, ensuring that the design is suitable for the context in which it will be used, and bearing in mind the personal, social, and environmental impact of the designed activities."[22]

In the beginning of this essay I pointed to one big difference that digital technologies make in our classrooms—they alert us to new ways of thinking about pedagogical challenges. Let me conclude by noting a reciprocal impact: digital technologies can make a huge difference in helping us, as theological educators, to align our Christian convictions and our pedagogical strategies more effectively. They can do so in at least these six ways that I have described: providing a richer, more multiply intelligent environment within which to learn; providing more opportunities for real collaboration; giving teachers a better angle of vision on the challenges their students are facing and the specific assumptions with which they enter courses; providing better access to primary source materials; overcoming constraints of geography and time; and attending to the meaning-making contexts of our students and our communities of faith. Each of these differences plays a role in making more visible and tangible the deep and enduring ways in which we truly know as we are known by the One who creates, redeems, and sanctifies. To the extent that we embody the community of truth, then our teaching and learning will make a huge difference. To the extent that theological education can support that community using digital technologies, then digital technologies can make a real difference.

NOTES

1. Some of the weblogs on digital technology and education which I read regularly include Stephen Downes' "OLDaily" (http://www.downes.ca/news/OLDaily.htm), Will Richardson's "Weblogg-ed" (http://weblogg-ed.com/), the Tomorrow's Professor blog (http://amps-tools.mit.edu/tomprofblog/), and the MacArthur Foundation's "Spotlight on Digital Media and Learning" (http://spotlight.macfound.org/).
2. If these terms are unfamiliar to you, they are well defined and illustrated in the Wikipedia, an online resource available at: http://wikipedia.org. This online encyclopedia is entirely user-generated, so not always authoritative. On the other hand, since its basic information about digital tech is generally of very high quality and frequently updated, it's a great resource for basic learning about digital tech.
3. Here the Wabash Center on Teaching in Theology and Religion is a great resource, particularly their Internet Resource guide (http://www.wabashcenter.wabash.edu/resources/guide_headings.aspx).
4. This process is described at length in chapter 4 of the current volume, and the image is found on p. 51.
5. See chapters 1, 3, and 4 for more on these techniques.
6. See, in particular, David Weinberger, *Small Pieces Loosely Joined* (New York: Perseus Books Group, 2002); James Paul Gee, *What*

Video Games Have to Teach Us About Learning and Literacy (New York: Palgrave Macmillan, 2004); Henry Jenkins, *Convergence Culture* (New York: New York University Press, 2006); and Renee Hobbs, *Reading the Media in High School* (New York: Teachers College Press, 2007).

7. Details available at: http://www.digitallearning.macfound.org/. The white paper is entitled "Confronting the challenges of participatory culture: Media education for the 21st century," by Henry Jenkins.
8. Ron Heifetz describes these distinctions in much of his work, and I illustrate the terms more fully in chapter 1 of *Engaging Technology in Theological Education* (Lanham, MD: Rowman & Littlefield, 2005).
9. There are several famous essays online about why NOT to use presentation software, but for good ideas on how to do so well, visit the PresentationZen weblog (http://www.presentationzen.com/).
10. A wonderful example of this on the web can be found at the journal *Kairos* (http://english.ttu.edu/kairos/8.1/binder2.html?http://www.hu.mtu.edu/kairos/CoverWeb/anderson/index.html). Recent research into how the brain functions is also particularly pertinent here, and an excellent introduction to that literature in the context of teaching and learning is James Zull's *The Art of Changing the Brain* (Sterling, VA: Stylus Publishing, 2002).
11. More information on how to do this (including several templates for use with specific software) can be found at: http://facstaff.uww.edu/jonesd/games/.
12. That site is "Into the New Testament" and can be found at: http://www.readnew.net/. Look, in particular, at the activity grid found at that site.
13. "A Private Universe" was produced by the Harvard-Smithsonian Center for Astrophysics and documents the sometimes startling ways in which people learn. The video documents the problem of countering enduring misconceptions with traditional teaching practices (read: instrumental notions of information transfer). Information on accessing the video, and a wealth of additional learning resources are available online at: http://www.learner.org/resources/series28.html.
14. Richard Nysse, "Online Education: An Asset in a Period of Educational Change," in Malcolm Warford (ed.), *Practical Wisdom:*

On Theological Teaching and Learning (New York: Peter Lang, 2004), 205.

15. Some of my own favorite examples include O'Donnell's Augustine site (http://ccat.sas.upenn.edu/jod/augustine.html), the Jesuit Plantation site (http://www.georgetown.edu/departments/amer_studies/jpp/coverjpp.html), Hymnuts (http://hymnuts.luthersem.edu/), and the War Posters site (http://digital.lib.umn.edu/warposters/warpost.html).
16. This repository is available online at: http://www.atla.com/digitalresources/.
17. More details at: http://crossroads.georgetown.edu/vkp/
18. Jason Byassee, "Book Review," in *The Christian Century*, February 8, 2005.
19. http://www.netimperative.com/2005/04/25/youth_abandoning_old_media
20. "Heeeeeeere's Democracy!," in *Chronicle of Higher Education*, April 19, 2002.
21. A good basic introduction to RSS news feeds can be found at the Digital Divide website: http://www.digitaldivide.net/blog/marniewebb/view?PostID=929.
22. Andrew Brown and Bradley Voltz, "Elements of effective e-learning design," in the *International Review of Research in Open and Distance Learning*, March 2005. Taken from the web on 31 December 2006: http://www.irrodl.org/index.php/irrodl/article/view/217/300.

CHAPTER 13

"How Do We Connect Classroom Teaching to Institutional Practice?" Sustaining a Culture of Reflective Practice in Teaching

Mary E. Hess and Stephen D. Brookfield

The foregoing chapters in this collection have not been prescriptive narratives but rather stories that invite readers to reflect on their own teaching practices and learning processes. We want to continue this reflective theme in this final chapter by examining some of the dynamics that assist theological educators to build a culture of reflective practice in their own institutions. We also want to explore the ways such practices seek to open hearts and minds to God's ongoing presence. Although theological educational institutions might be thought to incline naturally to valorize the contemplative aspects of pedagogy, and thus to be natural sites for reflective practices, our contention is that this is not necessarily so. There is more that unites the working conditions and institutional imperatives of a proprietary college of business and a seminary than there is that divides them. Consequently, theological educators can build profitably on reflective practices evident in nontheological contexts.

I. WHAT IS REFLECTIVE PRACTICE?

Reflective practice is the constant effort by theological educators to unearth and investigate the assumptions they make about the conditions that best foster learning. These assumptions are the taken-for-granted beliefs about education, and the significance teachers' actions have for students, that seem so obvious to us as not to need to be stated explicitly. In a very real sense we *are* our assumptions. Assumptions give meaning and purpose to who we are and what we do. Becoming aware of the assumptions that frame how we think and act is one of the most puzzling intellectual challenges we face in our lives. It is also something we often instinctively resist for fear of what we might discover. Who wants to clarify and question assumptions we have lived by for a substantial period of time, only to find out that they don't make sense?

Every reader of this book will act according to personal assumptions made about theological teaching. The way we sequence curriculum, the evaluative measures we choose to gauge how and what students are learning, the questions we pose to stimulate or deepen conversation, who we call on next in a discussion, which example we use to illustrate a complex concept, even something as simple as when we call a break—all of these actions are based on assumptions we make regarding what will most help students learn. Teaching reflectively means we constantly check whether or not these assumptions are well grounded, and consequently we raise our chances of taking informed action. By informed action we mean action that is based on assumptions that have been carefully and critically investigated. Such action can be explained and justified to ourselves and others. If a student or colleague asks us why we're doing something, we can show how our action springs from certain assumptions we hold about teaching and learning. We can then set out the evidence (experiential as well as theoretical) that undergirds these practices and we can make a convincing case for their accuracy.

Becoming aware of our assumptions, however, is a puzzling and contradictory task. Very few of us can get very far doing this on our own. No matter how much we may think we have an accurate sense of ourselves, we are stymied by the fact that we're using our own interpretive filters to become aware of our own interpretive filters! This is the pedagogic equivalent of a dog trying to catch its tail or of trying to see the back of your head while looking in a mirror. To some extent we are all prisoners trapped within the perceptual frameworks that determine how we view our experiences. A self-confirming cycle often develops whereby our uncritically accepted assumptions shape actions that then only serve to confirm the truth of those assumptions. We find it very difficult to stand outside ourselves and see how some of our most deeply held values and beliefs lead us into distorted and constrained ways of being, or into inauthentic practices. To undertake reflective teaching we need to find some lenses that reflect to us a stark and differently highlighted picture of who we are and what we do. Our most influential assumptions are too close to us to be seen clearly by an act of self-will.

One of the problems of using colleagues and peers to stand outside ourselves and help us realize our assumptions, however, is that the people we find to serve as mirrors often share our assumptions. This is perhaps even truer for teachers within communities of faith than for many others. If our conversational partners are similar to ourselves, then talk with them can easily become an unproductive loop in which the same prejudices and stereotypes are constantly reaffirmed. Just as we tend to read authors we already agree with, or have some affinity for, so we tend to seek out colleagues whom we know are sympathetic to and familiar with our orientations. Rare indeed are the people who deliberately seek out books, conversations, and practices that they know will challenge or even undercut much of what they find to be comfortable and familiar. This is one of the reasons interfaith dialogue is often so difficult to conduct. The whole idea of systematically searching out and challenging our assumptions is also often deliberately avoided for fear of what it might lead to. No one likes to discover that ideas he has lived by for much of his life are somehow inaccurate or invalid.

Sooner or later, however, something happens that forces teachers to confront the possibility that they may be working with assumptions that don't really fit their situations. Students might express religiously grounded beliefs that we find bizarre or distasteful. Biblical texts might be interpreted by a new group of learners to justify in their eyes practices that we believe are abhorrent or that belie what we regard as Christ's teachings. Perhaps we find that a humorous, ironic aside we voiced is taken as Gospel truth by some of our students. All these events are examples of what Mezirow calls disorienting dilemmas—moments when we realize a discrepancy exists between what is and what we believe should be that is often the beginning of the reflective journey.[1] Theological teachers who embark on this journey have four lenses through which they can view their teaching: their autobiographies as learners, their students' eyes, their colleagues' experiences, and theoretical literature. Viewing what we do through these different lenses alerts us to distorted or incomplete aspects of our assumptions that need further investigation.

The first of these lenses—our autobiographies as learners—comprise both recollections of our past history in this role and also our current learning activities. Our experiences as learners, particularly those concerned with faith development and spiritual learning, are felt at a visceral, emotional level much deeper than that of reason.[2] The insights and meanings for theological teaching that we draw from these deep experiences are likely to have a profound and long-lasting influence. They certainly affect us far more powerfully than methods or injunctions that we learn from textbooks or hear from superiors. We may think we're teaching according to a widely accepted curricular or pedagogic model only to find, on reflection, that the foundations of how we work have been laid in our autobiographies as learners. In the face of crises or ambiguities we fall back instinctively on memories from our times as learners to guide how we respond.

For example, teachers who were underestimated as students when they were in college are careful not to make the mistake of underestimating their own students. This predisposes them to allow students second chances, to renegotiate course requirements and deadlines, or to give students the benefit of the doubt when they are unable to do what they had promised. Teachers who were reluctant discussion participants in their own student days are not likely to dismiss non-contributors to classroom discussions as mentally negligible, disengaged, or hostile. They may well interpret a student's silence as evidence of her being engaged in reflective analysis. Remembering the cultural and psychological inhibitors to their own discussion participation, they are more inclined to create ground rules that acknowledge the value of silence and that create space for equal participation.

Seeing ourselves through students' eyes—the second reflective lens available to us—constitutes one of the most consistently surprising elements in any teacher's career. Each time we do this we learn something. Sometimes what we find out is reassuring. We discover that students are interpreting our actions in the way that we mean them. They are hearing what we wanted them to hear and seeing what we wanted them to see. But often we are profoundly surprised by the diversity of meanings students read into our words and actions. Comments we made incidentally that had no particular significance to us are heard as imperatives. Answers we gave off the cuff to what seemed like inconsequential questions return to haunt us. Long after we've forgotten them students quote them back at us to prove that now we're contradicting ourselves. What we think is reassuring behavior on our part is sometimes interpreted as overprotective coddling. What we regard as an inspired moment of creativity, when our awareness of new possibilities causes us to deviate from the plan for the class, is perceived as arbitrary, inconsistent, or confusing behavior. A joking aside appreciated by some leaves others insulted.

Colleagues' perceptions of our practice is the third reflective lens we can use. Talking to colleagues about what we do unravels the shroud of silence in which our practice is wrapped. Participating in critical conversation with peers opens us up to their versions of events we have experienced. Our colleagues serve as critical mirrors reflecting images of our actions that often take us by surprise. As they describe their own experiences dealing with the same crises and dilemmas that we face, we are able to check, reframe, and broaden our own theories of practice. For example, if we ask colleagues what they think are the typical causes of students' resistance to learning we will likely hear a variety of responses. Some of these we will have discovered ourselves. Others, such as teachers making false promises, teachers being perceived as dishonest, the white privilege we possess that we have never acknowledged, or students' fear of questioning previously unchallenged ways of thinking and behaving, may never have occurred to us. When we ask our colleagues how they have dealt with each of these causes of resistance we may encounter reactions that surprise us and that suggest new readings of this problem in our classrooms. It may never have occurred to us, for example, to apologize for something we have done or said, to find new ways to model the learning behaviors we want students to exhibit, or to make a deliberate effort to focus on racial dynamics.

Talking to colleagues about problems we have in common and gaining their perspectives on these problems increases our chances of stumbling across an interpretation that fits what is happening in a particular situation. A colleague's experiences may suggest dynamics and causes that make much more sense than the explanations we have evolved. If this happens we are helped enormously in our effort to work out just what we should be doing to deal with the problem. Without an accurate reading of the causes of a problem (are these embedded in our own actions, in our students' past histories, in the wider political constraints placed on our learning and teaching, in the predictable rhythms of faith development, or in a particular intersection of all of these?) we are crippled in our attempts to work through it.

Checking our readings of problems, responses, assumptions, and justifications against the readings offered by colleagues is crucial if we are to claw a path to critical clarity. Doing this also provides us with a great deal of emotional sustenance. We start to see that what we thought were unique problems and idiosyncratic failings are shared by many others who work in situations like ours. Just knowing that we're not alone in our struggles can be a life-saving realization. Although critical reflection often begins alone it is, ultimately, a collective endeavor. We need colleagues to help us know what our assumptions are and to help us change the structures of power so that democratic actions and values are rewarded within, and without, our institutions.

Finally, theoretical literature is a lens that can help us "name" our practice by illuminating the general elements of what we think are idiosyncratic experiences. It can provide multiple perspectives on familiar situations. Studying theory can help us realize that what we thought were signs of our personal failings as teachers can actually be interpreted as the inevitable consequence of certain psychological, economic, social, and political processes. This stops us falling victim to the belief that we are responsible for everything that happens in our classrooms. Reading critical theory, for example, helps us realize that students' disinterest in learning is the predictable consequence of a system that forces people to study disconnected chunks of knowledge at a pace prescribed by curriculum councils and licensure bodies. Studying theories of cognitive and moral development helps us understand that much student anger seemingly directed towards us can plausibly be explained by the fact that students realize that they are on the verge of changing, or scrutinizing, aspects of themselves that are more easily left untouched. Faced with such an intimidating prospect it is no surprise that those seen as the catalysts of this process—teachers themselves—are the targets of such feelings. Critical ethnography warns us that our racial and gender identities can create misgivings and revive painful memories in students without us ever being aware that this is happening.

Teachers who have learned the reflective habit know something about the effects they are having on students. They are alert to the presence of power in their classrooms and to its possibilities for misuse. Knowing that their actions can silence or activate students' voices, they listen seriously and attentively to what students say. They deliberately create public reflective moments when students' concerns—not the teacher's agenda—are the focus of classroom activity. Week in, week out, they make public disclosures of private realities to their students and to their colleagues. They make constant attempts to find out how students are experiencing their classes and they make this information public. All their actions are explicitly grounded in reference to students' experiences, and students know and appreciate this.

II. BARRIERS TO CREATING A CULTURE OF REFLECTION

How can seminaries create a culture that values the kinds of reflective practices outlined in the first section? There is no doubt that teaching reflectively brings us into conflict with many of the taken-for-granted assumptions and practices that currently define seminary education. It challenges basic conceptions of how good teaching is evaluated and rewarded and it plays productive havoc with many of the political rules of the academic game. Although any number of mission statements incorporate values of reflective practice, their rhetoric is rarely matched by organizational conditions. For one thing, time is usually not organizationally allocated for reflection; instead, it is assumed that teachers will find the time themselves for this. Few colleges consistently honor and reward reflection as a crucial component of what it means to be a good teacher or scholar. And in the absence of this kind of cultural support, teachers in these institutions who want to challenge organizational assumptions, or to explore alternative pedagogic practices, will think twice before doing so. Those who do try to swim against the tide often find the currents too strong. Diverging from accepted practices incurs serious consequences. As Freire points out, "Acting alone is the best way to commit suicide."[3]

As we contemplate how to establish a culture of reflective practice we need to consider the obstacles that confront us. Prime amongst these is the fact that current campus culture frequently undercuts nascent attempts at reflection. First, we have to fight the culture of silence that surrounds us as teachers. Given the noise of a typical campus, it may seem strange to state that teaching is conducted in quiet. Yet, in a demoralizing though often unacknowledged way, many of us spend the greater part of our lives as teachers bound in chains of silence. This silence is a silence about the process and meaning of our teaching. It is a silence that acts subtly to prevent us from making talk about teaching a central element of our lives. Very few readers of this book, we would imagine, could say that the opportunity to talk about their teaching with peers in a sustained and serious way is recognized and fostered as a central element in their professional lives.

By talk about teaching we don't mean the daily carping about how unreasonable are the expectations that administrators place upon us, or our complaints about particular colleagues or students who seem to exist solely for the purpose of placing obstacles to our attempts to do good work. We mean, instead, talk about the dynamics and rhythms of classroom processes and the daily struggle to confront what we know are irresolvable dilemmas and contradictory pressures. We mean, too, talk about the meaning that teaching has in our lives; the way we draw strength or suffer humiliations in doing it; the moral, social, and political purposes we attribute to it; and the importance that it has for our sense of ourselves as contributors to the flow of human experience. Purposeful, deliberate, and extended conversation about these things is rare. For many of us there is a sense that teaching is a secluded activity conducted in private fiefdoms over which we hold sway. We visit colleagues' classrooms only when required to do so for purposes of reappointment, promotion, or tenure observations.

Why should this privatization of practice be so common? One reason is that to ask for help with teaching is often felt as a public admission of one's powerlessness or incompetence. In institutions where teaching ability is a major determinant of whether or not we will be reappointed or promoted, it is not unnatural for us to think twice before talking publicly about our pedagogic struggles in front of colleagues who may be voting to decide whether or not we will be employed or what we will be paid a year or two hence. Teachers soon learn that talking about teaching is often the last thing that their colleagues expect of them.

Living in silence reinforces a demoralizing sense of isolation that saps any momentum teachers might have for raising critical questions. Knowing that asking awkward questions could result in one's being excluded from all kinds of networks and conversations guarantees self-censorship. If the questioning of conventional wisdoms is seen to be punished by professional ostracism, then the critical spirit is crushed before it gathers strength. If teachers who question the decisions and justifications of those in authority are passed over for promotion, or are always assigned to the most boring or most tiring duties, then no one can be surprised if teachers remain publicly servile while privately venting their anger and frustration through different kinds of workplace sabotage.

A second cultural barrier is the culture of individualism. As we examine the cultures of seminaries we can see how frequently they employ reward systems that work against the spirit of collectivism. Time, space, and money are denied for teacher collaboration while academic excellence is measured in terms of individual effort. This is true for students, where group projects are sometimes dismissed as soft options and group dissertations disallowed. But it is just as true for teachers. In the quest for tenure one sole-authored article is worth five co-authored and ten multi-authored pieces. Not surprisingly, teachers get the message that collaboration is viewed as evidence of intellectual inferiority (you could only write this article because you were helped by two or three colleagues) or laziness (team teaching is a way of getting out of work by piggybacking on colleagues' efforts).

The rhetoric of collaboration, especially of team teaching, is often present in seminaries, but its power is subtly destroyed by the toll collaborative work takes on teachers. The conditions under which team teaching is introduced almost always ensure its failure. If you're team teaching, so the argument goes, your job is easier. After all, you're dividing one person's labor amongst several. Since your job is easier, you can take on more hours, more students, and more sections to compensate for the lack of solo instruction in your life. In reality, as anyone who has involved themselves in it seriously knows, team teaching that is properly planned, conducted, and monitored is far more time consuming than working alone where you answer only to yourself for the decisions you make.

Finally, a strong cultural inhibitor to critical reflection is the culture of secrecy—the way in which self-disclosure that reveals the discloser as something less than perfect leads to her being chastised, even punished. For critical reflection to happen there has to be a trustful atmosphere in which people know that public disclosure of private errors will not lead to their suffering negative consequences. A precondition of critical conversation is a willingness to make public one's private dilemmas, uncertainties, and frustrations. Too often, however, the institutional rhetoric that emphasizes the importance of "learning from our mistakes" is contradicted by the penalties that accompany admissions of failure. If owning up to fallibility does nothing more than earn you a reputation for incompetence (with all the organizational injuries that implies), then you are going to present yourself as always being in total control. Only saints or idiots draw attention to their errors in cultures where maintaining the mask of command is prized above all else.

Crucial to creating a climate that encourages the public disclosure of private errors is the modeling of this behavior by those in positions of symbolic or actual power. Unless senior and respected figures in the organization (deans, department heads, program chairs) take the lead in this kind of self-disclosure—with all the risks to their professional standing this entails—there is no chance of this happening among rank-and-file teachers. Osterman and Kottkamp show how principals' public declarations of error were of greatest importance in nurturing the reflective spirit among junior teachers.[4] Sharon Parks makes a similar point in her most recent book.[5] This same relationship between senior administrators and teachers holds true in seminary education.

Where a culture of secrecy exists, reflection is doomed. Those who believe that knowledge is power often use a form of communicative nepotism to retain their positions of privilege. They dole out little bits and pieces of knowledge as selected favors to a chosen few. Information is used to ensure allegiance or bestow patronage. This privatization of knowledge is reinforced by the reward system that exists in some colleges where merit payments are made according to the ratings students give to their teachers. If a teacher has worked up a great technique that makes difficult content accessible to students, captivates their curiosity, and therefore earns her high marks on her end of course evaluations, why should she share this technique with a colleague and thereby risk losing her shot at one of the few merit payments available that year? For critical reflection to become an institutional habit the privatizing instinct must be challenged. People must trust each other enough to share information with the assurance that this won't adversely affect their institutional standing.

III. CREATING A REWARD SYSTEM FOR CRITICAL REFLECTION

Myles Horton was an adult educator who spent his life working with grass roots organizations in the Appalachian region and who worked out an approach to social change that relied on making people aware of their own experience and knowledge and then using these to solve the problems that confronted them. One of his maxims as an adult educator was that if you want to change people's behavior you don't reason with them about why they should act differently—you change the system to ensure these changed behaviors. In his own words, "It doesn't make a great deal of difference what the people are; if they're in the system, they're going to function like the system dictates that they function."[6] Instead of telling people why they should change, Myles believed you should devote your energy to changing the structures within which they live so that these structures create a different set of expectations about behavior. As he put it, "If you want to change people's ideas, you shouldn't try to convince them intellectually. What you need to do is get them into a situation where they'll have to act on ideas, not argue about them."[7] Once structures are changed and old patterns of behavior are untenable, people are forced to act differently.

Interpreting this approach in the context of encouraging reflection among seminary teachers suggests the creation of institutional expectations and procedures that imply that reflection is a normal and desirable professional habit. The most important place to start is with the reward systems that are in place. Reward systems drive a great deal of organizational behavior. If we log the ways in which teachers spend their days in seminaries where the "publish or perish" syndrome reigns, the greatest amount of teacher time is devoted to scholarly research and writing. If we compile a similar record of teachers' behaviors in seminaries that prize good teaching, we find, not surprisingly, much more emphasis on teachers participating in faculty development, designing new materials, or experimenting with different approaches.

A reward system that encouraged reflection would make a demonstrable commitment to this process the chief professional behavior that was rewarded. An eagerness to become critically reflective—and a minimal understanding of what this involved—would become important criteria for deciding which applicants were appointed to vacant positions. Job announcements and descriptions would name reflection as a professional attribute sought after in candidates. Application forms would ask for evidence of past engagement in this process and for a statement of how it would be pursued in the position being sought. Those teachers who demonstrated a more or less continuous effort to question assumptions and explore alternatives would be those who would be promoted, given merit payments, and honored with "Teacher of the Year" awards.

Student evaluation forms would be redesigned to take account of the cognitive and emotional complexities entailed in teachers becoming reflective. Instead of teachers being evaluated only on how or if they pleased students (through forms that ask students whether or not they liked the teacher or the course) there would be items on end-of-course evaluations that would probe the extent to which students felt they had been stretched, challenged, questioned, and introduced to alternative perspectives. A culture of reflection would support involvement in conversation groups by giving teachers release time to participate in such groups during the normal workday. This would involve senior administrators agreeing to hire substitutes to cover for teachers who choose this activity. Every two or three weeks part of the college day would be devoted to a troubleshooting session in which teachers would come together to talk about dilemmas and critical moments in their practice. These conversations would be about events that had caused them to recognize, challenge, or reframe familiar assumptions or to look at habitual behaviors from a new perspective.

A reward system for critical reflection would also encourage teachers to engage in the kind of professional development in which they agreed to learn something new and difficult on a regular basis as a means of gaining new insights into their teaching. Making the deliberate attempt to view their own practice through the lens of learning would become the norm for faculty development activities. An attempt to help colleagues negotiate their own critical journeys—to be critical friends or mirrors—would be regarded as one of the most collegial kinds of behavior possible. Watching one's peers at work would become named as a professional expectation, a sign that one was acting as a scholar should.

At the end of each year (or at other points in the faculty review and appraisal process) teachers would be asked to submit a reflective portfolio. This portfolio would constitute a major piece of evidence consulted in decisions regarding promotion and tenure. It would document not only the teacher's own involvement in critical reflection, but also her efforts to encourage this in colleagues through various forms of mentorship or peer review. Items to be included in the portfolio might include extracts from teaching journals, letters of thanks from colleagues, video vignettes from classroom teaching, taped discussions from critical conversation groups, new statements of purpose and rationale in course outlines, and narrative evaluations given to students on their work in progress.

One way that the administration would show that it took reflection seriously would be through its granting of sufficient release time for the preparation of these portfolios. Honors recognizing pedagogic excellence (such as "Teacher of the Year" awards) would be bestowed on those individuals who had owned up to what they saw as their own failures and mistakes and who had demonstrated how they had learned from these. Those willing to make their struggles public, rather than those who seemed to have resolved all possible problems, would become acclaimed professional exemplars. Teachers would think of peak experiences as those times when they made an error that was particularly productive in prompting new learning, rather than those times when everything went so well that they received only favorable evaluations.

IV. ADMINISTRATORS AS EXEMPLARS OF A REFLECTIVE CULTURE

Studies of how teachers practice reflection time and time again stress that the factor most likely to encourage this in teachers is their seeing this behavior modeled by senior administrators.[8] It takes a while for teachers to trust administrators, just as it does for students to trust teachers. But if those who have the most to lose are seen to be inviting and welcoming of a public critical scrutiny of their actions, the effect is undeniable.

One way administrators could send a message concerning how seriously they took reflection would be for them to make their perceived readiness to engage in this process an important indicator of administrative effectiveness. In some institutions administrators regularly invite faculty to appraise their work. Asking faculty how well the administrator is exemplifying reflective process would ensure that there is no perception of a double standard operating where teaching and administrative effectiveness is concerned. Both groups would be seen to be held to the same criterion of good, reflective practice.

Modeling reflection seriously would mean that deans, department chairs, and even presidents and principals would find themselves going public with their own learning. In college newsletters, faculty meetings, and in speeches they would recreate in public the private reasoning behind their decisions. They would pay particular attention to talking about those times when events had caused them to rethink their basic assumptions, or to see things from an entirely different viewpoint. They would invite critique of their actions and, when this critique was not forthcoming (as it would not be at first given the level of mistrust in most educational institutions), they would play the role of devil's advocate in offering alternative perspectives on what they had done.

Administrators would also take pains to ensure that their words and actions were perceived as being as consistent as possible. They would do this by soliciting regular anonymous commentary on how they were doing (the anonymity being crucial to make faculty feel safe in being honest) and then by making this commentary public. Several times a year faculty would receive written summaries of the anonymous comments they had given, and they would be invited to discuss these at a faculty meeting. Administrators would also do their best to build a case for reflection by using their autobiographies to illustrate the benefits of the process in their own lives. They would start faculty development days by talking about the role that reflection plays in their own practice. They would invite faculty and administrators from other institutions where reflection was valued to come and talk about its importance.

V. TAKING OUR THEOLOGICAL COMMITMENTS SERIOUSLY

Finally, as with all else in theological education, all of us—faculty, administrators, students, staff—need to take our theological commitments seriously as both nourishment of and challenge to our reflective practice. Indeed, some might argue that theological work is, essentially, work of reflection. Many of the most recent books that have been published on topics of teaching in theological schools have quite deliberately chosen to step aside from particular theological commitments, hoping in part to make the texts more accessible across a wide variety of theological positions. Such a desire is laudable. But refusing to engage directly the theological commitments that lie at the heart of our contexts also teaches, and not necessarily in the ways we would expect.

Throughout this book we have tried to place ourselves very

clearly in our specific settings and have spoken from those locations with as much particularity as we can manage. We hope that in doing so we have invited you, the reader, to consider your own settings, commitments, and practices. We also hope that we have modeled taking seriously the theological assumptions upon which our specific settings rest. We hope in doing so to have been descriptive rather than prescriptive and to have been a catalyst for reflection in your own setting. We also hope that we have shared some of the ways in which the challenges of teaching have been supported and sustained by the commitments we bring into the process. At the heart of this process has been reflective practice, and at the heart of our reflective practice lies both our personal and our communal sense of how God lives in relation with us and sustains us in our learning and in our teaching.

More than anything we hope that this book provides a way into reflective practice in your own context and that the One who sustains us might also sustain you on that path.

NOTES

1. Mezirow, J. *Transformative Dimensions of Adult Learning* (San Francisco: Jossey-Bass, 1991).
2. English, L, Fenwick, T. and Parsons, J. *Spirituality of Adult Education and Training* (Malabar, FL: Krieger, 2003); and Tisdell, E. *Exploring Spirituality and Culture in Adult and Higher Education* (San Francisco: Jossey-Bass, 2003).
3. Shor, I., and Freire, P. *A Pedagogy for Liberation: Dialogues on Transforming Education* (Westport, CT: Bergin and Garvey, 1987), 61.
4. Osterman, K. F. & Kottkamp, R. B. *Reflective Practice for Educators: Professional Development to Improve Student Learning* (Newbury Park, CA: Corwin Press, 2004).
5. Sharon Daloz Parks, *Leadership Can Be Taught: A Bold Approach for a Complex World* (Cambridge, MA: Harvard Business School Press, 2005).
6. Horton, M., and Freire, P. *We Make the Road by Walking: Con-*

versations on Education and Social Change (Philadelphia: Temple University Press, 1990), 103.

7. Horton, M. *The Long Haul: An Autobiography* (New York: Doubleday, 1990), 16.
8. U. C. Reitzug, "A Case Study of Empowering Principal Behavior." *American Educational Research Journal*, 1994, 31 (2), 283–307; W. G. Webster, Sr. *Learner-Centered Principalship: The Principal as Teacher as Teachers* (New York: Praeger, 1994); J. Blase, J. R. Blase, G. L. Anderson, and S. Dungan, *Democratic Principals in Action: Eight Pioneers* (Thousand Oaks, CA: Corwin Press, 1995); and K. F. Osterman, and R. B. Kottkamp, *Reflective Practice for Educators: Professional Development to Improve Student Learning* (Newbury Park, CA: Corwin Press, 2004).

REFERENCES

Adams, Maurianne (ed.). *Teaching for Diversity and Social Justice.* New York: Routledge, 1997.

Alexander, Hanan. *Reclaiming Goodness: Education and the Spiritual Quest.* Notre Dame, IN: University of Notre Dame Press, 2001.

Allen, K. R., Floyd-Thomas, S. M., and Gillman, L. "Teaching to Transform: From Volatility to Solidarity in an Interdisciplinary Family Studies Classroom," in *Family Relations*, *50*, 4 (2001).

Anderson, Chris. *Teaching as Believing: Faith in the University.* Waco, TX: Baylor University Press, 2004.

Anderson, L. W. *Classroom Assessment: Enhancing the Quality of Teacher Decision Making.* Mahwah, NJ: Earlbaum, 2002.

Angelo, T. A. (ed.). *Classroom Assessment and Research: An Update on Uses, Approaches, and Research Findings.* New Directions for Teaching and Learning, no. 75. San Francisco: Jossey-Bass, 1998.

Apps, J. *Teaching From the Heart.* Malabar, FL: Krieger, 1996.

Banks, Robert. *Reenvisioning Theological Education: Exploring a Missional Alternative to Current Models.* Grand Rapids, MI: Eerdmans, 1999.

Banner, Jr., James M., and Cannon, Harold C. *The Elements of Teaching.* New Haven, CT: Yale University Press, 1997.

Baptiste, I. "Beyond Reason and Personal Integrity: Toward a Pedagogy of Coercive Restraint" *Canadian Journal for the Study of Adult Education*, (2000) 14/1, 27–50.

Beyond Borders: Ministry in a Multi-Cultural World (CD-ROM). Produced by JMCommunications, and available through the Mexican American Cultural Center in San Antonio, TX (http://www.maccsa.org/).

Bischoff, Claire. "Truth-centered Communities: Taking the Trinity Seriously in Religious Education." MA thesis, Luther Seminary, 2004.

Blase, J., Blase, J. R., Anderson, G. L., and Dungan, S. *Democratic Principals in Action: Eight Pioneers*. Thousand Oaks, CA: Corwin Press, 1995.

Blyden, E. W. "Philip and the Eunuch. Discourse delivered in the United States in 1882," in E. W. Blyden, *Christianity, Islam and the Negro Race*. Edinburgh: U. P., 1967.

Bonhoeffer, Dietrich. *Ethics*. Minneapolis, MN: Fortress Press, 2005.

Boomershine, Thomas. "How to Be a Faith Witness in the Communications Media? Conditions Requisite for the Public Communications Value of Faith Witnesses." Paper presented at the *Witnessing to the Faith, An Activity of the Media* conference, St. Paul University, Ottawa, ON, May 30, 1999.

Brady Williams, R. "The Vocation of Teaching: Beyond the Conspiracy of Mediocrity." In M. L. Warford (ed.), *Practical Wisdom: On Theological Teaching and Learning*. New York: Lang, 2004, pp. 15–28.

Branson, Mark Lau. *Memories, Hopes and Conversations: Appreciative Inquiry and Congregational Change*. Herndon, VA: Alban Institute, 2004.

Bridges, D. *Education, Democracy, and Discussion*. Lanham, MD: University Press of America, 1988.

Brookfield, Stephen. *Becoming a Critically Reflective Teacher*. San Francisco: Jossey-Bass, 1995.

Brookfield, Stephen, (ed.). *Learning Democracy: Eduard Lindeman on Adult Education and Social Change*. New York: Routledge, 1988.

Brookfield, Stephen D. *The Skillful Teacher*. San Francisco: Jossey-Bass, 1990.

Brookfield, S., and Preskill, S. *Discussion as a Way of Teaching: Tools and Techniques for Democratic Classrooms*. San Francisco: Jossey-Bass, 2005.

Brookhart, S. M. *The Art and Science of Classroom Assessment: The Missing Part of Pedagogy*. ASHE-ERIC Higher Education Report Series, Vol. 27, No. 1. San Francisco: Jossey-Bass, 2000.

Brown, Andrew and Voltz, Bradley. "Elements of Effective E-learning Design," in the *International Review of Research in Open and Distance Learning*, March 2005. Taken from the web on 31 December 2006: http://www.irrodl.org/index.php/irrodl/article/view/217/300.

Brown, Laura. *Subversive Dialogues: Theory in Feminist Therapy*. New York: Basic Books, 1994.

Brueggemann, Walter, Placher, William C., and Blount, Brian K.

Struggling with Scripture. Louisville, KY: Westminster John Knox, 2002, 68.

Bruffee, Kenneth. *Collaborative Learning: Higher Education, Interdependence and the Authority of Knowledge.* Baltimore: Johns Hopkins University Press, 1993.

Bultmann, Rudolf. "Is Exegesis Without Presuppositions Possible?" in *Existence and Faith: Shorter Writings of Rudolf Bultmann.* Translated by Schubert M. Ogden. Cleveland, OH: World Publishing, 1960, pp. 289–298.

Bultmann, Rudolf. *Jesus and the Word*, trans. from the German (*Jesus*, 1926), by L. P. Smith and E. H. Lantero. New York: Scribner's, 1934 [1962].

Burbules, N. *Dialogue in Teaching: Theory and Practice.* New York: Teachers College Press, 1993.

Bush, Melanie. *Breaking the Code of Good Intentions.* Lanham, MD: Rowman & Littlefield, 2004.

Butler, S. M., and McMunn, N. D. *A Teacher's Guide to Classroom Assessment.* San Franicsco: Jossey-Bass, 2006.

Campolo, Anthony, and Battle, Michael. *The Church Enslaved: A Spirituality of Racial Reconciliation.* Minneapolis, MN: Fortress Press, 2005.

Christensen, C., Garvin, D., and Sweet, A. (eds.). *Education for Judgment: The Artistry of Discussion Leadership.* Boston: Harvard Business School Press, 1991.

Cladis, George. *Leading the Team-Based Church: How Pastors and Church Staffs Can Grow Together into a Powerful Fellowship of Leaders.* San Francisco: Jossey-Bass, 1999.

Coakley, S. "Kenosis: Theological Meanings and Gender Connotations," in J. Polkinghorne, (ed.). *The Work of Love: Creation as Kenosis.* Grand Rapids, MI: Eerdmans, 2001.

Conde-Frazier, E., Kang, S., and Parrett, G. *A Many-Colored Kingdom: Multicultural Dynamics for Spiritual Formation* (Grand Rapids, MI: Baker Academic, 2004).

Conn, Walter. *Christian Conversion: A Developmental Interpretation of Autonomy and Surrender.* New York: Paulist Press, 1986.

Cooperrider, David, Barrett, Frank, and Srivastva, Suresh. "Social Construction and Appreciative Inquiry: A Journey in Organizational Theory" in Hosking, Dachler, and Gergen (eds.), *Management and Organization: Relational Alternatives to Individualism.* New York: Ashgate, 1995.

Copeland-Carson, Jacqueline. "Black Philanthropy Today: Embracing the New Diversity," in the *Minnesota Council of Foundations* newsletter: http://www.mcf.org/MCF/forum/2005/newdiversity.htm (taken from the web on 070102)

Cranton, P. *Becoming an Authentic Teacher in Higher Education.* Malabar, FL: Krieger, 2001.

Daloz, et al. *Common Fire: Lives of Commitment in a Complex World.* Boston: Beacon Press, 1996.

Davis, J. R. *Interdisciplinary Courses and Team Teaching: New Arrangements for Learning.* Phoenix, AZ: ACE/Oryx, 1995.

Dean, Kenda Creasy. *Practicing Passion: Youth and the Quest for a Passionate Church.* Grand Rapids, MI: Eerdmans, 2004.

DeYoung, Emerson, Yancey, and Kim, *United by Faith: The Multiracial Congregation as an Answer to the Problem of Race.* New York: Oxford University Press, 2003.

Edwards, Mark. "Characteristically Lutheran Leanings?" in *Dialog: A Journal of Theology*, Vol. 41, #1, Spring 2002.

Eisen, M. J. "The Many Faces of Team Teaching and Learning: An Overview," in *New Directions for Adult and Continuing Education*, (2000) 87, 5–14.

Eisner, Elliot. *The Educational Imagination: On the Design and Evaluation of School Programs.* Columbus, OH: Merrill/Prentice Hall, 2002.

English, L, Fenwick, T., and Parsons, J. *Spirituality of Adult Education and Training.* Malabar, FL: Krieger, 2003.

English, L., and Gillen, M. *Addressing the Spiritual Dimensions of Adult Learning.* San Francisco: Jossey-Bass, 2000.

Farber-Robertson, Anita. *Learning While Leading: Increasing Your Effectiveness in Ministry.* Herndon, VA: Alban Institute, 2000.

Farley, Edward. *Theologia: The Fragmentation and Unity of Theological Education.* Philadelphia: Fortress Press, 1983.

Foss, Sonja K., and Griffin, Cindy L. "Beyond Persuasion: A Proposal for an Invitational Rhetoric" in *Communication Monographs*, 62 (1995): 1–18.

Foster, C. R., Dahill, L. E., Golemon, L. A., and Wang Tolentino, B. *Educating Clergy: Teaching Practices and Pastoral Imagination.* San Francisco: Jossey-Bass, 2006.

Foucault, Michel. *Power/Knowledge: Selected Interviews and Other Writings, 1972–1977.* New York: Pantheon Books, 1980.

Fra-Molinero, Baltasar. "Juan Latino and His Racial Difference," in J. F. Earle and K. J. P. Lowe, *Black Africans in Renaissance Europe.* Cambridge: Cambridge University Press, 2005.

Frederick, P. "The Dreaded Discussion: Ten Ways to Start" in D. Bligh (ed.), *Teach Thinking By Discussion*. Guildford, England: Society for Research into Higher Education/ NFER-Nelson, 1986.

Freire, Paulo. *Pedagogy of the Oppressed*. New York: Continuum Publishing, 1985.

Fretheim, Terence. "Theological Reflections on the Wrath of God in the Old Testament" in *Horizons in Biblical Theology*, Vol. 24 #2, 2002.

Gee, James Paul. *What Video Games Have to Teach Us about Learning and Literacy.* New York: Palgrave Macmillan, 2004.

Gensichen, Hans-Werner. *Glaube fuer die Welt: Theologische Aspekt der Mission*. Guetersloh, Germany: Mohn, 1971.

Gladwell, Malcolm. *Blink: The Power of Thinking Without Thinking.* New York: Little, Brown, 2005.

Gladwell, Malcolm. *The Tipping Point: How Little Things Can Make a Big Difference*. New York: Little, Brown, 2000.

Gonzalez, Justo L. *Acts. The Gospel of the Spirit*. Maryknoll, NY: Orbis Books, 2001.

Green, Thomas. *The Activities of Teaching*. Troy, NY: Educator's International Press, 1998 [1971].

Gregory, Marshall. "Curriculum, Pedagogy, and Teacherly Ethos," in *Pedagogy* 1/1(2001): 69–89.

Gunderson, Gary. *Boundary Leaders: Leadership Skills for People of Faith*. Minneapolis, MN: Fortress Press, 2004.

Habermas, J. *Autonomy and Solidarity: Interviews with Jurgen Habermas*. London: Verso, 1992. [revised edition]

Habermas, J. *Between Facts and Norms: Contributions to a Discourse Theory of Democracy*. Cambridge, MA: MIT Press, 1996.

Habermas, J. *The Theory of Communicative Action, Volume One, Reason and the Rationalization of Society*. Boston: Beacon Press, 1984.

Habermas, J. *The Theory of Communicative Action: Volume Two, Lifeworld and System—A Critique of Functionalist Reason*. Boston: Beacon Press, 1987.

Hall, Douglas John. *Confessing the Faith: Christian Theology in a North American Context*. Minneapolis, MN: Fortress Press, 1996.

Harnack, Adolf von. *The Mission and Expansion of Christianity in the First Three Centuries*. New York: Putnam, 1908.

Haroutunian-Gordon, S. *Turning the Soul: Teaching through Conversation in the High School*. Chicago: University of Chicago Press, 1991.

Hennessee, Sr. Paul Teresa, S. A., "Violence in the Household," in Susan Davies and Sr. Paul Teresa Hennessee, S.A., (eds.), *Ending Racism in the Church*. Cleveland, OH: United Church Press, 1998.

Hess, M., Horsfield, P., and Medrano, A. (eds). *Belief in Media: Cultural Perspectives on Media and Christianity*. Burlington, VT: Ashgate, 2004.

Hess, Mary. *Engaging Technology in Theological Education*. Lanham, MD: Rowman & Littlefield, 2005.

Hobbs, Renee. *Reading the Media in High School*. New York: Teachers College Press, 2007.

Hoppe, S. L. and Speck, B. W. (eds.). *Spirituality in Higher Education*. San Francisco: Jossey-Bass, 2005.

Horton, M. *The Long Haul: An Autobiography*. New York: Doubleday, 1990.

Horton, M., and Freire, P. *We Make the Road by Walking: Conversations on Education and Social Change*. Philadelphia: Temple University Press, 1990.

Hunter, George. *The Celtic Way of Mission: How Christianity Can Reach the West . . . Again*. Nashville, TN: Abingdon Press, 2000.

Huston, J. Dennis. "Building Confidence and Community in the Classroom," in *Teaching Excellence* 3/1 (1991).

Indigo Girls. "All That We Let In," from the compact disc *All That We Let In*, Sony, 2004.

Jablonski, M. A. (ed.). *The Implications of Student Spirituality for Student Affairs Practices*. San Francisco: Jossey-Bass, 2001.

Jacobson, Diane. "Hosea 2: A Case Study in Biblical Authority," in *Currents in Theology and Mission* 23 (1996) 165–72.

Jacobson, Rolf. "Teaching Students to Interpret Religious Poetry (and to Expand their Avenues of Thinking)," in *Teaching Theology & Religion* (January 2004), 38–44.

Jacobson, Rolf. [multiple entries] in Mark Roncance and Patrick Gray (eds.), *Teaching the Bible: Practical Strategies for Classroom Instruction*. Atlanta: Society of Biblical Literature, 2005.

Jenkins, Henry. *Convergence Culture*. New York: New York University Press, 2006.

Jenkins, Philip. *The Next Christendom*. New York: Oxford University Press, 2002.

Jones, Gregory L. *Embodying Forgiveness: A Theological Analysis*. Grand Rapids, MI: Eerdmans, 1995.

Juel, D., and Kiefert, P. "A rhetorical approach to theological education: Assessing an attempt to re-vision a curriculum," in David S.

Cunningham (ed.), *To Teach, To Delight, and To Move: Theological Education in a Post-Christian World*. Eugene, OR: Cascade Books, 2004.

Katz, Judith. *White Awareness: Handbook for Anti-racism Training*. Norman: University of Oklahoma Press, 1978.

Kegan, Robert. *The Evolving Self: Problem and Process in Human Development*. Cambridge, MA: Harvard University Press, 1982.

Kegan, Robert. *In Over Our Heads: The Mental Demands of Modern Life*. Cambridge, MA: Harvard University Press, 1995.

Kegan, Robert, and Lahey, Lisa. *How The Way We Talk Can Change The Way We Work: Seven Languages for Transformation*. San Francisco: Jossey-Bass, 2001.

Kelsey, David. *Between Athens and Berlin: The Theological Education Debate*. Grand Rapids, MI: Eerdmans, 1993.

Kitchener, Patricia, and King, Karen. *Developing Reflective Judgment: Understanding and Promoting Intellectual Growth and Critical Thinking in Adolescents and Adults*. San Francisco: Jossey-Bass, 1994.

Kivel, Paul. *Uprooting Racism: How White People Can Work for Racial Justice*. Philadelphia, PA: New Society Publishers, 1996.

Klimoski, Victor. "Evolving Dynamics of Formation," in Malcolm Warford (ed.), *Practical Wisdom: On Theological Teaching and Learning*. New York: Lang, 2004.

Klimoski, V., O'Neil, K., and Schuth, K. *Educating Leaders for Ministry: Issues and Responses*. Collegeville, MN: Liturgical Press, 2005.

Lai, Alan Ka Lun. "Educating Chinese Seminarians in North America: A Cross Cultural Understanding of Teaching and Learning," in *Consensus* (1999) 69–91.

Lightfoot, Sara Lawrence. *Respect: An Exploration*. New York: Perseus Books Group, 2000.

Limburg, James. *Psalms for Sojourners*. Minneapolis, MN: Augsburg, 1986.

López, Ian Haney. *White by Law*. New York: New York University Press, 1996.

Lose, David. *Confessing Jesus Christ: Preaching in a Postmodern World*. Grand Rapids, MI: Eerdmans, 2003.

Lutheran Book of Worship. Minneapolis: Augsburg, 1978.

Malcolm, Lois. "Teaching as Cultivating Wisdom for a Complex World," in L. Gregory Jones and Stephanie Paulsell (eds.), *The Scope of Our Art: The Vocation of the Theological Teacher.* Grand Rapids, MI: Eerdmans, 2002.

Malony, H. N., and Spika, B. (eds.). *Religion in Psychodynamic Perspective: The Contributions of Paul W. Pruyser.* New York: Oxford University Press, 1996.

Marcuse, H. "Repressive Tolerance," in R. P. Wolff, B. Moore, and H. Marcuse, *A Critique of Pure Tolerance*. Boston: Beacon Press, 1965.

Matsuoka, Fumitaka. *The Color of Faith: Building Community in a Multiracial Society*. Cleveland, OH: United Church Press, 1998.

McIntosh, Peggy. "Working Paper #189: White Privilege and Male Privilege, an Account of Coming to See the Correspondences through Work in Women's Studies." Wellesley Center for Research on Women. 1988.

Mezirow, J. *Transformative Dimensions of Adult Learning*. San Francisco: Jossey-Bass, 1991.

Meyer, Paul W. *The Word in This World: Essays in New Testament Exegesis and Theology* (ed. John T. Carroll; Louisville, KY: Westminster John Knox, 2004): 15.

Miller, V. M., and Ryan, M. M. (eds.). *Transforming Campus Life: Reflections on Spirituality and Religious Pluralism*. New York: Lang, 2001.

Moltmann, Jurgen. From a Capps lecture, given April 27th, 2005 at the University of Virginia, *In God We Trust, In Us God Trusts: On Freedom and Security in a "Free World."* Available online at: http://www.theologicalhorizons.org/documents/CAPPStranscript1.pdf.

Newell, W. H. *Interdisciplinary Essays from the Literature*. New York: College Entrance Examination Board, 1998.

Nysse, Richard. "Online Education: An Asset in a Period of Educational Change," in Malcolm Warford (ed.), *Practical Wisdom: On Theological Teaching and Learning*. New York: Lang, 2004.

Osterman, K. F., and Kottkamp, R. B. *Reflective Practice for Educators: Professional Development to Improve Student Learning*. Newbury Park, CA: Corwin Press, 2004.

Palmer, P. *The Courage to Teach: Exploring the Inner Dimensions of a Teacher's Life*. San Francisco: Jossey-Bass, 1998.

Palmer, P. *To Know as We Are Known*. San Francisco: HarperCollins, 1993.

Parks, Sharon Daloz. *Leadership Can Be Taught: A Bold Approach for a Complex World*. Boston: Harvard Business School Publishing, 2005.

Paterson, R. W. K., "The Concept of Discussion: A Philosophical Approach" in *Studies in Adult Education* (1970, 1 [2]).

Pattison, S. "Health and Healing," in A. Hastings (ed.), *The Oxford*

Companion to Christian Thought. New York: Oxford University Press, 2000.

Patton, Kimberley C. "'Stumbling Along between the Immensities': Reflections on Teaching in the Study of Religion," *Journal of the American Academy of Religion* 65/4 (1997): 847–48.

Peart, Norman. *Separate No More: Understanding and Developing Racial Reconciliation in Your Church*. Grand Rapids, MI: Baker Books, 2000.

Perkinson, James. *White Theology: Outing Supremacy in Modernity*. New York: Palgrave Macmillan, 2004.

Peters, R. S. (ed.). *The Concept of Education*. Boston: Routledge, Kegan and Paul, 1967.

Pruyser, P. "Anxiety, Guilt, and Shame in the Atonement," in *Theology Today*, *XX*, (2005) 15–33.

Reitzug, U. C. "A Case Study of Empowering Principal Behavior." *American Educational Research Journal*, 1994, 31 (2), 283–307.

Ricoeur, Paul. "Appropriation," in *Paul Ricoeur: Hermeneutics and the Social Sciences: Essays on Language, Action and Interpretation*, edited, translated, and introduced by John B. Thompson. Cambridge: Cambridge University Press, 1981, pp. 182–195.

Robinson, A. B., and Wall, R. W. *Called to Be Church. The Book of Acts for a New Day*. Grand Rapids, MI: Eerdmans, 2006.

Rogness, Alvin. "Centennial Article: Marcus Olaus Bockman," in *Luther Theological Seminary Review*, Spring (1975) 19–21, 45.

Schaff, Philip. *History of the Christian Church*, Volume IV: Mediaeval Christianity. A.D. 590–1073. New York: Charles Scribner, 1903–1912.

Schein, Edgar. *Organizational Culture and Leadership*. San Francisco: Jossey-Bass, 2004.

Schwarz, Hans. *Christology*. Grand Rapids, MI: Eerdmans, 1998.

Searle, John R. *Expression and Meaning: Studies in the Theory of Speech Acts*. London: Cambridge University Press, 1979.

Shor, I., and Freire, P. *A Pedagogy for Liberation: Dialogues on Transforming Education*. Westport, CT: Bergin and Garvey, 1987.

Shults, F. L., and Sandage, S. *The Faces of Forgiveness*. Grand Rapids, MI: Baker Academic, 2003.

Shweder, Richard. *Thinking through Cultures: Expeditions in Cultural Psychology*. Cambridge, MA: Harvard University Press, 1991.

Snyder, Will. "Roundtables: A Way for Students to Develop Their Internal Sources of Motivation to Learn and to Act," in *International Research in Geographical and Environmental Education*, 14, 2, (2005), 150–154.

Spencer, F. S. *Journeying through Acts*. Peabody, MA: Hendrickson Publishers, 2004.

Sullivan, W. M. "Introduction." In C. R. Foster, L. E. Dahill, L. A. Golemon, and B. Wang Tolentino, *Educating Clergy: Teaching Practices and Pastoral Imagination*. San Francisco: Jossey-Bass, 2006, pp. 1–16.

Svinicki, Marilla. "If Learning Involves Risk-taking, Teaching Involves Trust-building," in *Teaching Excellence* 2/3 (1989).

Tait, Lewis. *Three Fifths Theology: Challenging Racism in American Christianity*. Trenton, NJ: Africa World Press, 2002.

Talvacchia, Kathleen. *Critical Minds and Discerning Hearts: A Spirituality of Multicultural Teaching*. St. Louis, MO: Chalice Press, 2003.

Thompson, Deanna. *Crossing the Divide: Luther, Feminism and the Cross*. Minneapolis, MN: Fortress Press, 2004.

Tisdell, E. J. *Exploring Spirituality and Culture in Adult and Higher Education*. San Francisco: Jossey-Bass, 2003.

Tracy, David. *Plurality and Ambiguity: Hermeneutics, Religion, Hope*. San Francisco: Harper & Row, 1987.

Van Ments, M. *Active Talk: The Effective Use of Discussion in Learning*. New York: St. Martin's Press, 1990.

Vigen, Aana Marie. "To Hear and to Be Accountable: An Ethic of White Listening," in Harvey, Case, and Gorsline (eds.), *Disrupting White Supremacy from Within*. Cleveland: Pilgrim Press, 2004.

Warford, M. L. "Introduction," in M. L. Warford (ed.), *Practical Wisdom: On Theological Teaching and Learning*. New York: Lang, 2004, pp. 1–14.

Webb, Stephen H. "Teaching as Confessing: Redeeming a Theological Trope for Pedagogy," in *Teaching Theology and Religion* 2/3 (1999): 151.

Webb, Walker, and Bollis. "Feminist Pedagogy in the Teaching of Research Methods," in *International Journal of Research Methodology*, 7, 5, (2003) 415–428.

Webster, W. G., Sr. *Learner-Centered Principalship: The Principal as Teacher of Teachers*. New York: Praeger, 1994.

Weinberger, David. *Small Pieces Loosely Joined*. New York: Perseus Books Group, 2002.

Welch, Sharon. "Ceremonies of Gratitude, Awakening and Accountability: The Theory and Practice of Multicultural Education," in Harvey, Case and Gorsline (eds.), *Disrupting White Supremacy from Within*. Cleveland: Pilgrim Press, 2004.

Wiggins, Grant and McTighe, Jay. *Understanding by Design*. Upper Saddle River, NJ: Merrill/Prentice Hall, 2001.

Winkelmes, M. "Formative Learning in the Classroom," in M. L. Warford (ed.), *Practical Wisdom: On Theological Teaching and Learning*. New York: Lang, 2004, pp. 161–180.

Zull, James. *The Art of Changing the Brain: Enriching the Practice of Teaching by Exploring the Biology of Learning* (Sterling, VA: Stylus Publishing, 2002).

INDEX